ACKNOWLEDGMENTS

I'm extremely lucky to have many wonderful people in my personal life. And I've had the pleasure of working with an array of talented artists in my professional life. While it would be impossible for me to acknowledge everyone who's had an impact on the writing of this book, on my career, or on *Thrill Me* over the past thirty years, I would like to extend my deepest appreciation to the following individuals who aren't otherwise named in the book:

Most importantly, my beloved Seth Arrobas, who's sat through almost as many productions of *Thrill Me* as I have. He was right there next to me on our trips to Seoul, London, Tokyo, and so many other places; squeezing my hand during the good moments—squeezing it harder during the bad ones. He's always championed me and just *listened* when that was all I needed him to do.

Adrian Bewley and Michael Patrick Walker, who performed in the first reading of *Thrill Me*—and on the demo. Broadway actors Danny Gurwin and Joe Paparella, and my longtime friend Sean McCall, who all performed in the later readings. "Theatre pal" from my youth, Sara Crowley, who was one of the recorded Parole Board voices in the very first production. Rob Harris and Richard Williamson who introduced *Thrill Me* to London.

My cherished pal, Nicole Del Percio, who's so generous with her insightful comments. Jason Rockwood, who's like a brother to me, for his beneficial input. Hyojin Kang, for help with the production list. Josh Rivedal, for his publishing industry advice. My crackerjack advance readers Danny Conover, Matthew Maslanka, and Erik Schneider. Leopold & Loeb expert, Erik Rebain. And extraordinary proofreader, Nathan Lichtenstein.

A few people, who are mentioned within the chapters of the book, deserve an extra thanks. So, with all my heart, a big shout-out to:

My biggest supporter for my entire life, my mother, Susie Dolginoff. For her, there just aren't enough words of thanks and gratitude.

My sister, Lori Dolginoff, the savvy world traveler. If she hadn't agreed to come along, I don't think I'd have gone to see *Thrill Me* in Seoul—which would've deprived me of an amazing once-in-a-lifetime experience.

My father, Eugene Dolginoff, who took me on my first trip to New York. And he splurged on tickets to all of the hit shows of the day.

My grandparents, the late Betty and Harold Levitt. Without their generous support, literally none of this would have ever happened.

My agent, Ron Gwiazda, who came to my apartment nearly thirty years ago to listen to the score of *Thrill Me* as I served him tea. He's been a crucial supporter and advocate for the show ever since. My other wonderful agent, Amy Wagner, for her fantastic representation, advice, and attention whenever it's needed.

Jim Kierstead, for reasons that this book will make abundantly clear. Jim Morgan, for his inspired casting idea. Michael Park, for having a bigger vision for the show than even I had. Joe Barros, for his incredible "instant musical" blocking and concepts. Mati Gordon, for all of the beautiful artwork that he's so skillfully created over the years.

The original New York "Nathan," Christopher Totten, for his brilliant performance. Matt Bauer, for his artistry. Joe Demerly, for his talent and perseverance. The very special Doug Kreeger and Shonn Wiley, for sharing their onstage magic with me Off-Broadway.

The talented Camille Diamond, who's always believed in me, and always laughs at my jokes! Miki Goto, Petra Knickmeyer, and Haemin Lee, for all of the important assistance they've each given me from so far away. The beautiful Melinda Berk, who was there from the beginning of my career. I couldn't even begin to list every way her legendary pep talks have helped me over these *many* years.

THRILL MAKER

To Laurent —

THRILL MAKER

— The Story of My Musical THRILL ME —

*thank you for your
support of all my shows
over the years'.*

Stephen Dolginoff

Thrillingly yours,

OFFSTAGE
DRAMA
PUBLISHING

OFFSTAGE DRAMA PUBLISHING
www.offstagedrama.com

Cover design by Mati Gordon & Guido Wain
www.drama.com.ar

Visit www.stephendolginoff.com
for *Thrill Me* photographs, video clips, reviews,
and updated information.

This memoir depicts the present recollections of actual past experiences in
the life of the author as truthfully as memory permits and/or can be
verified by research. Some events recounted within have been rearranged
or condensed for the purpose of clarity, and some dialogue has been
recreated. All persons mentioned are actual individuals; there are no
composite characters. The content reflects the author's personal
perspective and interpretation of the subject matter. His opinions,
perceptions, and conclusions are his own. They should not be construed
as being shared by any other person or entity.

All facts & figures included in the appendices of this book are accurate to
the best of the author's ability at the time of publication.
Handwritten notes have been recreated.

ISBN: 979-8-218-25544-2

FIRST EDITION

To all of those who put on shows…

CONTENTS

Finally, there are those left unnamed who are, nevertheless, very important to me: Every journalist and critic who's written about *Thrill Me* (even if they didn't like it). All of the authors who've honored me by mentioning *Thrill Me* in their own books. Everyone who's been part of the cast, crew, artistic staff, and producing team of any version of *Thrill Me*. And, of course, the loyal fans of the show all over the world.

Without *all* of these incredible people, there would be no *Thrill Me* and certainly no *Thrill Maker*.

INTRODUCTION

*"I'm sorry if I stumble. / Though I'm tense, /
I'll try to give you what you're after, / tell you more."*

That's the first sung line in my musical *Thrill Me: The Leopold & Loeb Story*. And right now it seems very prescient—because it describes exactly how "tense" I'm feeling as I attempt to "tell you more." I suppose it's comforting that I'm currently in exactly the same place where I actually wrote that line.

The *same place*. That makes it sound like I haven't made much progress since then. But that couldn't be further from the truth. While I may still live in the same *apartment*, after all the experiences I've had my life couldn't be more different now than it was then. The furniture is also a little nicer.

It's hard for me to believe that I started writing *Thrill Me* all the way back in 1994. But since I dutifully scrawled the date at the top of my long-since-yellowed, original handwritten notes, I know that it's true. *Thrill Me* has been an integral part of my life now for thirty years. *Thirty years*! How could that be possible?

It's even harder for me to believe that, since it was first produced in 2003, it's pretty much never been out of production. Or, at least, *pre*-production.

As of this writing, there have been over two hundred stagings spanning twenty-five separate countries and seventeen different languages. *Thrill Me* has been mentioned in over two dozen published books, has been the subject of several college theses, and has won or been nominated for numerous awards and honors.

I still contend with various aspects of *Thrill Me*-related business nearly every day. Sometimes it's an interview request or a contract negotiation along with my agents. Other times I'm answering questions posed by directors and actors while they're in rehearsal.

And I'm practically always promoting various productions of the show on social media. The truth is that I never know what's going to happen from one day to the next—or what exciting new prospects might suddenly arrive in my e-mail or my DMs.

I've had the pleasure of traveling to see versions of the show all over the world. I've met literally hundreds of incredible producers, directors, actors, and fans. And I've been surprisingly forced to flex my theatrical muscles in ways I didn't think I ever could. Suffice it to say, *Thrill Me* has truly been "the gift that keeps on giving," and has led to so many opportunities and experiences that I never dreamed could possibly happen to me.

* * *

I took a look at the calendar not too long ago and realized that two significant milestones would be converging in 2024. It would be the thirtieth anniversary of when I first began writing *Thrill Me*, and the far more somber one hundredth anniversary of the incident that inspired it. For the former, I felt that I should do something to honor the occasion. As for the latter, it wasn't something to celebrate. But I was certain that it would be widely noted as a dark part of American history.

I thought back to the many interviews I had given to journalists over the years. For the most part they were an accurate reflection of my thoughts and insights about the show. But a few times, as might be expected, I was misquoted or felt I had my words taken out of context. And I often wished the reporters asked me different questions or that I gave better answers.

Thus, I decided that the best way to celebrate both anniversaries was to tell the entire story of my personal history with *Thrill Me* myself—the way I wanted it told. It was finally time to write a memoir.

I hadn't previously even considered the idea of such a book. There were some stories that I knew would be difficult to relive, and aspects of memoir writing that could be uncomfortable. But on the positive side, I would have the opportunity to definitively answer nearly every *Thrill Me*-related question that I've ever received.

So I opened up the computer and began writing this book exactly as I began writing *Thrill Me* nearly thirty years before—though with a much better computer this time. Wait, did I even *have* a computer in 1994? Hmm…well I do remember a giant metal vertical box, and a huge monitor…

This book shouldn't be considered a comprehensive history of every single production of *Thrill Me* because I wasn't personally involved in most of them and would have no stories to tell. But I do believe that it will shed light on my early writing process.

It will explain why I wrote what I wrote, why I strayed from certain facts—yet kept others—and what the actual real-life details were that I felt needed to be simplified and condensed for the stage.

I've also done my best to disclose the most important things that stand out in my mind once *Thrill Me* finally got on its feet. Every *Thrill Me* cast member, director, producer, musician, and designer that I've mentioned by name has also been written about in *Thrill Me* press stories, reviews, or interviews at least once.

How *I* personally perceived certain situations may not be how others did. Some people may remember things differently than I do. And while sometimes specific details from long ago can be fuzzy, I've been as truthful and accurate as possible, to the best of my recollection.

I really wish that I'd kept a detailed journal to document the entire journey. But I didn't. So there are surely events that happened that I simply don't recall, some that I might not have even been aware of at the time, and some that I recollect—but just couldn't fit in. And, of course, all the opinions I express are my own and they shouldn't be interpreted as being shared by any individual or entity that I've written about.

I truly hope that sharing my personal stories, memories, and anecdotes will be of interest to fans of *Thrill Me*, musical theatre enthusiasts, writers, actors, directors, or even Leopold & Loeb scholars. And if I'm lucky, perhaps some of my experiences will be universally appreciated by *anyone*.

* * *

I know that many readers of this book will already be familiar with the plot of the musical. But I want it to be accessible for those that have never seen it, never listened to the score, or perhaps never even *heard* of it. So before you read about everything that has truly thrilled *me* during the last few decades, let's start with a complete synopsis—with song titles in parentheses—of my musical, *Thrill Me*:

> It is 1958 at Joliet Prison in Illinois. Fifty-four-year-old Nathan Leopold faces a Parole Board for the fifth time. He tells them the facts of the "crime of the century" that sent him to prison thirty-five years earlier ("Why"). But this time he reveals more than ever before, hoping it will finally lead to his release.
>
> In his memory, he goes back to 1924 Chicago, where as a nineteen-year-old, he anxiously meets up with Richard Loeb, a classmate with whom he has shared friendship, sex, and participation in minor crimes.
>
> Richard, who has been away at college, treats Nathan indifferently. Nathan begs to renew their relationship before separating again after the summer to attend different law schools ("Everybody Wants Richard").
>
> Richard relents and allows Nathan to join him in his activity for the evening: setting an abandoned warehouse on fire. In front of the blaze, which arouses and exhilarates Richard, Nathan finally gets what *he* wants ("Nothing Like a Fire").
>
> The next day, Nathan implores Richard, who is voraciously reading Nietzsche, to stop the criminal

activity. But Richard, now empowered by Nietzsche's theory of the "Superman," threatens to shut out Nathan completely unless they make a formal deal ("A Written Contract"). Their agreement stipulates that Richard will satisfy Nathan's sexual needs only in exchange for Nathan's expertise as his accomplice in petty crimes. Reluctantly, Nathan agrees.

They sign in blood and their crime spree continues until Richard fails to live up to his end of the agreement ("Thrill Me"). Richard explains that he has become bored with the misdemeanors and wants to commit a *superior* crime.

He suggests the murder of a young boy, and a sham ransom scheme *after* the killing ("The Plan"). Richard insists that their intellect and meticulous plotting will prevent them from being caught. Nathan has no choice but to agree or risk Richard's wrath.

Back in 1958 at Joliet before the Parole Board, Nathan explains his feelings ("Way Too Far") as he recalls how Richard prepared the set of murder weapons which consisted of a coil of rope, a crowbar, and a bottle of acid. In 1924, Richard lures the victim by promising him a ride ("Roadster"). While the shaken Nathan helps clean up the murder scene, Richard extols the virtues of what they've just done ("Superior").

Having returned to Richard's house, they proceed with their plot to swindle the victim's parents ("Ransom Note"). The next day, the newspapers reveal that, despite their careful planning, the body has been found. As a few more days go by, Nathan's missing eyeglasses are discovered near the scene of the crime.

While Nathan panics, Richard tries to calm him over the phone ("My Glasses/Just Lay Low"). When the glasses are eventually traced to Nathan, Richard helps him concoct an emergency alibi and coaches him on how to answer the cops ("I'm Trying to Think").

After Nathan is successful with the police, Richard declares their relationship over so he can protect his own future as a lawyer. He reminds Nathan that everything would have been fine if the glasses hadn't been dropped.

Feeling betrayed, Nathan cuts a deal with the prosecutor by turning in Richard in exchange for a lighter sentence. When arrested, Richard realizes there is no way out. So he works his charms on Nathan by manipulating him into giving up his deal. Now they will both face the same punishment ("Keep Your Deal with Me").

While awaiting the penalty trial in his jail cell, Richard doesn't realize that Nathan can hear him muttering his fears to himself, despite his strong facade ("Afraid"). Thanks to the cunning strategies of their lawyer, Clarence Darrow, they escape the death penalty and are sentenced to prison, forever branded as *the thrill killers*.

On their way to prison, Nathan finally reveals his own shocking plan. He went along with the murder, but stayed one step ahead the entire time. He *deliberately* planted his glasses, knowing they would be all the evidence needed to eventually lead to their capture. Thus, his desire to be with Richard "in cage together like two rare birds" has been fulfilled ("Life Plus Ninety-Nine Years").

Now that the whole truth has at last been exposed, back at Joliet prison in 1958, Nathan is granted parole. But it's a bittersweet victory. Since Richard had been murdered by another inmate years before, Nathan must face the outside world alone ("Finale").

Got all that? Okay, here we go…

1

THE THRILL OF CREATION

"Don't bore me with details / They'll never impress me."

That's a lyric I wrote for the title song from *Thrill Me*. I hope I'm not actually about to "bore *you* with details." I'm shooting for the exact opposite of that sentiment. Whether or not I "impress you," I suppose will be open to interpretation.

I didn't always plan on being a writer. I thought I was going to be an actor. A famous one. I practically jumped out of the car, on a snowy New Year's Eve in the late 1970s, when my grandparents took me to see my very first professional play. It was the comedy classic *Arsenic and Old Lace*, the story of two murderous old ladies and their unusual relatives.

I was hooked instantly. And I truly wished that I could have left my seat and joined the delightfully bizarre "Brewster family" up there on that stage. In the following weeks, my grandparents bought me a copy of the script—which I would carry around with me like a teddy bear.

My "acting career" kicked off when I was cast in a television commercial for a popular magic kit. In it, I performed tricks from the kit on the stage of a big theatre. I was costumed in an adorable little white tuxedo. Not bad for a kid's first gig.

Then after seeing popular touring shows of the day like *Annie*, *They're Playing Our Song*, and *Evita*, I realized that *musicals* were really my thing. Eventually I started performing in summer stock at Starlight Theatre in my hometown of Kansas City (I lived on the Kansas side, the theatre was on the Missouri side).

I was in shows such as *Oliver!* with Christian Slater, *The Music Man* with William Katt, *Annie Get Your Gun* with Dee Wallace, and *Jesus Christ Superstar* with David Cassidy. Believe me, those were some big name celebrities back then. Even though I was usually just in the youth chorus, I paid close attention to everything and tried to learn as much as I could.

I was accepted into the Drama Department at New York University on a partial scholarship, and moved to the Big Apple immediately after graduating high school in the late 1980s. And that's when my *writing* career began. As an acting student at NYU, I came to the honest realization that my dreams of being a performer were likely not destined to be. In class, there was always someone better. Make that *several* who were better.

So to occupy myself, I decided to write a musical of my own. I had certainly seen and been in enough of them. Back in Kansas City I had also studied and performed at a professional children's theatre. The artistic director would have a hand in creating original musicals for the company, so I was exposed to the concept of writing and composing early on. Since I could play the piano, and had a pretty good ear for music, I figured "why not try?"

I was quite pleased with my first attempt, a musical called *Beauty Sleep*. It must have been pretty decent because it was produced by NYU the following year. I pretty much instantly knew that I had found my true calling, and I applied for a transfer into the highly competitive Dramatic Writing program.

For comparison's sake, the Drama Department had a class of a few hundred students. In Dramatic Writing, the entire class was less than thirty. I was accepted, and spent the next few years focused on getting that degree.

Upon graduating with my BFA in 1991, I started writing and composing my first professional musical, *One Foot Out the Door*. After a run in the basement of a restaurant on Bleecker Street, it was modestly produced at the famous Don't Tell Mama cabaret on 46th Street—not far from where I lived.

I even won the *Backstage* Bistro Award for Outstanding Book, Music, and Lyrics for the show. An elegant ceremony was held for the winners. I found myself sitting at a table in front of theatre personalities Mary Rodgers, the composer of *Once Upon a Mattress,* and Richard Maltby Jr., the lyricist and director of *Closer Than Ever* and *Baby.* Both of them also received awards that night.

I went out of my way to introduce myself to Mary Rodgers, who was known for her sharp wit. I told her that it was a great honor to be winning an award for my very first professional show on the same night that she was also receiving one. She tartly replied, "Congratulations. This is the first time *I've* ever won *anything!*" I had no doubt that my career was already off to a good start.

A few years later, a small theatre company in lower Manhattan presented a series of workshop performances of my next musical, *Most Men Are.* This led to a full production at a theatre on Waverly Place in Greenwich Village, which was very well received. It was later produced in Toronto.

* * *

I began writing *Thrill Me* in 1994 while still in pre-production on *Most Men Are.* At that time, I had two separate ideas for musicals swirling around in my head. The first would be a true crime story, with just about anything on the table in that regard. The other would be about some kind of unusual relationship between two people—a romance or a power struggle perhaps. But definitely something different than a standard love story. I had no idea which would come first, or if either concept would end up viable.

One day, as I was still in the midst of considering both, I walked up to Coliseum Books on West 57th Street, which was close to my apartment. I went to the true crime section and found a big shelf-worn paperback—one of the thickest books I had ever seen. It was titled *Bloodletters and Bad Men,* and it described itself as a narrative encyclopedia of American criminals.

I thumbed through the book. Billy The Kid...Al Capone...John Dillinger...finally I reached a chapter about Leopold & Loeb. It immediately struck a chord. I had heard of them, but I didn't know their story.

So I stood in the book store and read that Nathan Leopold and Richard Loeb were two teenaged geniuses and aspiring lawyers from Chicago in 1924. They had a sexual relationship with each other, and an obsession with Nietzsche's theory of the "Übermensch" or "Superman."

And to prove that they were superior to the rest of society, they committed a "thrill killing," certain they would get away with it. But Leopold & Loeb were very soon caught, pled guilty, and were represented by the legendary lawyer Clarence Darrow in a successful fight to receive a life sentence and not the death penalty.

As I read the pages, it slowly dawned on me that here was both a true crime story *and* a story of an intense power play between two people—an *unusual relationship*! Since I was careful with my spending back then, I didn't actually *buy* the book until sometime later (when a revised edition was published). So that day, I skimmed the chapter again to make sure that I knew the main details. Then I put *Bloodletters and Badmen* back on the shelf. Went home. And my life was never the same.

I did some investigation and found that while there had been a few stage and screen versions of the story, in my opinion there had never been anything truly definitive that the public would always have in their mind. If I had wanted to write about Bonnie & Clyde, for example, it would have been hard to top the Academy Award-winning movie that starred Warren Beatty and Faye Dunaway.

Also, I could find no record of the story ever being musicalized. I felt that I could truly put my own stamp on it. So I began doing further research, though books and other materials weren't so easy to come by back then.

But eventually, I felt that I had enough information. I wasn't too concerned with uncovering every possible detail ever written about the case and those involved. This was going to be a theatrical interpretation, not a nonfiction book or a biography.

I remember worrying at the time that it may be too difficult an undertaking to write the book, music, and lyrics all by myself for *this* intense of a story. I had always done it before, but my previous works were not nearly as ambitious. So I initially looked for a collaborator.

When that didn't work out, I realized I was just being silly and too cautious. There was no reason that I couldn't personally write the entire musical. I merely had to trust myself.

I knew I wanted the story to be intimate and straightforward, with nothing unnecessary or extraneous. So I immediately conceived it as a very small show. Two actors, one piano, no scenery, and no intermission. Something that could be done in a tiny East Village black box, a converted garage, or maybe a loft—any place with a grungy downtown vibe.

The first thing I imagined was what I wanted the experience for the audience to be like. Uncomfortable benches, which would force them to have to sit on the edge of their seats. The stage so dim with deep red lights that it could barely be seen. The room probably filled with smoke. No one's applauding or even moving—just sitting there riveted, leaning forward in shock by what's unfolding. Maybe with their hands over their eyes. In other words, something commercial and easily accessible to the masses was not *at all* what I had in mind!

So I threw caution to the wind, and dug in to write about a horrible crime and a bizarre co-dependency. If I was deft enough, I believed that I could make the characters relatable despite the plot, which I hoped would go well beyond being just a tale of manipulation and murder. I decided to go as far as I could with it and push as many boundaries as possible.

Sure, I knew people would question the concept of a musical about two notorious killers who were also teenaged lovers, but I didn't care. If I had thought about it harder, I might have had concerns. But I was very fearless back then. And had I known that the show would become a popular worldwide hit, I probably would have censored myself and written it far more conservatively. So I'm glad that was never even a sliver of a thought.

* * *

I always like to start a musical by having the title decided. It helps me focus and motivates me to be more excited about the project. Instead of just mentally referring to it as "the musical" or "the project," it's much more fun to have an actual name. It took me a while to figure out what to call this show.

At first, I simply labeled the file as *Leopold & Loeb*—but I knew that I wanted it to have a more interesting title. I briefly considered *The Thrill Killers*, since that was the sensationalized moniker that they had been dubbed with in the 1920s—but I didn't think it sounded enough like a musical. And I thought it might be a bad idea to have the word "killer" in the title.

Thinking back, that actually might have been a decent title—but I'm glad I didn't go with it. *Crime of the Century* and *Trial of the Century* were terms used in connection with Leopold & Loeb back in 1924, but they seemed very cliché.

I kept thinking and thinking. For some strange reason, I have a very clear memory of being in a taxi cab on the way to Macy's department store on 34th Street in Manhattan, when the words *Thrill Me* just sort of popped into my head. I knew instantly that it was the perfect title. It was a play on the idea of the "thrill killing" and it sounded a little sexy, which couldn't be a bad thing, right?

Before I sat down to begin the script and score in earnest, I ruminated on it for a while. And once *Most Men Are* finished its run, I was finally able to devote most of my attention to *Thrill Me*. Come to think of it, I feel like I've never *stopped* devoting most of my attention to *Thrill Me*.

* * *

Just like most musical theatre writers, I'm often asked which comes first—the music or the lyrics. For me, the answer is simple. Both. When I sit down to start writing a song lyric, the music comes right along with it in my head. So as I'm writing down the words, I'm also mentally writing the music. Once the lyrics of a song are finished—or at least roughed in—it's just a matter of going to the piano and transcribing the tune.

However, sometimes I may need to extensively rewrite the words, or perhaps even totally discard them, and then reuse an entire piece of music as the basis of a brand new song—perhaps in a different context. In those instances, it's much more challenging to fit lyrics—that need to rhyme and "scan" correctly—into a pre-existing melody. But when I accomplish that, it's extremely fulfilling.

As for writing the book, also known as the libretto or the script, I usually do it in chronological order. Sometimes I will leave space for the eventual song. Sometimes I won't move forward until the song is written in. Occasionally I will skip around and just write a few songs ahead of the script.

For *Thrill Me*, I started by writing some "test" songs, just to be sure I could musicalize the characters. I knew I didn't want the music to sound like standard music of the 1920s. I was going for something that would sound darker and more emotional, with mainly minor chords and a lot of bass notes.

It would have made perfect sense to have written the characters themselves as high tenors to reflect their youth, or as a tenor and a baritone to have contrast. But I decided to place both roles in the baritone range.

That way, when the songs began they would be in the register of both actors' natural speaking voices. This would make them seem more conversational and less "musical theatre." I also thought that when the harmony sections went high, they would really stand out dramatically.

Luckily, the songs were very easy for me to write. I was truly inspired. Among the very first words and music that I wrote for the show was a verse that began with the plaintive warning *"Perhaps there was a witness near the lake. / Perhaps we left a foot print in the mud…"* and continued with the fearful realization *"Suppose we weren't too careful with the blood. / Or maybe made some other huge mistake!"*

Although it was originally meant to be part of a different song, and didn't make it into the very first draft, I worked hard to find a place for it. With a few tweaks, it ultimately ended up in the song "My Glasses/Just Lay Low," where it has forever remained.

* * *

I figured that the natural first scene of the story should be when Nathan and Richard are reunited for the summer after spending a school semester apart. So I wrote it to begin with Richard startling Nathan, who is birdwatching in the park. Even though it began with Nathan being "scared," I came to worry that just wasn't an interesting enough or a *big* enough way to start the musical.

So instead, I decided to begin with a prologue that would immediately capture the audience's attention. The real Richard Loeb was stabbed to death in prison in 1936. That seemed like an interesting way to start the show. Then I would have the rest of it unfold as one big flashback before returning to that first scene as an epilogue at the very end.

I tried this two different ways. In the first version, the lights would come up on a bloody, naked Richard, alone on the floor of a prison shower, having just been stabbed. Nathan would rush in with a towel, and as Richard lay dying in his arms, they would begin to recount their story.

The scene featured a song called "A Little Boy," which tied into the fact that their victim was indeed "a little boy," but the little boy in this instance was Richard himself. Nathan started the song with the line *"Remember when I met you, as a little boy..."* It was a haunting number, with what I thought was a beautiful, carefully composed melody. But considering the subject matter, I decided that starting with a naked shower scene might have really been pushing it.

In the second version, the prologue started in the prison infirmary where Richard would be discovered lying in bed, near death, as Nathan rushes in to be with him in his final moments. They would still sing "A Little Boy," and from there, the flashback plot would begin.

But neither of these prologues seemed to work for me. I kept weighing the pros and cons of whether we should know that Richard was already dead before the show even started. I decided that the answer to that was "no."

A courtroom scene as the verdict was announced seemed like a possibility. A *clichéd* one. I wanted something unexpected. But what?

I finally wrote a draft that had no prologue at all, but ended with a short epilogue in which Nathan, about a decade later, learned that Richard was killed. This was conveyed through a monologue he spoke as he listened to an unseen warden who gave him the information. The capper was when he mused that Richard probably engineered it on purpose so that Nathan wouldn't "win."

This would stand in stark contrast to the final version of the script which would end with a mostly triumphant Nathan. At least this epilogue was simple. I went with it for a while, but I knew deep down that my early instinct was right. That first birdwatching scene in the 1920s didn't have enough "oomph." I tried to start the overture with a big musical jolt to compensate, but that was a just a temporary fix.

I promised myself that I would eventually come up with a new prologue and a way to tie the whole show together. I just had to wait for the inspiration to hit. It took a while, but I ultimately landed on a prologue that was centered on Nathan's 1958 parole hearing.

The real Nathan Leopold wrote a book in which he detailed his long quest for parole, so it seemed fitting that I take my cue from Leopold himself. I decided that the young actor playing Nathan would also appear as "Older Nathan," just by a change in his posture or vocal tone, and would address an unseen Parole Board to plead his case. Then the story would unfold from there.

But it would be more than just a prologue and an epilogue, this would become the through-line of the entire show. As I first wrote it, Older Nathan had three separate monologues to the board, one at the beginning, one in the middle, and one at the end which culminated with his actual parole.

I later felt that pattern was a little obvious, so to make it more surprising, I eventually added a fourth. In these monologues, he conveyed both the questions and the answers—like when an actor does a telephone call in a play.

It focused the show more squarely on Nathan's point of view. He was now unquestionably the "me" in *Thrill Me*. Richard would now be a presence that only existed in Older Nathan's mind as he told the Parole Board his story.

In basic dramatic terms, Nathan became the protagonist while Richard was clearly the antagonist. Much better than two protagonists or two antagonists—depending how you looked at it. This also gave the character of Older Nathan a very clear objective: he wants out of prison. That's what we writers call "stakes."

If I could pull it off, I hoped this would give the audience something to "root for." It would also be a great opportunity for an actor to take on the challenge of playing the same person at two different ages.

This meant that the first scene with the Parole Board needed a new song for Nathan (as Older Nathan). Goodbye to "A Little Boy." This was going to be a challenge. I certainly didn't want him to just sing "let me out!" But I also didn't want to wait and have "Everybody Wants Richard," which Nathan would sing in the next scene, set it 1924, as the first song. I've always felt that singing should be established as early as possible in a musical. He *had* to sing in the prologue.

For my original attempt at this, "Everybody Wants Richard" was expanded and re-written so that Older Nathan started singing it to the Parole Board. Then the lights would change, the song would get faster, and he would transform into young Nathan and then continue the song in the new context. But this meant Nathan and Richard's first scene would have to be radically changed, and I was so pleased with how it unfolded that I hated to alter it.

Still, I tried it this way for a while, but I eventually wrote a new song called "Why," which used the melody of "A Little Boy." It was a response to a question from the Parole Board. I felt that it effectively set up what was to come, and was a good way to lead us into the 1920s flashback that would take place in Jackson Park.

* * *

After the Jackson Park scene with Nathan and Richard came the first crime to be depicted in *Thrill Me*, the arson scene. It featured the seduction song, "Nothing Like a Fire." I had originally put a long musical interlude within it. I described that it was where Nathan and Richard were to "get intimate."

Fearing that someday there might be a truly vulgar interpretation, I took it out. As the song exists today, there is hardly time for anything "intimate" to happen within the confines of the music. Though the more prurient among us may disagree, I think it was for the best.

Originally there were to be two versions of the title song. Richard would have a version about how he is thrilled by crime; Nathan would have a version about how he is thrilled by Richard. Then the two songs would very cleverly intertwine in an exciting musical tour de force. Oh, how thrilling it would sound at its climax! Well…it didn't work out that way. I realized that "Nothing Like a Fire" was essentially already Richard's "thrill song" and anything else would have been redundant.

One story that I came across many times while researching *Thrill Me* was about how the real Leopold & Loeb broke in to Loeb's fraternity house and stole a typewriter. So I wrote a scene where they came back from having just stolen it. Thus, returning from this robbery represented a second crime.

It led into a song that was called "We Signed a Contract." In it, they sang about how the fraternity full of "snobbery" deserved the "robbery," and then revealed the terms of a contract that they had *previously* created at some point in the past. It filled in important information, but since it was reiterating something that had supposedly already happened, it didn't have forward movement. That was a problem.

As I continued working it out on paper, I found yet another issue. Two scenes in a row were about a crime of some kind. I knew that I wanted to have a scene where they plot the murder to come soon after, and I felt it should specifically follow a crime.

But I didn't want to have *three* different crimes at this point in the show. I also had to get to the scene with the very important title song to fit in somewhere. Ugh! It was a challenging puzzle.

Finally, I had to drop the idea of them arriving with the stolen typewriter. Instead I had Nathan just mention how he remembered Richard had stolen it in the past. So that freed me to create a new sequence of scenes after the first crime ("Nothing Like a Fire"). The scene that immediately followed the fire contained a new song called "A Written Contract."

In this version of the song they actually *create* their "sex in exchange for crimes" contract on the typewriter. That was clearly how it should have been all along. It was no longer a song about something that had occurred beforehand. Now it actually dramatized a key element of the story.

I also felt that the onstage use of the typewriter itself would add variety and visual interest. For obvious theatrical reasons, what was merely a verbal contract between the real Leopold & Loeb became a blood-signed physical document for my Nathan and Richard.

Next came a scene that depicted them coming back from the robbery of a neighbor's house (now the second crime). It led into the title song. The original version of "Thrill Me—the song" had very sexually suggestive language. I eventually toned it down considerably.

This was followed by the scene where they plot the murder ("The Plan"). I wanted Richard's lyrics for this song to be as gruesome as I could possibly make them. But the music, while still in a minor key, would be jaunty, light, and almost cheerful.

Here would be the point when the audience starts to realize that Richard is serious and dangerous. As *Nathan* realizes this, the tone of the entire musical shifts and the plot starts moving forward much faster. I used to call it "the runaway train moment."

In "The Plan," Richard first suggests his younger brother as the victim. In 1994, before there was an internet (or I guess I should say before there was an internet in *my* apartment), it was very difficult for me to figure out if that brother, Tommy Loeb, was still alive. If he was, I felt it would be disrespectful to use his name in a such a dark, yet semi-humorous way, by calling him out as the potential victim of his brother, the notorious killer.

So I decided to essentially create a fictional younger brother named John. The moniker was based on the name of John Levinson, one of the potential "random kids" that fit the profile Leopold & Loeb created after deciding it wasn't a good idea to kill Tommy.

Not only did this solve the problem of possibly infringing on Tommy Loeb's privacy, but it gave me many more options for rhymes in the song. It would have been very different if I had to use the name "Tommy," or even just "my brother." I later discovered that Tommy Loeb had died in 1991 at the age of seventy-seven, and I also learned that Tommy himself actually had a son named John—so it all ended up *sort of* accurate. There was a John Loeb after all!

The real Leopold & Loeb ended up coming upon young Bobby Franks on that fateful day. He, sadly, became their victim. In *Thrill Me*, Bobby Franks would be unseen but referred to in the scene preceding the murder as if he was there. In some publications that I read, Bobby was referred to as a "distant cousin" of the real Richard Loeb.

I decided very early that it wasn't necessary to include that fact in the script. I thought it would introduce an unnecessary association. The most important fact was that Bobby was indeed a *random* victim.

Years later I would discover that the Franks and Loeb families were actually not really related at all. They shared relatives in common by marriage, but had no blood between them. The families had no connection to each other aside from living in the same neighborhood. The reporting in 1924 never boasted headlines like "Loeb! Kills! Cousin!" or anything like that. So I know I ended up making the right decision in that regard.

For Richard's next song (eventually titled "Roadster"), in which he lures the unseen victim into a car to meet his fate, I did a total juxtaposition of "The Plan." This time, I made the music very dramatic, driving, and almost frightening. But Richard's lyrics weren't scary or murderous at all, just innocuous words about his car.

I initially planned to set the song during a storm to make it more atmospheric, with the music punctuated by thunder. But this would have meant that an umbrella would have probably been required on stage—that would have added a complication. And if the lyrics were about getting the victim into the car to escape the rain, I felt that it would have made it too easy for Richard. The moment needed *tension*. So no musicalized thunder.

To make it more exciting for the character of Richard, and enticing for the victim, I altered a real-life fact. Instead of the basic rented vehicle that the real Leopold & Loeb used in conjunction with the crime, I turned it into Richard's personal shiny Packard roadster. Somehow that just seemed appropriate.

* * *

The entire first half was quite easy for me to write. All I had to do was follow the facts about the relationship and the murder, which all pretty much happened between Nathan and Richard *alone*.

And because of that, no one could ever assess how accurate I might have been in their dialogue. No one else was in the room. Maybe I was right on the money, maybe not even close. But it all worked dramatically.

Dramatizing the events *after* the murder wouldn't be as easy. At this point, in real life, there were police investigations, arrests, upset families, lawyers, reporters, a trial, etc. It was harder to make the story unfold with just Nathan and Richard themselves on stage.

So, for the second half, I had to make a lot of adjustments. I adapted the true facts in such a way that I could keep the story moving while it was being told only through scenes between Nathan and Richard. That meant switching things around, and reconceiving a story element here and there.

I tried to use the fact that after they were caught in real life, they each implicated the other as the one who actually did the hands-on committing of the murder. I worked on a song where they separately pondered *"If I implicate him..."* But it brought everything to a standstill because Nathan and Richard were just sullenly singing their internal thoughts.

Fully dramatizing the plot point would have meant either more unseen characters or yet another argument between the two of them. No matter what I wrote, it got me nowhere—because no matter who did what, they were *both* guilty. So in the end, it didn't seem important enough to keep working on. And that aspect of the story never became part of *Thrill Me.*

Instead, I created a song called "I'm Trying to Think." It was originally a solo for Nathan, sung to an unseen police officer. It was meant to counterbalance Richard's solo, "Roadster," which was sung to the unseen victim. But I felt I could make it into a stronger moment.

So I changed it into a back-and-forth duet with Richard coaching Nathan on what to say to the cops. This wasn't like anything else in the show. I felt that it really helped reveal more aspects of the characters and their relationship.

It also gave the actors more to "play with." I've seen versions where the actor playing Nathan mimics Richard's voice and mannerisms as he repeats back the commands, and other versions where Richard instead imitates Nathan's voice and mannerisms as he sings his instructions to him. Either way, it works.

As I worked toward the conclusion of the script, I decided to take a pretty significant liberty. It was regarding the real Nathan Leopold's infamous eyeglasses, which had been dropped right at the scene of the crime.

In real life, the finding of them is what eventually led the police straight to Leopold, and by extension, Loeb. If those glasses were never found (or never dropped in the first place), they very likely might have gotten away with the crime. But as it happened, those glasses helped send them to prison.

In my version, it would be revealed at the end that Nathan actually left his glasses at the murder scene *on purpose,* so he could ensure that he and Richard's fate would be forever entwined. Even in prison...or worse. Though I made all of that up myself, it was at least based on the possibility that it *could* have happened that way.

After all, no one could ever know what was going on in the mind of the real Nathan Leopold. Maybe he dropped them on purpose, maybe he didn't. But I figured the idea would make a wonderful surprise ending, and help the show feel more like a "thriller."

Despite what they might have been like in real life, I had conceived Richard as a dominant narcissist and Nathan as his submissive hanger-on. We think poor Nathan was led down the horrible path by Richard. But Nathan, due to his eyeglass scheme, ends up being the true sadistic mastermind after all, duping Richard. The manipulator would become the manipulated.

By turning the tables in this final reveal, I felt that audiences might leave the theatre mostly remembering being fooled by the "twist." My thought was that it would cushion the horror of watching the story of two murderers. And that would be a good thing.

When it was time to put together this ending of the show, along with the song "Life Plus Ninety-Nine Years," I sure had a lot of fun. I put myself in Nathan's shoes as he metaphorically stuck the knife in Richard's back. It probably took me less than forty-five minutes to write the first rough version of the song.

* * *

In my first pass at both the dialogue and the lyrics, I figured that since the real Leopold & Loeb were prodigies, I should use "big words" to make them sound smart. This was most apparent in "Everybody Wants Richard." I had Nathan declare to Richard that *"You live amongst a faceless multitude, lacking those who share your aptitude."*

Ultimately, I realized that lyrics like that were just too hard for the listener to comprehend. The characters needed to just sound like normal people, so the lyric became *"You've played around with lots of losers, who ended up as cheats and users."* Simpler, right?

Early on I also wrote a lot of dialogue about sado-masochistic (or master-slave) games between the two of them. This was based on the fantasies that Leopold had about Loeb in real life. I put all of this in because I really wanted to be provocative. But I felt it ended up making the characters seem too sexually sophisticated and much more mature than what I thought 1920s teenagers would be like.

Accordingly, I took most of this content out because I wanted my Nathan and Richard to feel like real young guys of the time. But a few remnants of this remained in the script, and those remnants are still there to this day. If anyone ever wondered about the meaning of lines such as "You'll enjoy a little pain" and "But that's what you like, isn't it?" and the song lyric *"But I told myself that this was all a game"*—well, now you know.

I also went back and forth with the use of profanity in the dialogue. There was a draft that was laced with it, and a draft that had none (did I think that would make the material somehow G-rated?). Ultimately, in the final version, I used four-letter words judiciously. But never in lyrics, because I've always felt that they sound too jarring in songs.

And, when toying with various possibilities, I had a draft where the characters were known only as Nathan and Richard, with no mention of their last names. The time period and location was intentionally vague. Even Bobby Franks would be referred to in the song "Superior" as *"a nameless kid with no face"* and in another draft as *"a useless kid with no name."* Well…that was a series of dumb ideas, and they didn't last long.

* * *

Many of my ideas, however, *did* make the cut. Throughout the script I decided to put in a few specific character-defining touches. For example, "Babe" was a nickname given to the real Nathan Leopold by his family, and it was used by just about everyone. But in *Thrill Me*, I thought it would be more effective if "Babe" was more of a private nickname given to Nathan by Richard, which he would deploy strategically. Nathan would melt whenever he heard it, and it would cause him to lower his defenses. Thus, Richard would know exactly when to call him "Nathan" and when to call him "Babe."

As for the real Richard Loeb's nickname, "Dickie," which he was often called, I just couldn't give that name to a character. To me it made him seem juvenile. Using the more formal "Richard" would definitely be a better choice for my version of him.

I chose to make Richard more of the Nietzsche fan, who introduces the concept of their supposed superiority to Nathan, though in real life it very well may have been the other way around. The switch would better define the differences between the two, and make Richard clearly the leader in the relationship, while Nathan would appear to be the follower.

But to give Richard a little sympathy, and perhaps a bit of jealousy towards Nathan, I drew occasional attention to Nathan's close relationship with his "dad," while clearly giving Richard animosity against his "father." This was loosely inspired by the real-life fact that, unlike the senior Mr. Leopold, the then-ill Mr. Loeb was unable to attend the trial. This caused speculation in the press that he may have simply refused to be there.

There were a few other plot alterations that true Leopold & Loeb aficionados would surely notice. For example, to make it easier to follow, I streamlined the sequence of all the various schools they attended, and the timeline of Older Nathan's parole quest.

I also switched one of the three murder weapons. Along with acid and rope, a chisel was used by the real Leopold & Loeb. Although their intention was to use it as a bludgeon, just the sound of the word, and the thought of what was *usually* done with a chisel and its sharp edge seemed so grisly to me. So the chisel became a crowbar.

Immediately after the murder, my Nathan and Richard retreat back to Richard's bedroom to type the phony ransom note. When in reality, Leopold & Loeb literally went out for hot dogs and root beer! I couldn't have even begun to imagine how *that* would have played on stage.

But for the most part, I kept everything at least in the *spirit* of historical fact. Sometimes people would question why I "changed" the actual story. Well, I didn't go back in time and alter history. I merely *dramatized* it—because I was (and still am) a dramatist. Not a biographer. Not a documentarian.

* * *

When all was said and done, I completed the first draft in about six weeks. This draft had no "My Glasses/Just Lay Low," which would eventually be a big dramatic number depicting Nathan and Richard on telephones. Instead, there was a brief Nathan solo simply titled "My Glasses." It had actually first started life as a ballad called "Loyalty," sung in a slightly different context. But that version never actually made it in.

There was also no actual "Ransom Note" song. But, once it was written, it was sung to the same melody as "The Plan" because in both songs Richard is creating diabolical instructions. This would continue a thematic throughline of repetition for Richard, since his "Roadster" and "Keep Your Deal with Me" songs also shared a melody. In the former, he's luring the victim; in the latter, he's "luring" Nathan. And Richard's climactic jail cell song, "Afraid," was the farthest thing from my mind at that point.

However, some songs that appeared in the draft such as "Nothing Like a Fire," "The Plan," "Superior," and "Life Plus Ninety-Nine Years," were very close to what would ultimately be their final versions. Only a few early lyrics of these were ever changed.

There would certainly be many revisions made as the life of *Thrill Me* progressed. But that first draft I wrote in such a short period is pretty close to the same script being performed today. And I'm still as proud of it now as I was then. But, needless to say, writing it was only the first step on what would prove to be long and winding road to an actual theatre.

2

DEVELOPMENTAL THRILLS

"Who's in control now? / Who's got resources?"

You get the idea now. That's a lyric from the show with a meaning that's thematically relevant to this chapter. Clever, right? From here on out the lyric quotes should be self-explanatory. Anyway…

I now had what I believed to be a producible musical. Now came the hard part—getting it produced. The theatre company that had done the workshop of *Most Men Are* was no longer in business. And, since I didn't think *Thrill Me* would be appropriate in a festive cabaret showroom, my contacts from *One Foot Out the Door* wouldn't be helpful.

So I needed to find either an independent producer who had (or could get) the funds to rent a theatre and put it on, or a theatre company willing to present it in their own space. Even getting it *read* in the first place would be a challenge.

But before any of that could be attempted, I had to at least hear the script out loud in voices other than the ones in my head. So the first thing I did was personally put on a non-staged reading of *Thrill Me* for a small invited audience. This was the version without the prologue—only the short epilogue.

The reading was held at the Dramatists Guild, the trade organization for playwrights, composers, and lyricists—of which I was a member. Their offices were located right above Sardi's, the storied New York restaurant that was famous for its celebrity caricatures. Located right in the heart of Broadway on 44th Street, it was not too far from my apartment.

In the Guild's beautiful lounge room, I played the score on a grand piano once owned by legendary composer Richard Rodgers. *Richard Rodgers!* The man who literally invented the modern musical, along with lyricist Oscar Hammerstein II. He wrote the music of *Oklahoma!*, *Carousel*, *South Pacific*, and *The King and I*, among others. And here I was playing *his* piano, this "kid" from Kansas City. It was totally surreal.

On the strength of the well-received reading, I had a demo recording of the score made. The first version was highlights only. But later, with a partial grant from the ASCAP Leonard Bernstein Composers Fund, most of the rest of the score (as it existed at that point) was added.

I commissioned a set of orchestrations for the demo, which were performed on a synthesizer. They were fine, but I worried that they made the show sound too large. And the drums were totally wrong— much too "razzmatazz." These orchestrations were never used again. *Thrill Me* seemed to "want" to be a piano-only musical.

* * *

There came a point when I took a brief break from *Thrill Me* to write a musical adaptation of Jules Verne's *Journey to the Center of the Earth*. It was commissioned by that previously mentioned professional children's theatre in my hometown. There was even a song in *Journey* that used a melody that I had first written for *Thrill Me* (shhh!).

I went to Kansas City to be on hand for the rehearsals. It was so much fun seeing the show produced at the place where I got my start. I had left that theatre as a teenager, and came back as a professional myself. Even though they were now producing my script, I felt like I was just a kid again among the theatre's staff. They had all watched me grow up.

While it was certainly nice to visit home, my first priority was to leave the quick foray into children's theatre behind and continue to focus on my "grownup" work. I couldn't wait to get back to New York, where Leopold & Loeb would be metaphorically ready to welcome me.

* * *

After some refinements, it was time for a *staged* reading of *Thrill Me*. I rented a nearby Manhattan studio to serve as the rehearsal and performance space. Since I felt quite confident, a much larger audience was invited. Seeing it "on its feet" for the first time gave me a few new ideas that I incorporated into certain scenes to make them stronger. But otherwise, the reading proved to me that the script was ready to be sent out.

My agent, Ron Gwiazda, who had represented me since *One Foot Out the Door* at the beginning of *both* of our careers, began submitting scripts and cassettes to various theatres and producers. We both crossed our fingers and hoped they would take a look and a listen. Thankfully, the submissions were very well-received for the most part. Feedback was always good.

But it was clearly apparent that no one was brave enough to actually take *Thrill Me* on. It was heartbreaking for me at first, but I didn't stop trying. Eventually a few prospects popped up, but nothing ever really panned out.

An Off-Broadway theatre group in New York was interested in putting on a modest developmental reading. It was to be part of a program that they were regularly doing at the time. Unfortunately, the terms and conditions didn't sit right with me.

In a meeting, their intended director pointed out that in real life Richard Loeb tempted the victim by discussing a fancy tennis racket, and not by the promise of seeing a fancy car as I had written in Richard's song. Yeah, I knew that. She actually insisted that I would need to rewrite the lyrics to make it "accurate." It's just my opinion, but something like *"Can we talk about your racket?"* would have been a really unusual way to start the song in question.

And she was just getting started! I could only assume that requests for the hot dog and the root beer would be coming next. So I decided to decline the offer. Did she think she was going to direct a documentary? Apparently, she never heard of dramatic license.

I also talked to the artistic director of a very small theatre company in Manhattan. He was interested in presenting *Thrill Me* as some kind of special event or fundraiser. Unfortunately, we were never able to make it happen.

Ron got the idea to send the material to the prestigious Manhattan Theatre Club (MTC), a major not-for-profit theatre company in New York. They had produced many notable Off-Broadway shows—several of which moved to Broadway, such as *Ain't Misbehavin'* and *Love! Valour! Compassion!* After MTC's director of musical development read it and listened to the demo, he asked Ron to set up a meeting with me. I was extremely excited. I figured he must have been interested in some way, or why would he want to meet?

I went to his office in midtown. It had stacks and stacks of scripts piled high on a desk and practically falling out of the surrounding shelves. He was as nice as he could be, and was very complimentary of my work. But almost immediately he questioned the entire concept of *Thrill Me* being a "two-hander," the industry term for a two-character show. He asked why I didn't want to tell a bigger story. He suggested that I add more characters, such as Clarence Darrow, police, and perhaps even members of the Leopold & Loeb families.

While I was sure that he was attempting to be helpful, his suggestions simply weren't my vision. I was dead set on an unencumbered story that focused squarely on the two main characters and nothing else. Though it might have been vaguely implied, it's not like he promised that if I wrote this new interpretation then Manhattan Theatre Club would be interested in producing it, or even in seriously considering it. I frankly didn't know why I was there.

But I thanked him profusely. Then I went straight home and reported everything back to Ron. I made it clear to him that *Thrill Me* would remain a "two-hander." MTC was clearly not the break we had both hoped for.

* * *

A significant opportunity arose in 1997. The Dramatists Guild asked me to submit *Thrill Me* to be considered for their Musical Theatre Development Program. The program had been founded by the great Broadway composer-lyricist Stephen Sondheim many years earlier.

Each year, it gave creators of three musicals a professional mentor, free rehearsal space at the Guild, and various other resources. The writers would assemble their own director, cast, and any necessary musicians. This would all then culminate in a modest staged reading of the show in front of a group of Broadway writers and composers. They would give their very valuable expert opinions and critiques.

A few months later, after all the many applications were considered, I was informed that an esteemed panel, including Sondheim himself, chose the three winners. *Thrill Me* was among them. I was now a member of the program.

The professional mentor assigned to me was Martin Charnin, the renowned director/lyricist of the musical *Annie*. Coincidentally, I had attended the opening night of the first Broadway revival of *Annie* the night before I met him! At our meeting, Martin really seemed to "take" to the material. His interest seemed to be far outside the scope of a mentor.

By the time I got home from that meeting, Martin had called Ron's office and told him he wanted to option the script to produce and direct himself after the program was finished. This was pretty much one of the most exciting things to ever happen to me at that point, and the first major break for *Thrill Me*.

One of the very first national touring productions I had ever seen was *Annie* when I was in Junior High, and now I was about to start working with its creator! Junior-High-Stephen would have never believed it.

Several weeks later, as Martin closely watched, the official Dramatists Guild staged reading ended up being a very successful showcase of the musical. In fact, it couldn't have gone better. Not long afterward, Ron and I went to the office of Martin's lawyer to finally sign the formal option papers. I was paid five hundred dollars up front, which felt like five million. I couldn't believe I had finally made *any* money from *Thrill Me*.

* * *

Once Martin and I began officially working together, we had several meetings in his Park Avenue apartment. His office had a shelf full of his many awards, and a long wall covered all the way across from top to bottom with framed window cards (posters) from the shows that he had been associated with in one way or another. At the end of the room was an oversized photograph of Martin in his onstage days as the character "Big Deal" in the original production of *West Side Story*. It would be fair to say that I was a bit star-struck every time I was there.

As we went over and over the script, Martin would occasionally propose cuts or make small suggestions which were generally quite helpful. For example, he assured me that the term "mafia" was not in use in 1924, but "the mob" was. I took his word for it. So in the song "Superior," I had to change *"And we're far more efficient than the mafia"* to *"And we're far more efficient than the mob is, Babe."* It was also around this point when I added in Older Nathan's monologues for the Parole Board scenes.

After a few months Martin decided it was time to do another reading of *Thrill Me*. It would be mostly private with just a few close confidants in attendance. While preparing for it, Martin shocked me by requesting that we try doing the Parole Board scenes with actual onstage actors and a separate performer as Older Nathan.

Like any theatre writer, I couldn't be *forced* to change my script. But Martin's request was sincerely made, and there was no ultimatum. So, in the spirit of cooperation, I went ahead and turned all of the monologues into dialogue—just as a test. Thankfully, Martin didn't ask for an actual onstage "Clarence Darrow" like the guy at MTC did.

After the reading, Martin was encouraged. He envisioned producing a small version of the show first, with the hope of a transfer to a larger venue. We looked at several little theatres in New York City, but he never made a commitment.

A short time later, Martin was obligated to go to London to direct yet another revival of *Annie*. Once there, he told me that he decided it would be better to stage the show in London first before moving it to New York. It was frustrating for me because sometimes it seemed like months would go by without a word from him.

But every now and then he would send me information about venues he'd been scouting. One was the King's Head, which was London's oldest pub theatre (that literally means a theatre within a pub), and another was the then relatively new Jermyn Street Theatre, a small space in the heart of the West End. Martin would also share various budgets for the show that had been drawn up.

When he got back to New York, he decided to produce and direct another reading of *Thrill Me*. It would ultimately be the fifth one overall. Martin invited many of his colleagues and industry contacts. I made sure several of my friends would be there to support me. We sent out invitations that Martin had designed to look like ransom notes with all the letters appearing to have been cut out of magazines and newspapers. He was clearly very enthusiastic.

This time Martin had even bigger thoughts regarding the onstage three-member Parole Board. Now he wanted them all to have a *dual* role—each with their own private scene with Older Nathan, who was still to be a separate actor. As if that wasn't enough, he also wanted them to have their own group song. Since I'd agreed the first time, a can of worms had now been opened.

Martin knew I was reluctant, but he asked me to at least try it. He reminded me that *all* of the 1920s Nathan and Richard scenes, which were the real crux of the piece, would still remain completely intact. So I *very* grudgingly wrote new scenes that took place "in the present" to be interspersed throughout.

The first was with a publisher offering Older Nathan a book deal that he refused. The second was with a young lawyer to whom Older Nathan actually sang an early version of "Why" in the middle of the show (this was back when "Everybody Wants Richard" started in the first Parole Board scene.) The third was with a photographer for *Life* magazine. As the Parole Board, the three of them were even given a scene where they sang a song called "Point of View"—the less said about that, the better.

These additional scenes really padded out the story of Older Nathan, which I didn't think improved anything, they just made the show more convoluted. *Much* more. And it wasn't my vision. Older Nathan just didn't interest me the way he clearly interested Martin.

I couldn't confidently endorse my own musical if it had substantial scenes in it that were based on someone else's ideas. Sure, I *wrote* them myself. But they were scenes that I didn't even like. Constructive suggestions were one thing, but all of this went way beyond that.

So I promised myself that—barring some earthshattering revelation—once the reading was finished, I would remove everything peripheral and restore the script back to my original two-character intention. There would be nothing Martin could do to stop me. I had to take back control.

This was something I personally found very important. I knew if I was lucky enough for the show to make it to the stage, being *collaborative* would be essential. So, moving forward, whenever there was anything I could legitimately *control*—such as the actual material and other overall decisions, I seized the opportunity.

Unfortunately, after the reading, Martin was slow to get anything happening. In the meantime, West Coast Ensemble, a Los Angeles-based theatre company, wanted to do a small production. They had been sent the two-character script by Ron months earlier.

Since Martin now held the exclusive rights, it could only be done with his permission. When he and the theatre couldn't come to an agreement, which likely included a stipulation that Martin had to direct it himself, it all fell apart.

As it ended up, Martin was never actually able to put his own production together. Eventually, his option expired and the rights reverted back to me. While I was thankful for all he had done, I wasn't exactly heartbroken to no longer be working with him. But I wondered if I'd ever get such an opportunity again.

By that point *Thrill Me* had been a part of my life for five years. But with no other leads on the horizon, the script—now back in its two-character format—went into the proverbial "drawer" for a while. It was time for me to move on to other projects.

* * *

Around this period, I was contacted by various rights holders about writing musical versions of the book *The Fan*, which had also been made into a slasher film starring Lauren Bacall; the novel *The Man Who Fell to Earth*, which was the basis of a sci-fi drama starring David Bowie; and the movie *Homicidal*, which was directed by William ·Castle—and was basically a rip-off of *Psycho*.

I was always flattered to be asked, so I dabbled for a bit. But my heart was in none of these. I wanted to work on something of *my own*. So I decided to tackle another true piece of the darker side of American history, this time set in the 1930s.

I titled my new musical *Panic*. It told the behind-the-scenes story of the infamous *War of the Worlds* radio broadcast. I put on a few readings, recorded some demos, and continued to work on it as the 1990s came to end and a new century began. But I had to pause when a huge opportunity fell in my lap—practically out of nowhere.

I was commissioned by a Tony and Grammy Award-winning producer to write a Broadway musical! This was an offer I couldn't refuse. It was to be about a then-current celebrity-turned-politician, from whom the producer had purchased his "life rights."

What an adventure that was, to say the least. I was interviewed by *Variety* and *The New York Times*. I taped a segment for *Good Morning America*. I was featured on the *NBC Nightly News*—the national version! And I was even invited to a few of the producer's star-studded parties, where I stood at the buffet line alongside everyone from Sidney Poitier to Henry Winker.

Frustratingly, getting the required approval on every word of the script and every note of the music from the subject of the show proved to be far more difficult than anyone initially assumed. I was told that the situation grew untenable for the producer, who remained squarely in my corner and told me that he was very pleased with my work. My final required draft of the musical was turned in, but the show never went into production.

* * *

During all of this, *Thrill Me* was never far from my mind, and it remained my true passion. I never stopped believing that if I could just get it in front of an audience, it would be successful. I felt it in every fiber of my being. And because of that, it wouldn't take long for that "drawer" to be opened once again.

3

THRILL ME'S FIRST TRIAL

*"Now our lives will be entwined completely. /
Our friendship's now redefined, rethought, and revised."*

In 2002, I met Jim Kierstead. He was a very ambitious aspiring theatre producer. Jim would eventually win Tony, Emmy, and Olivier awards for producing. But at this point he was looking for his first real project. I told him about my previous musicals, and then about *Thrill Me*, which piqued his interest almost immediately. That was when I opened the drawer again! He read the script, listened to the score, and told me that he loved it. It really seemed to "speak to him" and was very much in line with his tastes.

Right around this time, we read about the Fourth Annual Midtown International Theatre Festival in New York City. It seemed like a good prospect to get the show on stage under the auspices of an established organization. Applications were being accepted for the festival's 2003 summer run at the Abingdon Theatre Complex on West 36th Street. Jim filled out the forms and formally submitted the script.

We waited for what seemed like forever, but finally Jim got the word that *Thrill Me* was accepted. We were given a slot to do six performances that July in the Abingdon's tiny fifty-seat black box theatre, which I thought would be perfect for the show. I actually couldn't believe it. After years of disappointments, the show would finally make it to the stage in just a matter of months. Now came the rush to put it all together.

The first step was to find a director. Ron, ever the agent, suggested a few of his clients and we had serious discussions with one of them,

36

whom I was very enthusiastic about. Having told Jim the entire story about Martin Charnin and his unrealized plans, we wondered if *he* might be interested in directing this version of the show.

It certainly was a long shot. Martin previously had an option to produce it, and essentially be in full charge. But this opportunity would solely be a directing gig. Would he be willing to just be a member of the team?

I contacted Martin to test the waters. He was interested. He told me that he still thought fondly of the material. I made sure he understood, however, that *Thrill Me* was back to being a two-character show, and in no uncertain terms would that change. He said he was fine with it—I believed that he *knew* I was right all along on that front. I also thought he must have believed that there could be more in store for *Thrill Me* than just the Midtown Festival, and he was potentially being offered a second chance to be a part of something bigger.

He and Jim had discussions, and Jim told me that he felt that it would be more interesting to work with Martin than with the other potential director. But the decision was ultimately mine. Remembering a few moments of conflict with Martin, I wasn't sure.

In terms of the actual directing, I felt that with such a small stage space and limited resources, either of the two choices would do a capable job. One would probably be easier to work with, the other more challenging. You can probably guess who was who. But the one thing Martin had going for him was that he was well known in the theatre industry. And *that* could potentially bring us publicity.

Every single show in the festival would be fighting for press. With Martin on board, we believed it would likely be easier to get coveted mentions in newspapers round-up stories about the festival, and perhaps even feature articles on websites like *Playbill* and *Theatermania*.

I also thought Martin's name might help attract critics—whom the festival could not otherwise promise would attend. I knew that garnering (hopefully) good reviews would be crucial for the future of the show. With that in mind, I crossed my fingers and chose Martin Charnin.

I was right about the publicity. *Thrill Me* was one of only a few shows mentioned in nearly every feature written about the festival. Journalists apparently couldn't resist the story about how the man who created the hit musical about Annie—the red-headed young orphan, was now working on a show about Leopold & Loeb—the cold-blooded young murderers.

We even got a very substantial segment on the popular NY1 network television show *On Stage*. They showed rehearsal footage along with on-camera interviews with Martin, Jim, and myself. It was a major coup, and it helped ticket sales significantly.

* * *

But before all of the publicity happened, our next task was to cast the show. The actors who had played the parts in the final readings a few years earlier now were regularly working on Broadway and wouldn't be available. So Jim put out a casting call in *Backstage* newspaper, and booked audition space at Ripley Greer Studios, which wasn't far from my apartment.

While the turnout was a little smaller than we had hoped, several talented guys auditioned. For Nathan, a young actor named Christopher Totten impressed us immediately. Chris sang like an angel, was totally adorable, and read the scenes from the show almost perfectly. He didn't know it yet, but he was definitely going to be our Nathan.

The problem was finding a Richard. No one seemed right. The closest candidate was an actor with dirty blonde, curly hair, who paired nicely with Chris, and gave a good first audition. I think Martin was sold on him. But at his final callback, I realized that just about everything he did had a bit of a country twang to it.

Though my exact memory is a bit foggy, his audition song was probably something from *Big River*, the Huckleberry Finn musical. And when he was asked to sing another song, it might have been something like a bluegrass ballad. I just had a very hard time picturing him as a wannabe lawyer from Chicago. So he was out, and we had no one.

I believe Martin made a few calls to some agents he knew, and an actor named Matthew S. Morris was recommended to come to our very final callback session. He was good. Handsome, with an aloof, devilish quality that we all felt was right for the part. When Matthew read a few scenes with the very warm and open Chris, they had a great contrast and a suitable chemistry. They were soon offered the roles. My Nathan and Richard were finally about to come to life.

* * *

Because I enjoyed dabbling with graphic art on my computer, Jim agreed that I could design the logo for the show. I based it on a design that had earlier been created by my friend, Jim Story Jr., as artwork for the demo recording. It featured the shadowy naked torsos of two men embracing. They were rendered in tones of black and grey with the title of the show presented in blood-red, all lowercase letters, in an antique typewriter font. When looking at it, you almost felt like a voyeur peering at the men through a window.

Since the revival of the musical *Chicago* was still a huge hit on Broadway, and the Oscar-winning movie version had recently been released, Jim and I decided to put a tag line at the top which compared the two sets of characters. It read "If you thought Roxie & Velma turned Chicago upside down, wait 'til you meet Nathan & Richard…" I thought it was inspired. Martin liked it too, but he wanted us to reword it a little and make it shorter. We didn't.

After Jim had the posters printed, he hired a professional service to put them up. One day, he surprised me by taking me on a tour of their placements all around the city. I was overwhelmed and extremely grateful to him.

If I do say so myself, my logo looked quite striking on walls and windows everywhere from Times Square to Chelsea to Greenwich Village. One copy was even on the poster wall at Sardi's! And as far as I know, it still remains in their rotating collection to this day.

* * *

One of the last changes I made to the script before we started rehearsing was to take out all references to specific furniture or set pieces. Even though I would be there to express my intentions, I felt that there was no reason not to start setting up the script for potential future productions. So "Nathan grabs a chair" became "Nathan sits" and "Richard is discovered in bed" became "Richard is resting and reclining."

This way, the abstract concept would be more clearly expressed in the text. And it would be apparent that there were practically no actual scenic requirements for *Thrill Me*. I even removed references to any props that weren't absolutely necessary. I wanted no clutter, nothing extraneous.

It's a good thing there wasn't too much required, because pretty much every aspect of the production was DIY. Unable to acquire period-specific candlestick telephones, Jim and I made them ourselves. We used dowel rods, black shoelaces, and other tidbits that we bought from a large craft store.

Jim had to saw the dowels by hand to make them the correct size, which took a lot of time, and was much harder to do than either of us expected. Then, in his backyard, we spray-painted them black and used hot glue and black electrical tape to put them together. Once in use for the show, they constantly needed to be repaired because the mouth pieces didn't want to stay connected. Why didn't we think to just look on eBay for real ones?

The acid bottle was actually vanilla extract that I bought at Williams-Sonoma, the high-end kitchen store. The bottle had an old-fashioned apothecary look to it—which I thought was perfect. The crowbar was really a pry bar that I bought at a hardware store, because I didn't know the difference. And I have no memory of where we got the rope.

Jim bought the typewriter at the Chelsea Flea Market on 23rd Street. It wasn't an Underwood like the one that the real Leopold & Loeb used. It had a very unusual design with high type bars split on each side. They would swing inward to strike the paper, but would often stick together when Chris (as Nathan) was typing—a real pain for him! I would watch him try to separate them as he kept singing. Sorry, Chris.

For some reason, I had always imagined the characters to be costumed in a way that wasn't period-specific, but more stylized. I thought they should wear all black—like turtlenecks and slacks. Sort of dressed as cat burglars. Martin insisted on clothes that looked like traditional 1920s outfits. I had a hard time picturing them that way, but I realized that it made sense. Once I got used to the concept, I liked the look very much.

Jim and I ended up buying most of the costume pieces at Macy's one night after rehearsal when we were so tired, hot, and cranky that it was a miracle we could even see straight. A few pieces were also bought at Daffy's, a discount clothing store on 57th Street. Daffy's just so happened to be on the site of the former Coliseum Books, where I first discovered the story.

Though it may have seemed to be a simple task, it actually wasn't easy finding the perfect ties, vests, suspenders, shirts, or pants that would fit the actors and look appropriate, but we managed. A necktie for Nathan was the final piece we needed. Luckily, street vendors selling neckties on sidewalk tables was something quite ubiquitous in New York in the early 2000s. I ended up finding a decent one for about a dollar!

We had no particular game plan or color scheme in mind. But we ended up with costumes mainly in tones of light grey and beige. They contrasted nicely against the black walls of the theatre.

* * *

Putting together the physical production for the Midtown Festival was a fairly easy task. I wasn't always quite sure Martin had a particular game plan or a vision for the staging. But either he did, or he got lucky, because the show ended up looking fantastic.

Our set was made up of standard-issue theatrical black cubes, which the Abingdon had on hand. They were arranged in a fixed configuration. The blocking looked almost like the actors were moving around and on top of a big black Rubik's Cube. It was very simple, yet very imaginative. The audience would be seated on three sides. The pianist and electric keyboard was positioned within the audience section, which necessitated the removal of a few seats.

There wasn't much by way of lighting equipment. But Thom Weaver, our lighting consultant, made the most of what we had. He wisely added a gobo, which is a little metal plate that goes inside a light, causing it to project a shape onto the stage. In this case, it was the silhouette of prison bars that would be displayed during the Parole Board scenes.

The only bad part was that since we were sharing the theatre with other shows in the festival, the gobo had to be installed before every performance. Then it had to be taken out afterward. Our brave stage manager had to climb a very tall ladder to do it.

* * *

While we were in rehearsal, there was some strategic cutting and editing of the dialogue, but otherwise there were no major changes. That is until Martin and I discussed the Parole Board scenes once again. The script we went into production with had those original monologues spoken by Older Nathan. But Martin strongly felt that it wasn't the right approach and there should be actual voices heard— recorded ones. At least he had given up on actual *people*.

I pushed back a bit. But I eventually came to agree with Martin's conclusion that the scenes would be easier for the audience to grasp if Older Nathan was just answering the questions without having to also relay them. And the voices would give the actor something to play against.

The overall dramatic content would simply be an expansion of what I had written and conceived on my own. So I went ahead and converted the monologues into dialogue that was somewhat similar to what was in the readings from a few years earlier. Though, in hindsight, I guess I could have simply insisted on rewriting the monologues to make them stronger and clearer, but that's not where my head was at the time.

We went to a studio and recorded a Parole Board of three voices. Martin himself was one of them. I'll never forget the hacking cough he added during one of his lines just to make it sound "more real."

While I didn't dislike the finished recording, I lamented that a technical complication was now added. And I've regretted agreeing to it ever since. I had always wanted to keep the show as simple as possible. But suddenly my easy-to-produce, two-character, one-piano musical now required "sound." Not the end of the world, but productions would never be quite as easy as I first envisioned.

Since the recording could theoretically come in early, late, or not at all, there would always be the potential for a snafu. To alleviate this, Chris was required to time his dialogue perfectly because each scene was recorded as one long cue with blank space for him to perform his lines.

With the door already opened, we also added in a recorded voice-over during "My Glasses/Just Lay Low," which I started to refer to as "the telephone song." As it was originally written, Nathan and Richard were to hold large prop newspapers with headlines that cued the various verses of the song. But because we weren't able to create convincing versions of those, the voice of a radio newscaster revealed the discovery of the body, his identification, and finally, the finding of Nathan's glasses.

Sometime in the middle of our rehearsal period, all of us concluded that it would be a good idea for the score to be arranged in such a way that there would be no opportunity for "applause breaks." I knew the audience would applaud the musical numbers by rote at first. But as the show went on, it would get harder and harder for them to keep clapping for murderers.

By never having a musical "button" or a final resolving chord after each song—just the direct flow into the next section of underscoring—the option was taken away completely until the very end. Though I would occasionally observe that some people just couldn't resist the urge to applaud—which made it a bit awkward because the music just kept plowing through. But I still think it was a smart adjustment.

What would end up being a very major component of *Thrill Me* wasn't added in until about three days before we opened. The staging had ended up being very abstract in the black box theatre with black cubes as the only scenery. Because of this, Martin and I worried that the audience may not quite grasp exactly where and when things were taking place, even though the story was told in a linear fashion.

So I added short individual speeches for Nathan as Older Nathan to say to the Parole Board at the end of most scenes. They would essentially set up where the following scene would take place and how much time had passed, along with filling in additional details. Lines like "I met him at the warehouse that night. Richard got so excited when we started the fire. We used Diamond Matches—they always lit on the first strike!" and "We went back to his house...I was shaking the whole way...he got out the Underwood..."

I had to write all of these quickly one night so they could be given to the actors the next morning—as the clock was ticking towards opening. They were initially conceived to be just a series of off-the-cuff, temporary fixes. I thought that there would never be such an *extremely* abstract version again. The plan was to cut them for future productions.

But after one rehearsal with these lines implemented, the musical was unquestionably easier to follow. *Much* easier. Suddenly the fact that the show was from Nathan's point of view was even clearer. And as he told the story to the Parole Board, he was telling the story to the audience—more opportunities to gain their sympathy.

It was the final piece of the puzzle that unified the entire show. I never even revised or rewrote any of those hastily written lines. Not a single word. They became a permanent part of the script.

* * *

Unfortunately, and I hate to have to admit it, I had issues working with Martin that went beyond disagreements about the Parole Board.

Sometimes he was friendly and approachable, other times, in my opinion, he would snap for the strangest reasons. He had what I felt was an inexplicable attitude about treating the whole enterprise as if we were *literally* doing a Broadway show.

I suppose it made sense that he wanted us to all be as professional as possible. I wanted that too. But it *wasn't* a Broadway show. It was a non-union festival production that no one was being paid for. He seemed to think we should be following some set of strict rules and regulations, and adhere to Broadway-style hierarchies.

I remember one afternoon during a break from rehearsal, I asked Chris Totten if he wouldn't mind singing some new lyrics for a verse of "My Glasses/Just Lay Low" that I was toying with unofficially. Suddenly, Martin came in and flew into a rage—at least that was how I perceived it. As he put it, I was "rewriting the show and rehearsing behind his back."

Both were completely untrue. I was doing nothing behind his back—he just didn't happen to be there at the time. There was nothing wrong with my asking an actor to try something during a break. While I was only testing out the new lyrics, and not quite ready to make the change, it was *my* script and *my* score. To put it bluntly, it was my *property* and I had *every right* to rewrite it however I saw fit. Well, Martin's ranting caused me to come very close to pulling the rights entirely or refusing to allow him to continue as director. Jim really had to talk me off the ledge.

Later that day, assumedly having realized he'd overstepped, Martin asked to hear the new verse. I played it for him. Then I told him that I felt it was an improvement and should definitely go in—now that I had thought about it for a while. *"The Herald says they found a pair of glasses. / I think that it's a very scary sign. / They gave it seven paragraphs. / And printed lots of photographs. / The glasses look an awful lot like mine!"* were definitely better, clearer lyrics than *"I'm convinced I must have dropped my glasses. / Somewhere in the woods or on the ground. / I think it's a coincidence, / I hope it's a coincidence. / The Herald says a pair like mine were found!"* Martin agreed and the ordeal was never spoken of again.

I know he loved the show. And as challenging as it was, I would have worked with him again in a heartbeat. If the situation was right.

After he passed away in 2019, Jim and I went to watch the traditional dimming of the Broadway marquee at the theatre where Martin's *Annie* had originally played. I personally wore the necktie that I bought on the street for Chris Totten to wear as Nathan so many years earlier.

As we stood in silence, I mentally thanked Martin for all he had done for *Thrill Me* and for *me*. Difficult as I found him to be sometimes, I think it was all for a reason. He, unwittingly, gave me the resolve to *always* stand up for myself. It made me stronger.

* * *

On July 16, 2003, the very first public performance of *Thrill Me* occurred. It had been nine years since I first began writing it, and my perseverance was finally about to pay off. Before the show, we all gathered together in the lobby of the Abingdon.

For opening night gifts I gave out black varsity jackets and sweatshirts with the red and grey *Thrill Me* logo embroidered on the back. Jim presented everyone with framed *Thrill Me* posters. And Martin—who was actually out of town for the opening—had custom coffee mugs created for the occasion. We all exchanged break-a-leg wishes. Chris and Matthew went to their dressing room as Jim and I went into the theatre.

I was already pleased with the final dress rehearsal earlier that day. I thought the whole thing was really working well. But this would be my first time seeing it with a real audience. I was nervous, but also very excited.

The "Prelude," which was what I titled the short overture, began. The lights dimmed. Chris appeared in his prison uniform. I thought back to what I wanted the audience's experience to be like when I first started writing the script.

The opening night crowd was indeed sitting on the edge of their seats. Barely moving. Riveted for the entire ninety minutes. And while there were no red lights or smoke, it was otherwise nearly exactly as I imagined. The dark humor got the hoped-for laughs, the horrific moments got the desired gasps. Since there had been none throughout, after Chris sang the last words of the finale, the cathartic applause was loud, enthusiastic, and sustained.

To say that I was thrilled beyond belief would be an understatement. It was what I had dreamed of for almost a decade. The difficulties of working with Martin paid off. *Thrill Me* had turned out just as I had always hoped.

I thought back to Manhattan Theatre Club, the "tennis racket" director, all the theatres that sent rejection letters, and I felt totally vindicated. At that moment, I wouldn't have cared if it was the one and only performance of the show ever. I was *that* satisfied.

But there would be at least five more. Due to the festival schedule, the second performance wouldn't be until a few days later. So that meant it was time to clear the space by taking the entire physical production temporarily apart.

It wasn't easy for any show to be part of the Midtown Theatre Festival. There was only a tiny little corner to store our props and electric keyboard. We had to wait for one show to end so we could rush in and set up ours.

Then we had to break everything down after the show in just a few minutes for the next group. This was standard operating procedure for just about any kind of fringe or theatre festival, but it sure caused a lot of stress.

If I recall correctly, the very first published review of *Thrill Me* came out the night before the second performance, which was on a Saturday. It was written by critic Matthew Murray of *Talkin' Broadway*, a very popular and well-read theatre website. While Matthew had a few reservations, it was an undeniably fantastic review.

We had a celebratory lunch at the now long-gone Thalia restaurant on 8th Avenue, not far from my apartment. Jim beamed as he read the entire review out loud to a big group of our friends and families.

This was just one example of what a natural born producer and leader Jim was (and *is*). He treated us all like gold. There were cast parties on his dime, catered lunches, and reassuring, calming words whenever they were needed. Even though it was very small and no-frills, every aspect of the production was as first-rate as he could possibly make it.

Soon more reviews came in, including one by the very popular critic, theatre columnist, and author, Peter Filichia. Peter actually had to leave the show before it was over, so he could rush to another production. But even without knowing how it ended, he raved.

Every performance of the show was sold out almost instantly. And each one had a long waiting list. The head of the festival wanted Jim and me to give up our reserved seats in the back row—comps that we were entitled to as part of the overall agreement—so he could sell them. We refused. After all that hard work, we wanted to be there to enjoy every performance.

To help with the demand for tickets, the Abingdon started squeezing in a few extra chairs at our performances. One was even behind a column—offering only an obstructed view. Then after a lot of finagling with everyone's availability, we added an extra matinee performance. Once it was publicized, it practically sold out within hours.

There also would have been a second added performance. The festival wanted to actually cancel someone else's show, which hadn't sold many tickets, and put *Thrill Me* in their slot instead. When the creator of that show personally called Jim and begged him not to accept the offer, this second additional performance fell through. Apparently, that was the only performance the other guy's family could attend. Jim and I discussed it and we simply didn't have the heart to take it away from him.

So, when all was said and done, there had been a total of seven performances of *Thrill Me*. The run was incredibly well-received. Many important theatre people including producers, general managers, directors, and agents attended.

Naturally, I hoped it would lead to something bigger, or at least something *more*. I know Martin tried to make something happen. But he had been out of town during the majority of the run, so he didn't have much of a chance to schmooze or "work the phones."

* * *

My prayers were answered immediately after our closing performance on the afternoon of August 3rd. The head of the Abingdon Theatre itself asked us if we would be interested in having an actual full run at the theatre, totally unaffiliated with the Midtown Festival. I believe Jim was told that we could restart performances as soon as we'd be able to start promoting them.

I was very enthusiastic about this exciting opportunity, and I was positive that the actors and Martin would be too. Later that same night, Jim and I sat at John's Pizzeria on 44th Street, right across from the Majestic Theatre, where *The Phantom of the Opera* was in its fifteenth year. I would have been happy if *Thrill Me* could run fifteen weeks!

Jim started to scribble out some numbers to see if he thought he could make this whole prospect viable. The theatre rent might have been free—but Martin, the actors, the pianist, the stage manager, the lighting designer would all have to be paid. There would be marketing and promotional costs, and certainly lots of other expenses as well.

We calculated out some estimates against potential ticket revenue, and Jim said he just couldn't see how it could be done. He told me the felt numbers just didn't work. I tried to get him to change his mind and scrambled to think of ways that it could be more affordable. I offered to waive or reduce my own royalties.

But he wouldn't budge. And it was *his* decision to make. He was the producer. He would be responsible for the budget.

I was frustrated, but I respected Jim's reasoning. And I knew that from a producer's point of view, he was right. So just like in Nathan's song "Way Too Far," *"I tried to stay calm, I tried to stay sane."*

Eventually, it would be clear that it was all for the best. Had we continued at the Abingdon, the trajectory of the show might have been completely different. Maybe we could have run a few months in that fifty-seat theatre. We might have then been perceived by the public— and the industry—as just a little Off-Off-Broadway show forever.

I was thankful for everything that Jim had done, but for now, his time with *Thrill Me* had come to an end. Perhaps only temporarily, but he soon moved on to his next project. This meant that the responsibility of getting *Thrill Me* back on stage was all mine once again.

* * *

I began an aggressive campaign. I sent out clippings, and corresponded with theatres and producers in the United States and other English speaking countries. There were some people who actually reached out to *me* after reading about the show on their own.

I made sure they each received a promotional package of everything they could possibly need. This not only included the script, but also a brand new demo recording that was made shortly after closing. This second demo featured most of the score as it existed by that point.

Of course, Ron did his fair share as well. And we both chased every possible lead. Soon I would discover there were opportunities in store for *Thrill Me* that I never could have imagined that night at John's Pizzeria.

4

VISITING AND REVISITING *THRILL ME*

"So don't give last night a second thought. / Let's plan next time!"

In 2004, I was flattered to be asked by the Chicago Historical Society, which is now known as the Chicago History Museum, to donate materials from *Thrill Me* to be used as part of their upcoming exhibit on Leopold & Loeb. It would commemorate the eightieth anniversary of the crime. The museum had culled together artifacts from their own collection and also borrowed items from other institutions.

I sent them the original black, grey, and red poster that I'd designed, some printed sheet music, a few pages of my original handwritten notes, a program, production photos, and a copy of the script. It would all be in good company. The museum also commissioned local artists to create original works such as paintings, woodcuts, and mixed-media pieces. The alternative rock band *The Smashing Pumpkins* even gave permission for a video of their song "Bobby Franks" to be played over onscreen images. I never imagined I'd be sharing the bill with *them*!

In coordination with the museum, The TimeLine Theatre Company of Chicago produced a staged concert version of *Thrill Me*—which was performed in the museum's auditorium—as a special event. This would be the very first licensed production after the Midtown Festival. I was very relieved that, no matter what, at least I could always say that there had been "more than one" production of *Thrill Me*.

I didn't get a chance to see the concert, but I was briefly in Chicago later during the run of the exhibit, and I was given a private tour. The Museum staff was incredibly gracious as they showed me all the displays. Needless to say, it was quite an honor to see my *Thrill Me* items in a big glass case next to posters from classic movies such as *Compulsion*, which was based on the first comprehensive book about the crime. I was practically shaking.

But then I was chilled to the bone when I laid eyes on the original ransom note that Leopold & Loeb typed as part of their horrible scheme. I stood in front of it and read their words. Of course, the text was totally different than my fictionalized, sung, version. And it certainly didn't rhyme. I was struck by how tiny the piece of paper was.

Then I turned to see the real Nathan Leopold's actual eyeglasses just a few feet away. *They* weren't tiny. To me, they looked huge, like he must have had a head the size of a watermelon, but maybe that was just my perception.

My tour culminated with a visit to the auditorium where *Thrill Me* had been performed only a few weeks earlier. It was quite an upgrade from the tiny Abingdon Theatre black box. This time, there was a real stage with real theatre seats. I could only hope that the audience leaned forward with their hands over their eyes as Richard sang *"I'll lure him to my car, / then strike with something sizable. / We'll drive out extra far to dump him."*

* * *

In April of 2005, there was a full-scale production in Melbourne, Australia, which was the first international staging. How I wish I could have gone to see that one. But luckily, a friend of the producers visited New York City later in the year, and brought a video that they had asked my permission to record. So I got to see the whole thing.

This version was staged in a black box theatre similar to the Abingdon, but much larger, and with extremely high ceilings. Utilizing a film-noir style, the lights would cause gigantic silhouettes of the actors to loom large on the back walls. It was especially chilling during "Roadster," which included bright beams from a pair of strategically placed headlights. There were many moments where I just watched the hypnotic movement of those huge shadows.

A few months later came a production of *Thrill Me* at the Orlando International Fringe Festival. *Thrill Me* in the city of Walt Disney World. Now that I would have really loved to have seen! At least they sent me pictures.

Their costume design contained a chilling concept that I don't think has ever been equaled. During "Superior," the actors wore t-shirts that had small bloody handprints all over them. You know why. Richard even had a bloody handprint on his arm! Boy, that must have been a very brutal offstage murder. Theatre people in Orlando are clearly very daring. At least the audience had the option to go to a theme park afterwards to shake off the memory of all that blood.

* * *

After giving it some careful thought, at this point I decided to officially retitle the show *Thrill Me: The Leopold & Loeb Story*. I made this change because I felt that it was only fair that ticket buyers understood that they would be seeing a true-crime story. I was worried that they might be offended if they innocently thought that *Thrill Me* sounded like a romantic comedy or something—and would then be shocked by what they saw.

What can I say? I was being cautious. Though "The Leopold & Loeb Story" had been used as a tagline, or as a description under the title, in every production thus far, there was no way to ensure it would always be there in the future. That's why I thought it was best to effectively make it mandatory.

As the years would go on, I regretted the decision to use an ampersand in the new title because so many productions would incorrectly use the word "and" instead. *And* it drove me crazy. I used to insist on corrections, but eventually, I would often just let it be.

A production in Boston, at what was then known as The Stoneham Theatre, was the very first to use the new title, and the very first regional production that I traveled to see. It was an invitation that was hard to refuse, since it was so close to New York. I was also asked to take part in an onstage talkback after the show.

On a very cold winter day, I took the train to Boston. Upon my arrival, a member of the staff picked me up and brought me to the theatre. I met the director, and she told me that the actors didn't want to meet me before the show because they were nervous. So even though I arrived quite early, I wouldn't get to see them until afterwards. Trust me, I was much more nervous than they possibly could have been.

It felt very strange to be sitting in the theatre actually *watching* a production that I wasn't personally involved in (had no control over) for the very first time. But I ended up enjoying it very much.

The Stoneham had a large proscenium stage. And despite the standard setup, there was a lot of creativity all around. I especially loved how they staged the song "Roadster" by having large panels that opened to reveal the car headlights, as if in a garage.

Afterwards, during the talkback, the director very dutifully kept referring to the show as *"Thrill Me: The Leopold & Loeb Story," "Thrill Me: The Leopold & Loeb Story"* over and over again. It was a bit of overkill, but I appreciated that she was striving for accuracy. She knew that I had just made the change.

* * *

There were other things that I changed or considered changing along the way once *Thrill Me* went into production. My *least* favorite song in the show was, and always will be, "Way Too Far," which comes right before the murder. It was rethought, retitled, and rewritten during rehearsals for the Midtown Festival in 2003.

I would have cut it, but I couldn't think of anything better, and it would have left a big hole in the show. The rest of the original team disagreed, with most everyone else claiming that they loved the song. It was even the *favorite* of some of them.

Originally titled "What Makes Me Feel This Way," it was just a standard love song for Nathan. In at least one earlier draft it was actually sung *after* the murder, and I considered moving it back to that spot. But I thought that would only exacerbate the problem.

When I realized it could stay where it was and be reconceived to be sung by Older Nathan in "the present" as if to the Parole Board, while Richard was simultaneously speaking to him as young Nathan in "the past," I decided I could live with it. And while I have softened on it over the years, I've never really enjoyed listening to it, watching it, or singing it.

"Afraid" was the final song I wrote. It wasn't in the original readings or on the original demo. Since so many of the songs seemed to favor Nathan—because he was the focus of the show—I felt that I should put in an "eleven o'clock" number for Richard to help balance things out.

It was based on a melody I had originally written for a different scene, but discarded. I didn't really love how "Afraid" turned out, and the song was almost cut after the Midtown Festival production. Because of that, it wasn't even recorded for the second demo.

I planned to write a new similar song for future productions. But since I couldn't quite figure out what angle to take, I decided to let it remain for the run in Boston. This way I would be able to see it again for myself, and perhaps get some fresh ideas for the revised version.

When I saw how well "Afraid" played there, and how grippingly it was performed, I decided to keep it in. I realized that it was actually the interpretation and staging of it in the Midtown Festival that I didn't like. Future Richards seemed to be pleased with my decision not to cut it.

Richard's "Roadster" song got some even earlier scrutiny. In initial versions of the script, it was called "Sports Car." But back during my critique session at the Dramatists Guild Musical Theatre Program presentation in the late 1990s, Tony Award-winning lyricist Lee Adams, whose *Bye Bye Birdie* I had always adored, told me he was certain that there was no such phrase used in 1924. He suggested that I change the title to the period-correct "Roadster."

I did a little research just to make sure he was right, and indeed I couldn't find the term in use until around 1928. So, in the end, the man who wrote "Put on a Happy Face" helped me with the title of my "murderer song." Thank you, Mr. Adams! Years later, I would occasionally hear the words "sports car" find their way back into translated versions of the song in other countries. It would always make me smile.

But Lee Adams didn't know *all* the details of old cars. Sometime after the Midtown Festival production, I decided to consult a book about the automotive history. That way I could further vet the lyrics to "Roadster."

Originally, I had a line that went *"We could roll down all the windows."* I discovered it was unlikely that windows could actually roll down in cars of the time, so I changed it to *"We could open up the windows."* There was also a reference to *"the key to start the engine"* but my research revealed that keys back then weren't used in that manner. Luckily, I read that there would often be some sort of ignition apparatus that was unlocked with a key. So the lyric became *"the key to the ignition."*

After the Midtown Festival, I could have easily taken out all of the voice-overs and gone back to monologues for the Parole Board scenes, and newspapers for the "telephone song." But I figured that ship had already sailed. The show clearly worked and I was afraid to tamper with success. Despite my fears, I never heard one complaint about the recording being required, or heard of any production that *didn't* happen because of it. Frankly, it was a nice way for theatre groups to involve more people.

When further analyzing the script after the first few productions, I worried that some of the slang and other terminology I used may not have existed in 1924. So I searched through a fascinating slang dictionary and made a few changes in various places. For the life of me, I just can't remember what they were anymore. But I do remember that I always strived to make the script as perfect as it could possibly be.

But things are rarely perfect. Sometimes my insecurities would come into play. I used to often worry that if a line in the script wasn't said in just the right way, my words would seem ridiculous and I'd come across as an untalented hack. But hopefully that's never been true. And even if it was, I obviously would have no way of controlling other people's opinions.

* * *

It was very exciting and extremely fulfilling that *Thrill Me* was being performed in major cities. That was more than many other writers and composers *ever* achieved. And I was very grateful.

But there was still another goal clearly in my sights. I knew that to make it happen I would have to be focused and relentless. Perhaps I was being "greedy," but I was dead set on getting the show back on stage in New York City.

5

OFF-BROADWAY'S LICENSE TO THRILL

"What a way to make your mark!"

The theatre scene in New York City has always been extremely competitive. That said, it also has a lot of opportunities. More so than probably anywhere else in the world. So I did everything possible to bring *Thrill Me* back. I researched New York theatre companies, wrote to producers, and, of course, sent scripts, demos, and review packets to just about everyone I could think of. Ron was on standby to negotiate with anyone who showed interest.

In 2004, among the many email queries I sent, one was to Jim Morgan, the artistic director of The York Theatre Company. Founded in 1969, it was the only professional Off-Broadway theatre company in New York City that was dedicated solely to musical theatre. Jim wrote back that he had heard about *Thrill Me* at the Midtown Festival and was very receptive to receiving the script.

Once he read it, he asked me to come to his office for a meeting. Just a few days later I rode a very slow elevator down to the York's basement-level space on 54th and Lexington Avenue. I was excited, but I thought back to the meeting at Manhattan Theatre Club years before—so I went in with a bit of trepidation.

I shouldn't have worried, because from the moment I sat down, the incredibly gregarious Jim Morgan gushed about the script and made it clear that, if all the details could be worked out, he wanted to produce *Thrill Me* at the York. It would be a high-quality, full-scale, Off-Broadway production! I played it cool, but I was practically jumping up and down inside while listening to him.

Though he said it would ultimately be my choice, I felt that he gave a strong indication that he would prefer a different director than Martin Charnin. I had reluctantly granted Martin a temporary "right of first refusal" to direct another potential New York production, but the agreement had expired. It was not a difficult decision to move on to a new director. But if the York *had* wanted Martin, I would have definitely let it happen.

The York penciled in the show for the following season. But it wasn't guaranteed. In keeping with a common practice for theatre companies, they told me they would need "enhancement money" from outside investors, and additional assistance to help make it all happen.

That gave Jim Kierstead the chance to come onboard to co-produce the Off-Broadway production. Having Jim be part of the team was the icing on the cake. He knew *Thrill Me* better than anyone other than myself—and it would make me feel more comfortable having an ally around.

* * *

In order to help establish the show at the York, we decided to present a one-night-only fully staged concert version of *Thrill Me*. It would feature the original cast from the Midtown Festival. Chris was onboard and enthusiastic, but the scheduling for Matthew was a little difficult to work out. He also had to take at least one of our very few rehearsals off due to illness. This worried me because there simply wasn't a replacement. But Matthew recovered and it all came together in the end.

For this concert—to keep everything as easy as possible—I personally made my *directing* debut. And so far, it was also my swan song. As much as I liked having my ideas and opinions at the forefront—not to mention the control of the blocking—I wasn't crazy about the *actual* job of a director. But I made it work.

On Sunday, August 1st, 2004, which was essentially the first anniversary of our final performance at the Abingdon, Chris and Matthew took to the stage at the York, this time with scripts in hand.

They performed the show just as splendidly as they had done a year earlier. I think my staging was adequate enough to get the show across overall.

I had the guys dressed mostly in black, sort of like how I had originally imagined. I bought a different vintage typewriter to use. This one looked a lot more like the actual Underwood from the 1920s. Since I didn't want to be nervous about a tape glitching, we had performers on microphones to voice the Parole Board and radio. We also had nice lighting—with cues for various looks throughout the show. And luckily, the then-current set at the York was very neutral, so it worked just fine for our purposes. There were even a couple of black cubes!

Fortunately, the concert drew an impressive crowd. I hoped that would help push things along for an eventual full production. But even if it didn't, it was an unquestionable success.

We had a modest reception afterward. I "pressed the flesh" with potential investors. And I was surprised to meet some fans of the show from the Midtown Festival who told me they were excited to have gotten the opportunity to see it one more time.

I was appreciative of Jim Morgan and everyone at the York for all they had done so far. I thanked the actors profusely for all of their hard work. It would be a while before I saw Chris Totten again. And, unfortunately, I never had the opportunity to work on another project with Matthew S. Morris.

* * *

It took quite a while to raise the entire budget and get all of the other necessary elements put in place. There were times that I thought it would never all come together. But finally, I got the word from the York that *Thrill Me* was scheduled to open in May of 2005, which was still several months away.

With Martin out of the picture, it was time to find a replacement. Jim Morgan suggested a rising director who had some previous experience at the York. After a constructive meeting, I signed off on her and we began our working relationship. But unfortunately, during the first round of auditions, it was clear that we weren't agreeing on casting. She decided to bow out. It surprised me, but I believe that she did it for the good of the show—and I've always appreciated it.

Someone less professional, who perhaps just wanted the paycheck, probably would have stayed and been unhappy. But she knew how important it all was to me and, in my opinion, she wanted *me* to be happy. Luckily it caused no major delays and didn't impact the production schedule at all.

She went on to direct several major plays and musicals, and I've sometimes wondered what her actual staging of *Thrill Me* might have been like. Maybe she'll eventually direct it someday, somewhere. I would love that!

I can't recall why Jim Morgan didn't take over as director himself—because I'm sure it was discussed. But a member of the team knew Michael Rupert, a popular Broadway performer, who had just begun directing. Michael was best known for his starring role in the various incarnations of the musical *Falsettos*. He had even won a Tony Award for his performance in the revival of the musical *Sweet Charity*, under the direction of Bob Fosse. It was the very first Broadway show I saw as an official resident of New York. That had to be a good sign!

Michael was very charming and affable. And he certainly knew plenty about theatre. We all decided it would be a smart move to hire him. The press release went out, and back into auditions we went. I remember that Michael and I were both surprised when an actor came in and sang one of Michael's signature songs from *Falsettos*—knowing that Michael would be in the room. That was a brave guy! But sadly, not right for either role.

Casting proved to be more difficult than anyone imagined. I sincerely assumed that Christopher Totten, the original Nathan from the Midtown Festival, would be asked to reprise the role. He was undeniably my first choice. But members of the production team felt we should look for bigger names or actors with major credits. There were also those who thought the main criteria should simply be "two sexy guys."

I suggested Randy Harrison, the young co-star of the popular TV series *Queer as Folk*. The final season would be airing during our run, and we thought it would be great for publicity. He could have fit either role, but we got word he wasn't interested. Unfortunately, many others either weren't available or weren't interested.

I circled back to Chris Totten, but one member of the team still wanted someone different in the role—even though Chris had been so great at the Abingdon. It broke my heart watching Chris's audition on the day of the "open call." He wasn't even given the courtesy of an appointment. Even though I had casting approval, I was powerless to make casting demands.

Since there was not even a glimmer of hope for Chris to play Nathan, or of attracting "names," we finally ended up casting the very gifted Matt Bauer in the role. At the time, he was temporarily in the ensemble of the Broadway musical *Dirty Rotten Scoundrels,* which starred John Lithgow.

In his audition, he was professional, poised, and sang with conviction. He read the scenes effectively. But Matt was very different from Chris. While Chris's Nathan was gentle and vulnerable, Matt's would be more confident and controlled. I was sure we would be in good hands with him.

We saw several guys for the role of Richard. My personal choice was a dynamic young actor named Doug Kreeger. Doug came in wearing a memorable white suit and a very big smile. His audition was marvelous. He sang his prepared song beautifully. Then after reading just a few lines from the script, I remember immediately thinking "that's him!" He literally spoke Richard's dialogue exactly as I had heard it in my head. But I had a hard time convincing the rest of the team.

While I don't know what was going on in their minds, I think he must not have been exactly the type that everyone else pictured. At the time of the audition, Doug's dark hair was shoulder-length. Maybe they all just couldn't imagine what he would look like in a proper 1920s cut. But, of course, everyone agreed that he was extremely talented.

There was talk of considering him for the other role instead. But I just couldn't wrap my mind around it. Why should the "perfect" Richard, be improbably cast as Nathan? He certainly had the ability to pull it off, but it just didn't seem right to me at the time.

Tall, blond, Shonn Wiley was a very close second as Richard for me. He had a beautiful singing voice and a relaxed stage presence. When all the relevant parties weighed in, Shonn Wiley got the majority vote. Even though I had originally imagined Richard as having darker hair and a slightly smaller stature, I was fine with it. I had actually cast Shonn in an early reading of my musical *Panic* a few years before and, though it was very brief, I remembered that he was a pleasure to work with.

Shonn received the first official offer to play Richard. But due to having a conflicting offer to play a leading role in the musical *Ragtime* at the prestigious Papermill Playhouse in New Jersey, he ended up declining. I understood completely.

With Shonn not available, I wanted the role to be offered to Doug Kreeger instead. I thought it was a no-brainer. But we ended up going with a different actor who the rest of the team had higher on their lists. At the time he was featured in a Broadway musical that was just about to close, and he gave an impressive audition for *Thrill Me*. He would be a more serious, larger, and brooding Richard.

Now the cast was in place and it was time to put the show together. Since the rehearsal room and stage at the York was booked, we rehearsed for the first few weeks in a studio space at the Irish Repertory Theatre on 22nd Street. After the first two days, I realized I had made an unfortunate mistake with the actor we cast as Richard.

It was my perception that his take on the role was that Richard would *always* be somewhat detached and callous toward Nathan. This was a valid interpretation, and was pretty much exactly how he had done it during his auditions and callbacks. Sinister, yet aloof. But once I saw his version of the character coming alive during rehearsal, in my opinion, it just wasn't appropriate for my vision of the show as a whole.

It was my fault, not his *at all*. I had signed off on him. Though it truly broke my heart, I felt I had to broach the subject of replacing him. While I will never know what anyone else truly thought, the entire team at the York gave me their full support. And we let him go. I've always wondered if he was actually relieved that it went down that way.

Regardless, he would go on to star in several Broadway shows and many other major productions. He and I would occasionally run into each other over the years, and when we did, he was always as gracious as could be. A real class act. I privately wished that someday he would get the opportunity to play Richard in a different production, where it would be based on someone else's vision. I bet he would have been spectacular.

At this point, as anyone could probably guess, I wanted to immediately go back to Doug Kreeger. But it was recommended by the York's casting director that we should look at a different young actor who was a real up-and-comer at the time. Incidentally, this actor would later go on to be among the stars of one of the most infamous flops ever on Broadway—and to be fair, a few hits too.

We gave him a private audition at the York. He sang for us, and then read a few of Richard's scenes. I read opposite him as Nathan. He did a nice job. There were some in the room who felt he should be given the part. But I stood my ground and let everyone know that I really felt that the role should finally be offered to Doug. The team eventually agreed.

Our casting director reached out to Doug's agent. We didn't even know if he was still in town or even still interested. When I found out that he accepted the job, I breathed a gigantic sigh of relief.

And just as I imagined on the day of his first audition, he looked extremely handsome and period-appropriate after the 1920s haircut he got from a stylist that the York hired during rehearsals. Later, when performances started, it was clear to me that Doug was giving a definitive performance as Richard. He was simply brilliant.

* * *

So, with Doug joining Matt, we continued putting the show together. The props were being acquired (no more DIY telephones!). The scenery was being constructed. The costumes were being gathered. The press agent was sending out releases.

An all-new logo and poster was designed for the show. It featured a vintage photograph of two unclothed young men seen from approximately chin to waist, rendered in sepia tones. In front of them, the title was presented in big red letters.

I was spending time making little tweaks here and there to the script and score. I specifically remember rewriting a few lines in the bridge section of "Afraid." And I may be wrong, but believe I even raised the key of the song to better suit Doug.

It was my observation that the actors seemed to love working with Michael Rupert. After all, he was one of them. Unlike Martin before him, who had started rehearsals with days and days of nothing but "table work," Michael started with the actors on their feet almost immediately. He had many good ideas and took the job very seriously.

So seriously that at one rehearsal he spent an extraordinary amount of time figuring out how one of the guys should move the typewriter from one place to another during "A Written Contract." I was a bit frustrated as I watched, but I supposed it was probably a good thing that he was letting the actors try out different variations. This way they could figure out what would be the most comfortable for them. He was undoubtedly trying to make the action look natural, and I think that it ended up looking perfect.

Overall, in my opinion, Michael's staging was very traditional, compared to Martin Charnin's more inventive version. But to be fair, Martin got to create his in a black box theatre that was far less conventional than the standard proscenium stage at the York. So what Michael accomplished was definitely appropriate.

* * *

When our tech rehearsals started and the spectacular lighting was fully designed and installed by the talented Thom Weaver, who joined us again after the Midtown Festival, everything finally came into focus. Since he told me he grew up listening to *Falsettos*, Thom seemed to be in total awe of working with Michael. I thought the show looked incredibly stylish and sophisticated. The lighting beautifully complimented the scenery, which was designed by Jim Morgan himself.

While abstract, the set sort of had the look of an abandoned warehouse—as in the one mentioned in the script for the "fire" scene. It featured a proscenium of dusty industrial windows, a shiny black floor, and a few strategically placed battered grey wooden crates of different sizes which would be used as a desk, stools, and a bench.

Upstage, in front of a black backdrop, stood three tall columns that were covered in black tiles. Though they looked great, sometimes under the hot lights the adhesive on the tiles would loosen. This would cause them to slide down the column or even fall off completely in the middle of a performance!

The pièce de résistance of the entire production was the near-constant cloud of ambient haze that enveloped the stage. It accentuated the concept that we were seeing the story unfold as a "memory play." It was absolutely exquisite.

That haze caused a battle with Actor's Equity Association later in the run. They actually insisted we had *too much* haze on stage and it was a health hazard for the actors. This was most likely due to an anonymous complaint from an AEA member in the audience one night. They forced us to cut the haze from the show for a few performances so the levels could be tested with a special machine that Thom had to order.

I felt it ruined Thom's entire design concept and the whole look of the show. Thom, for his part, appeared to take it in stride. I almost wanted to just close the production completely—furious that an outside party had the ability to control us. But when Thom did the official haze test, he discovered that the numbers were so far below the maximum allowance that it was almost funny. The haze was back. In full.

Among my other favorite features of the production were designer Jennifer Paar's brilliant costumes. She dressed the characters in the exact opposite color palette than I pictured, after I got over the all-black idea. She put Richard in light creamy yellow and white, while Nathan was in very dark blue. I had imagined Richard, the villain, as being dressed in dark colors, and Nathan, the sort-of-hero, in lighter, maybe even cheerful tones. But it said so much more about them by doing it her way.

Nathan looked like a stuffy, sullen, stick-in-the-mud, while Richard came across sportier and brighter with a devil-may-care attitude. Richard wore the most modern styles and cuts for 1924, such as a shirt with a then-new-fangled button-down collar. While, to me, Nathan was practically dressed in clothes that his *father* would have worn as a teenager in the 1800s.

For the prologue, Nathan as "Older Nathan" was given a cap with a brim to shadow his face. And as his prison uniform, a grey smock with his prisoner number stitched onto it. The smock had large snaps down the front so it could be quickly taken off at the beginning and put back on at the end. Jennifer also provided Richard with a fantastic vintage straw boater hat for his first scene, and a heavy tweed overcoat to wear during "Roadster."

As we had first decided back at the Midtown Festival, aside from the prison uniform, only one main costume would be created for each actor. The theory was that Older Nathan was thinking back to his younger self, so his younger look needed to be like a moment frozen in time. And since the Richard on stage would technically be the personification of Nathan's memory of him, it was almost as if he was the image in a favorite photograph come to life.

I could only imagine the chaos if there had to be different costumes for every scene that took place on a different day. Of course, that didn't mean Richard couldn't have various "looks." In some scenes he would leave his jacket off. Sometimes he would have no necktie, and later it would be put back on. He even revealed a period accurate undershirt at the end of the title song.

Older Nathan had to get back into that prison uniform and hat at the very end. And even *that* change was hard enough to figure out timing-wise. We had also decided back during the Midtown Festival that it wasn't practical for him to put it back on during the rest of the scenes and dialogue to the Parole Board. That would have probably required nearly double the underscore. No thanks!

* * *

As the final visual component, the upright piano was placed in view of the audience at a far corner of the stage. In rehearsals we had a few challenges balancing the sound. It sometimes drowned out the unmiked actors. Somehow, it eventually got solved.

During pre-production, Jim Morgan and I discussed the possibility of adding additional instruments. We thought about a string bass. Possibly some percussion. But that would have added costs to have the instrumentation commissioned and required the hiring of more players. Considering both the budget and my artistic concerns, I decided that it was best for *Thrill Me* to remain a one-piano show.

But I doubled down to be sure that the arrangements were grand enough to sound like a one-piano *orchestra*. The piano would essentially become the third character in the musical—almost always placed in plain sight of the audience. In many countries, the pianist even takes a separate bow during the curtain call.

Our musical director and pianist at the York, Eugene Gwozdz, was a true virtuoso. He helped me make my piano arrangements much more complex and powerful. This was accomplished by interpreting what he knew I wanted, but had a hard time notating on paper.

As we embellished it, the score became even more bass-heavy with very intricate flourishes abounding. I thought all of it ended up sounding absolutely impeccable—moody, atmospheric, and *very* dramatic. The only problem was that most future pianists would find the score very difficult to play. Sometimes it seemed like they needed a third hand!

Eugene also suggested a musical improvement at the big "kiss moment" in the show during the song "Keep Your Deal with Me." Originally the kiss was to be underscored by a vamp, which is a repeated section of music that doesn't have a specific end point, and relies on a cue to jump to the next sung section.

At one rehearsal, he told me that he had devised something more specific. He proceeded to play for me an elaborate underscored bridge section that used the melody of the title song which he had augmented in an almost-but-not-quite-over-the-top way. It sounded lush and romantic. And it flowed seamlessly into the next sung section.

I asked him what his motivation was to suggest it. He said that it was because he didn't want to have to worry about watching the scene for cue purposes, which he would have had to do if the section remained a vamp. It was a great idea, which definitely made the moment much more climatic. Also, it helped set the timing for the kiss—so it would be consistent at every performance.

I was also extremely impressed that Eugene played the whole show using a little electronic metronome, which would set the beat for each individual number. It sat on the stand next to the music. Since the underscore rarely stopped, I could never figure out how he found the moments to readjust the device to each song's tempo. Maybe it was his third hand.

* * *

For one of the voice-overs, we reached out to actor John Lithgow—since we had a bit of an "in" with him, thanks to Matt Baur. I was very hopeful that he would be interested. But Mr. Lithgow politely sent word back that, since he was inundated with so many various requests, he had to decline.

Our Parole Board—which I had now reduced down from three voices to only two—ended up being impressively cast, regardless. The distinctive-voiced John McMartin, who had starred in such Broadway shows as the fabled original production of *Follies* as Ben Stone, and as the narrator in the first revival of *Into the Woods*, was the first voice. As the second, we got Michael Rupert's friend and former co-star, the Tony-nominated actor Stephen Bogardus, who had a youthful, inquisitive quality. The radio voice was nicely performed by Michael himself.

This time, we recorded each individual line as its own separate cue, so Matt wouldn't be required to have the perfect timing that Chris needed two years earlier. But in the tech booth, that button on the sound board would need to be pressed with great precision.

* * *

After waiting and waiting, one of the most exciting moments for me happened during one of our final dress and tech rehearsals. The iconic white *Playbill* truck finally made its delivery to the York.

Since the 1930s, *Playbill* had been the official magazine and program for Broadway shows, and eventually for significant Off-Broadway shows as well. I used to collect them and tack them up on my bedroom wall as a kid.

I had always dreamed of having a genuine *Playbill* of my very own show, and that dream was finally realized. I grabbed a bundle, untied it, and at last held a copy of the *Playbill* for *Thrill Me*. I opened the cover, with its familiar yellow masthead over the show's logo, and excitedly thumbed through it until I saw my name and bio. It was a milestone for me. I kept so many copies—I still have a drawer full of them today!

On May 16, 2005, we finally started preview performances. I was excited but nervous. While everyone was working to the best of their abilities and wanted the show to be a big success, I felt that the stakes were highest for *me*.

Long after the director, designers, actors, and production team would move on to their next shows, I knew that I would be spending my life promoting, marketing, and trying to make a living from *Thrill Me*.

I was the one who had the most to lose—and, I suppose, the most to gain. So I was often on edge. This night was no exception.

During previews, the production received insightful critiques and helpful suggestions from several trusted people. That group included my college friend Melinda Berk, who was a very smart theatre professional—with a good eye for what worked and what didn't. My agent, Ron, also put in his two cents. There continued to be tweaks and improvements in the staging and the lighting until we were finally at our first critics' performance which, per the customary practice, was a few days before our official opening night.

For the first several weeks at the York, *Thrill Me* ran in repertory with a children's musical called *Captain Louie*. It had a score by Stephen Schwartz, the famed composer/lyricist of *Pippin*, *Godspell*, and *Wicked*. It would play early morning shows, while we played a typical eight-shows-a-week schedule of evenings and matinees. I thought it was in questionable taste to have a children's show playing at the same time as a musical about child murderers, but the "powers that be" didn't seem to mind.

When a passerby or a patron would come upon the marquee outside the York, they would see that it was essentially split in two. On one half was our sexy logo which bore the tagline "Relationships Can Be Murder," a phrase that Melinda came up with during a brainstorming session we had one night on the phone—after the York invited everyone to pitch in ideas. On the other half was the childlike, brightly colored, whimsical poster of the children's musical.

Sharing the theatre really didn't affect anything about our show, except for the fact that our set had to be broken down each night so the other one could be put up—and then vice versa—not unlike back at the Midtown Festival. But Jim Morgan made sure both sets were planned out strategically so the transition could be made as easily as possible. Once the children's show closed, we had the theatre and the marquee all to ourselves for the majority of our run.

* * *

After close to two weeks of previews, on May 26th, 2005, it was opening night for *Thrill Me* at the York. It was also an opening night

71

for Tony Walton, the Oscar, Tony, and Emmy-winning set and costume designer. He had worked on such Broadway musicals as the original *Chicago*, *Grand Hotel*, and *The Will Rogers Follies*, and films including *Murder on the Orient Express*, *Deathtrap*, and *All That Jazz*. Tony had donated a collection of his early drawings to the York to be used as a lobby exhibit during the run of *Thrill Me*.

He attended that evening and visited with me backstage before the show. We even shared a celebratory toast—at his insistence—which certainly helped calm my nerves. I was completely overwhelmed to meet him and share stories. It made for an even more special Off-Broadway opening night. I'll never forget how supportive and complimentary he was.

For gifts, I gave out miniature ceramic typewriters with a photo from the show pasted onto the front. I also gave Michael a small album of candid snapshots that I had taken during rehearsals. Michael gave me a bottle of vodka—which I definitely needed. Though he and I may have had a few disagreements, it was now time to celebrate. As the Richard character would later sing that night, *"We can let the past remain in the past. / And have no more reason to fight!"*

My mom, and my aunt and uncle, all flew into town for the occasion. My sister, cousins, and just about every friend I had were also part of the opening night audience. With their *Playbills* in hand, my nearest and dearest got to watch Richard lobby to become a murderer while singing *"If we killed my brother John, / then he'd never touch my things!"* and sex-obsessed Nathan exclaim "don't be unfocused, Richard!" I can only imagine what they must have thought of their "innocent" little Stephen!

The whole show went off without a hitch. Afterwards the entire company, along with all of our friends and family, went to the opening night party at the nearby restaurant Luna Piena. My mom was positively beaming with pride and joy. There was food, drink, and lots of photographs taken. Those photographs would be very crucial just a few weeks later. But for that night, all that was left was to wait for the reviews.

The first ones to appear online in the wee small hours were raves. And more would be published in the coming days. Most of them ranged from good to excellent, but as with just about any show, there were a few outliers that didn't receive *Thrill Me* as well as others did.

A notable negative review was in *Variety*. That really stung. As a kid in Kansas City, I actually had a subscription to the weekly edition— I was an atypical, but laser-focused, adolescent! How else would I have learned about what was playing on Broadway, how much money the shows were making, and all the latest showbiz gossip? So no *Variety* for the pull-quote ads. Luckily, the overwhelming response just about everywhere else was exactly what I had hoped for.

But there was still one review that hadn't yet been published: *The New York Times*. It was the only one that really mattered. If it was positive, the entire trajectory of *Thrill Me* could change overnight. We had no way of knowing exactly when it would land.

For Broadway shows, reviews are customarily published the day after opening. And nowadays, sometimes they are posted online within minutes of the curtain coming down. But for Off-Broadway, there's no set rule. All I could do was check every day.

After about five days I was getting impatient. I was at home late one night after a performance and I called Jim Kierstead to vent about the situation. It was getting close to midnight, and we both knew that the online version could very well appear on *The New York Times* website at any time since it would be a new day.

As anxious as I was for it, I was also nervous. What if it was negative? I was making myself worry—and my head started swimming with every possible scenario. I was exhausted and decided it was time to get some sleep and deal with it all in the morning. I said goodbye. Hung up the phone. And went to bed.

Sometime later my phone started ringing. I knew it had to be Jim, and I knew it meant the review must have been posted. I was literally too scared to answer the phone.

I could hear that Jim was starting to leave me a message on my answering machine. So I jumped up and quickly shut off the speaker!

Now I just tossed, turned, and stared across the room at my computer for the rest of the night.

Finally, in the early morning hours of June 1st, six days after our opening, I logged on and read what *The New York Times* critic Neil Genzlinger wrote. In his first paragraph was the line "Stephen Dolginoff's pocket musical about the Leopold and Loeb murder case lands like a well-placed punch, arresting and a bit breathtaking." I didn't even have to read any further. *Thrill Me* had gotten the *"Times* review" that I had always dreamed of.

* * *

Congratulations started pouring in. The staff at the York added quotes from the review to its marketing and ads immediately. Everyone was thrilled.

Either that same day, or perhaps a day or so later, Jim Morgan got a call from none other than Stephen Sondheim, who knew the script from years earlier when he was on the committee that selected *Thrill Me* for the Dramatists Guild Musical Theatre Development Program. Mr. Sondheim had read the review and asked for tickets.

Nathan's lyric *"What made me feel this way? / And made him so exciting?"* would prove to be quite relevant that night. Sondheim was such a giant in the industry—so we didn't want to tell the actors in advance that he'd be attending. We weren't sure if knowing would make them nervous, so we erred on the side of caution.

On the night he came, I excitedly sat in the back and literally watched Sondheim watch my show. I later found out that Doug had been tipped off that he would be there. And Matt actually spotted him sitting in the audience. It was an unforgettable night.

* * *

As I had hoped, after our great review in *The New York Times*—and the increase in ticket sales that it caused—the York decided to extend the show. There was just one problem. A big one. We were unable to retain Matt Bauer as Nathan. And I never could have predicted the incredible chain of events that would follow because of it.

6

THRILL ME'S UNEXPECTED TWIST

"I, Nathan Leopold, hereby swear to aid and abet."

We had to immediately spring into action to cast a new Nathan. I was sorry to lose Matt. He was a great actor, had a beautiful singing voice, and was giving a fantastic, powerful, performance. But to be honest, he was never quite the physical type that I had imagined for the role.

He was a handsome guy—but frankly, I thought he was almost *too* handsome in costume under the lights. I remember thinking that it looked like Nathan was being played by Cary Grant, the bygone-era Hollywood leading man. In my opinion, there simply wasn't as much physical contrast between him and Doug as I would have preferred—which certainly wasn't his fault. And *The New York Times* clearly took no issue.

Matt told the York that he was booked to do a regional production of *Gypsy* as Tulsa. It was a role he had understudied and performed on Broadway alongside Bernadette Peters as Rose. He couldn't stay one day past the originally planned six-week run.

An emergency casting call was arranged. At the top of the list was an interesting young actor who happened to be the son of famous parents. His mother was a very popular stage and TV star, and his father was a Broadway leading man. This actor gave a good audition for Nathan, but we weren't sure if he had quite the right vocal range.

Still, our casting director put him "on hold" which, in industry parlance, meant that he would know he was under serious consideration, and should keep himself available. When his agent started giving us ultimatums to either cast him or take him "off hold," we had no choice but to let him go. We just weren't ready to pull the trigger on him.

We also looked at a young actor who was starring in the York's *Captain Louie*. He had at least been around our production and had seen it, but he just didn't seem like a Nathan. I was seriously hoping that we could finally cast the original Midtown Festival Nathan, Chris Totten. But a member of the production team *still* wasn't interested in him.

A few other guys were considered, but no one seemed to have all the qualities we needed. What would be the use of recasting if it was someone that we weren't all happy with? Time was running out. And our musical director, Eugene, was getting ready to take a short vacation and wouldn't have much time to teach the score to a new actor.

Finally, one afternoon Jim Morgan called me into his office and told me he that he had a great idea of who should play the role. I said "who?" and he said "you!" I was in shock. Jim must have somehow thought I had it in me to do it, even though he had certainly never seen me perform—other than perhaps while demonstrating a song or two. And I'm also sure he was thinking that casting me could get some extra publicity. But the first word out of my mouth was "no!"

It was quite ironic that he even made the suggestion. Because only a week earlier, Jim had asked me to come and speak to a group of students at Marymount College, where he taught a summer theatre course. It was offered in conjunction with the York. I was honored to be on the bill with Harvey Schmidt, the composer of the longest running Off-Broadway musical in history, *The Fantasticks*. We were discussing alternative careers in the theatre—aside from acting.

The students had all seen *Thrill Me* a few weeks before as part of their curriculum. I told them the story of how I started out as an actor at NYU and then decided that I thought I would be more successful as a writer. One student asked if I had any regrets and if I ever imagined performing again. I immediately said "No! Never!" Jim had heard me clearly, but now he was asking me to eat those words.

Performing in the show myself was something that seriously never crossed my mind. I hadn't been on stage in years, and I'd never had a role as big as Nathan back in my acting days. In fact, I had hardly ever had a solo *verse* in a musical, much less dealt with the singing requirements of *Thrill Me*.

Even if I *had* pictured playing Nathan myself—which I hadn't—I was technically well past the age range of the character. Thanks to good genes from both sides of my family, I'd retained a youthfulness despite my actual age. But I was considerably older than Doug, and I wasn't sure if we would look right *together*.

Jim Morgan turned to his computer and opened up his file of the photos from our opening night party. We both looked at pictures of Doug and me next to each other. I conceded that we did *look* like we could pass as contemporaries. Still, I couldn't help but realize that I was just as close in age to the older version of the Nathan character as I was to the teenaged one.

Aside from the age issue, I was worried that people would think something like…"oh, he wrote the book, the music, the lyrics and now he is gonna *star* in it too—what an egomaniac!" Then again I felt I shouldn't care what people thought. It was my life. But, oh, those theatre chat boards could be vicious. I decided to at least consider the idea. I had the blessing of co-producer Jim Kierstead—who told me unequivocally that he thought I should do it.

But I still wanted to poll my friends and family. Ron Gwiazda thought that since the show had already opened and been reviewed, what harm could I do? Uh…the harm of the author being a total embarrassment, Ron! My dear friend Camille Diamond, an expert performer herself, thought that I should jump at the chance to play the part as we discussed it over lunch at our usual place, Tick Tock Diner on 34th Street. My family was understandably cautious.

I thought and thought about it and figured that if I had actually continued pursuing an acting career years back, Nathan was probably a part that would have fit me well. I was truly the right "type." Although, in real life, I was definitely more controlling—like the Richard character. But I highly doubt I ever would have been offered *that* part!

There was very little time left. It finally came down to the wire. Either I took over the role or the show would simply close as scheduled with no extension. I took a deep breath and decided to just go for it.

And I'm glad that I did. Many great things happened during the period when I was in *Thrill Me*. It was seen by a lot of people who would become very important later. Had I *not* taken over the role, there would have been no show for any of them to see. Because of that, I've always been grateful to Jim Morgan and his unanticipated casting idea.

* * *

Prior to officially announcing I would be taking over the role of Nathan, there was a publicity event scheduled for *Thrill Me* at the popular jazz club, Birdland. It was located in the Theatre District, just off of Times Square. Monday nights they hosted performances from many current shows, and we were invited to do a number. Matt was unavailable that night, so it was decided that I would personally join Doug to sing the song "Superior."

I was very tense. The last time I had performed in public had been over a decade earlier, when I played Lewis in a production of *Pippin* opposite Morgan Englund, the soap opera star, and son of Oscar and Emmy-winner, Cloris Leachman. Though Cloris herself was very complimentary of my performance, there really wasn't much to the role. I also knew that Doug would soon discover that I was set to play Nathan opposite him. This performance was almost like my audition for his approval.

"Now let's cap off one superior night" sang Doug, and I replied with *"This has gone way too far!"* I got through the song and felt it went very well. When I went back to my table at the club, I looked behind me. Sitting at another table nearby was actress/singer, Lucie Arnaz. I was a lifelong fan of both her and her mother, the great Lucille Ball. It was a good thing I hadn't seen her earlier. I probably would have fainted if I had known she would be watching my "comeback" performance.

After I calmed down, I went to Doug's table and broke the news that I would be his new Nathan. I hoped he would be on board with the idea. Would he want to be on stage with the actual author of the show—who was practically an amateur actor? Fortunately, he respected the idea and told me he thought it would be a very exciting journey for us both. Phew!

A day or so later, I found myself in one of the offices at the York signing an Actor's Equity contract to play Nathan. I had now temporarily joined the union that tried to take away my haze!

* * *

It was soon time for new publicity photos to be taken of Doug and me. I had just cut my hair very short the day before I was asked to join the show. Though my hair usually grows very fast, I was afraid there may not be enough time for it look like a 1920s style. For the shoot, it was still short, but I wet it down to try to give the illusion that it was long and slicked back. By the time performances began, it had grown long enough to achieve the look that I wanted.

As for my costume, Matt was much skinnier than I was. During my fitting, designer Jennifer Paar commented with a tactful euphemism, telling me that I "filled out the trousers better"—she would need to let them out a bit! She would also need to hem them since Matt was also taller than me. So in those first pictures, I was wearing my own dress slacks. But I did have to wear Matt's vest before it was altered for me—I could barely breathe because it was so tight! In some shots I wore it open. Jennifer also ordered me a pair of wingtip shoes in my size. They wouldn't arrive for a few days. Luckily, the photographer didn't need to capture my feet.

* * *

For my interpretation of Nathan, I first thought I would try to channel Chris Totten—since I was so fond of his performance. But I was nothing like Chris Totten, and it just didn't work. I had to find my own voice. And that was exactly what I did. Two voices actually.

I decided that, at least in my own mind, Nathan wouldn't *sound* like me. Young Nathan would have a slightly higher pitched quality, with a bit of a stammer sporadically. Older Nathan would have deeper voice with a slower cadence. Also, I wanted to have a more pronounced physical distinction between the two ages of the character than anyone I had previously seen in the role. So as the older version, I would be very still and hardly move a muscle, as opposed to the more frantic younger version.

As for my *singing* voice, it was clear that I would never be able to sound as good as Doug since I was basically untrained. But I could sing passably enough. Mine was more of a "character voice." It ended up giving the characters more contrast. Richard sounded smooth and confident; Nathan was a little rough around the edges.

Usually when I tried to make anything sound "pretty," I couldn't hit the notes, so I had to basically belt a few sections that Matt had been so beautifully nuanced on. But it worked. In later years I would occasionally see the show with actors who both had great voices— but, sadly, sounded almost exactly alike.

Luckily I had established that whenever the characters were harmonizing, Nathan essentially sang the melody. I'm not sure if I could have successfully navigated the more complex harmony parts. And I would have been very reluctant to have asked Doug to switch.

The one concession I did allow myself was lowering the key of my least favorite song, "Way Too Far." After struggling with it a bit while rehearsing, I decided that I needed to feel more comfortable singing it. The composer in me didn't mind the change, but it meant that we had to redo the underscoring that led in and out of the song.

The musical shift was a fortuitous one because it created a slightly more abrupt transition than anywhere else. It helped signal that the story was moving into darker territory. And, because of that, my new key became the official one in the permanent score.

* * *

For some reason, the York had *two* tech booths. And I watched Matt's remaining performances of the show every night from the empty one. I would move around to mimic the blocking while taking notes. I had to be in total darkness otherwise Matt and Doug would have been able to see me up there—and I can only imagine how distracting that would have been.

During the days, my living room became my own private makeshift version of the stage where I would act everything out and work on memorizing all of the lines and lyrics. Of course *I* wrote them. And, of course, I "knew them." But now I had to *really* know them.

It was all starting to click rather quickly. And that was a good thing. Because, due to union rules, I only had a few hours of actual rehearsal—which were just me alone with the Stage Manager. After watching nearly every performance, I was confident that I knew every move I had to make.

But once I got up on the actual stage, I couldn't believe how different the spacing actually was. What looked like a distance of three feet while watching from the audience, or from up in the booth, was actually closer to ten feet. In one specific moment, I dashed to a spot that I was certain was the right place, and I was told that I had to take five more steps downstage or I wouldn't be in the light! I had to adjust quickly.

After working with the Stage Manager, I had just two full run-throughs with Doug, known as "put ins." During the first one, with no costumes or lights, I was feeling pretty good about how it was going. I knew my lines, my blocking, and I tried my best to be sure Doug was comfortable with what I was doing. I knew how different I was from Matt.

When it came time to rehearse the big kiss scene towards the end of the show, I did everything exactly as staged. It was a very emotional, dramatic, moment in which Nathan ultimately concedes to make a big sacrifice. I thought it went perfectly. When rehearsal ended, Doug approached me in a very friendly manner and said something like "Stephen during the kiss you used your *tongue*."

Oh my God! I was *mortified*! I hadn't even realized it. Or thought about it. Or planned it. I must have turned about five shades of red. I told him that since I had never done a stage kiss before in my life— my brain must have just gone on "autopilot" to produce what it knew was "a kiss." I swore it would never happen again. Doug wasn't mad, he probably thought it was hilarious as he watched me squirm.

Needless to say, from that moment on, every time we did that scene I pulled my lips far back into my clenched mouth. I was determined to make sure it would feel like he was kissing a brick wall! But from the point of view of the audience, I think we really sold it.

For our dress rehearsal, I tried on my now-altered costume. With the structured vest changing my posture, I truly started feeling like the character of Nathan. But even more than the costume, it was those wingtip shoes. Since in real life I would almost never wear shoes with laces, with those on, I no longer felt like myself.

The only problem was that I was always paranoid that they would come untied on stage. Before every show I could often be found retying them over and over again just to be sure that the laces were tight enough.

And while I could certainly tie a pair of shoes, one thing I wasn't so good at was tying a bow tie. Since it was part of the costume, I figured that I could probably get it tied after a few attempts in my dressing room. But even more skill was required—I would need to be able to tie it with *no mirror*!

At the end of the title song, Doug would pull down his suspenders and partially take off his shirt—to reveal his sleeveless tank underneath. Then Matt would unbutton his vest and untie his tie. After the song, everything needed to be put back on. And Matt was able to retie the bow tie—live on stage.

I initially thought it would be impossible for me to replicate this. And I was told that I didn't *have* to. I thought perhaps I would just take my vest all the way off instead, and then put it back on—to help fill the moment. But I finally decided that "if he could do it, I could do it."

So I started practicing and practicing. I would walk to and from the theatre with a t-shirt on, tying and untying a cheap bow tie that I used to rehearse with. Finally, I was able to make it happen. I felt triumphant! And I personally thought it was a nice bit of "business" for Nathan in that particular scene.

Even still, it often made me nervous that I wouldn't do it correctly on stage. Sometimes I had to stop and start it all over again during the scene, all while saying the dialogue, in a very short amount of time. Sometimes Doug would see that it was crooked and, in character, he would straighten it out for me.

* * *

In my dressing room on my opening night, I put the final touches on my hair, which I had decided to wear in a style that would have seemed old fashioned, even in the 1920s. I created a very severe part straight down the middle, and applied a thick, waxy coat of American Crew Pomade. It looked great. But by the end of each performance, under the heat of the stage lights, the pomade would literally be dripping down my face. All these years later I can still smell it!

One thing was for sure, I looked vastly different that Matt. No one would have mistaken *me* for Cary Grant. I looked more like one of the old-timey guys on a box of Smith Brothers Cough Drops.

I kept checking my pockets to be sure I hadn't forgotten the pocket watch, cigarette lighter, or—most importantly—the eyeglasses. This was a ritual I soon would repeat before every performance. I also clutched a copy of the script which was opened to the page of dialogue right before "The Plan." For some reason I was worried I might mess up the sequence of lines in that particular scene. I'm pretty sure I double checked that page over and over again after getting dressed for my first few weeks.

The stage manager knocked on my door and called "five minutes." At that moment I saw myself in the mirror turn white as a ghost. Then I got major butterflies. But I took a deep breath and gave myself a pep talk right there into the mirror. I put down the script. I tightened my shoelaces again. And for probably the tenth time, I double checked that every prop hadn't somehow magically disappeared from my pockets.

Now it was "places." I was brought backstage, and led across the dark narrow gap between the back wall and the scenery. I went to my designated spot in the wings to await my entrance cue. There was no turning back now.

The "Prelude" started. During the first section, which is based on the melody of "A Written Contract," I breathed deeply and probably took one more tug at the shoelaces. Then the music shifted into the low bass notes of "Roadster." I went to my mark. The light hit me. And on I went. I was probably a little shaky at first, but I concentrated, relaxed, and quickly started enjoying myself.

My reveal from Older Nathan into his younger self felt particularly liberating as I stepped out of the shadowy lights of the Parole Board scene. I couldn't hide under the prisoner cap anymore. It was *me* up there, totally exposed. And it felt great. It felt right. It felt like I was where I had always belonged.

By the time I was lighting Doug's cigarette during "Everybody Wants Richard" as I sang the ironic line *"And God knows why I think you're so appealing,"* I was truly on a roll. For one thing, the lighter didn't malfunction as I feared it might, so that was one potentially unpredictable moment that I could stop worrying about. Doug, as directed, blew the smoke straight at me.

It seemed the audience was "buying" my very different interpretation of Nathan. More importantly, I was buying it myself. I endured performing "Way Too Far" (ugh!) and as soon as it was over, I mentally thought that it would be "smooth sailing from here on." As the evening progressed, I got the expected laughs, the gasps, and a big round of applause at the finale. Overall, I felt that I came across a bit more sympathetic than Matt had been.

A few days later, I read the first rave review of my performance, which was published by the news wire service, UPI. After that came an extremely complimentary notice by critic John Kenrick at

Musicals101.com. More positive reviews came soon. I was on cloud nine. Though to knock me back down to Earth, there was a least one write-up that…let's just say I chose not to ever read again. And I never put in my scrapbook or archives. But all press was good press, right?

There was also one notorious critic named John Simon who came to one of my first few performances. He later had a representative reach out to the York to explain that he had either forgotten to wear his hearing aids—or maybe that they weren't working properly… something like that. So he asked if he could be provided a copy of the script to help him write his review. Oh he needed help, did he?

Well, for decades, John Simon was very much loathed in the New York theatre community for his scathing personal critiques and over-the-top attacks. So much so that many actors on the receiving end of his poison pen considered it a badge of honor. It was common knowledge that he rarely enjoyed plays or musicals with gay themes.

There was no way I was going to *help* him write a negative review, so I asked if we could have just a little bit more information. Word came back that he "didn't hate it." Well, that still left plenty of room for his usual venom.

Though not I, nor anyone else, could know what he actually thought of *Thrill Me*—and while I was somewhat tempted to find out, I politely declined his request. Why should I give him the tools he needed to potentially trash me? If he was going to do it, he'd have to do it without a copy of my script. He never wrote the review.

* * *

Holding my own alongside Doug was challenging. The stage was his domain, not mine. And he didn't go easy on me. He expressed what *he* needed from his stage partner to make the show work. In those first few performances, after the sugar-high of my first night, well…I guess I wasn't exactly giving it. Doug made his dissatisfaction clear. He was very well trained in his craft and he knew what he was talking about.

He told me that he felt I wasn't "listening" enough, and that I was too busy "acting." That hit me in the gut. If there was one thing I remembered from back in drama class, it was that an actor has to be "in the moment" and not worry about merely giving a performance. Doug was right.

I appreciated the feedback. I was actually *grateful* for it because I wanted to learn from him, and be the best Nathan that I could possibly be—in a show that was the best *it* could possibly be. I've never forgotten how he pushed me to work harder and how he gave me several very clear objectives to apply.

An actor in his position could have easily just let me continue on the path I was going down—while he mopped the floor with me every night. But that wasn't Doug. He clearly wanted what was best for *Thrill Me*, not what was best for himself.

I highly doubt him doing *Thrill Me* with me changed *his* life, but me doing *Thrill Me* with *him* certainly changed mine. When he accepted the *second* extension of the show, obviously agreeing to keep performing with me, I knew that I must have ultimately pleased him.

* * *

We soon began an unofficial tradition. Both of us had our own dressing room, and we arrived at the theatre at different times. So we never actually saw each other until the moment Richard jumped behind Nathan in our first scene together on the stage.

Some nights I wouldn't even hear him next door. When "places" was called, I would have to confirm with the stage manager that Doug was actually there. It soon became a superstition for me. I was actually *afraid* to see him before the show—like a bride and groom before their wedding.

I think it helped establish the relationship between our characters. When *Thrill Me* begins, Nathan and Richard haven't seen each other in months and the tension during their reunion is palpable. By having our own "real life" version of this, it helped start the show with a lot of energy.

And I sure *needed* a lot of energy. As Richard, at least Doug had a few minutes off stage. He even had a glass of water hidden in one of the scenery crates, just in case he needed it. As Nathan, I was on stage the entire time and had no potential water breaks.

I only had about fifteen seconds at the beginning of Doug's "Roadster" solo where I was unseen by the audience, before being revealed upstage behind him. I had just enough time to take the glasses, pocket watch, and cigarette lighter props out of my pockets, take off my silver cufflinks, roll up my sleeves to look a little more disheveled after the "murder," and quickly pop an unwrapped pre-set Ricola lozenge into my mouth to soothe my throat.

Then on cue, I would run across the back of the stage and into the wings. I'd pull what remained of the lozenge out of my mouth and throw it to the side, then I'd grab a prop bloody rag and an empty leather case which would soon be used to hide the murder weapons. All of this had to happen in a few seconds so I could then land at my spot on stage just in time to meet Doug. Then I immediately started singing again.

One day, toward the end of the run, I happened to be in the wings when the work lights were on. I looked down and saw the graveyard of my sticky lozenges, now resembling gleaming amber jewels, piled in a corner. I hereby retroactively apologize to whomever had to clean them up.

As the days went by, I grew more and more comfortable. Doug and I had fun making the show "our own" by adding playful little bits into the staging. In several very serious moments Doug would tickle me and poke at me with a big smile on his face.

It truly caused me to giggle and sometimes even double over. This made both of us seem a little more youthful in our relationship— which was a significant contrast from the more emotionally intense version Doug had with Matt. The whole thing was just a little bit "lighter" now, at least until the ending.

I decided to try something different at the very last moment of the show. I wanted my Older Nathan to end up a little more surprising, and a little more *creepy*, than the solemn, dignified, man portrayed by Matt. The final direction in the script actually read "He smiles." But I took it a step further by giving what I called the "evil Nathan grin," which was big and wide—sort of like the Joker in *Batman*. Then I did a wicked little cackle as the lights went out. I felt this gave the ending a much bigger "payoff" and made it a little less grim.

The audience seemed to eat it up, and usually reacted in amused horror at my last-minute macabre shift. Unfortunately, the chairman of the board at the York, who was an enthusiastic supporter of the show, told me that he still preferred the more quiet ending that Matt did. With apologies to the chairman, I respectfully disagreed.

That said, I never changed or added to the direction in the script. It would be up to future directors and actors to decide how that moment should be played. Older Nathan could be more of a "Matt," more of a "Stephen," or just about anything in between.

* * *

The show was running smoothly and without incident until one night early in my run. We had a substitute player at the piano. Right as I started the first verse of "Life Plus Ninety-Nine Years," I could hear a giant whoosh of paper, followed by a thud. The score had fallen down. And since this was a sub, he didn't know the music well enough to even ad-lib with one hand while getting the book re-situated with the other. It was just dead silence.

Of course, since the piano was in full view of the audience, everyone knew what had happened. I had already gotten out my first words *"You thought that you used me,"* so I pretty much had no choice but to keep singing a cappella until the music started again. I could hear the poor guy struggling to get the music book balanced back onto the piano and find the right page.

So I slowed down as much as a I could to give him more time *"...and... thought... you...confused...me..."* In my mind it seemed like it was the longest verse ever sung in the history of theatre. But I kept going with no accompaniment other than the frantic shuffling of papers. *"I'll keep you focused...no outside forces for...life... plus...ninety-nine years."* I could just imagine that Doug, who was sitting beside me, was hoping that the piano would at least come back in time for his verse. I couldn't bear to look at him because I thought for sure I would start laughing. *"Not forever…but for life…plus…ninety-nine years…Life plus ninety-nine years."*

Right after I finished my section, the pianist found the right page, and sure enough the music came back just in time for the underscore that led into Doug's verse. Perfect. The amateur actor got thrown the curve ball while the professional was left unchallenged! The audience probably didn't give the whole incident a second thought. But maybe it was the moment where I truly paid my dues and became a professional actor myself.

* * *

When standing on stage at the York, nearly the entire audience was somewhat visible due to the way the lights were arranged high up on the grid. I believe this was called "light bleed." Many of my scenes were directed out front, as if talking to the Parole Board, and I could always see whatever was going on in the audience.

During the prologue, there was often late seating. Because of the bleed, I had to watch all the shuffling with the ushers and the patrons, and it was very distracting. After a few days, I requested that there be no late seating during the prologue because I felt it was really hurting my concentration. The York agreed.

Shortly after this policy was instituted, there was a rumor floating around that Joan Rivers might be attending an upcoming performance. The possibility alone was exciting. I had always been such a fan. She was a world-famous comedian, talk-show host, and actress who had also carved out a niche as a fashion reporter at celebrity red carpet events all over television.

One night, I was in the middle of performing the prologue, facing out front to address the Parole Board. Sure enough, there were people being seated late toward the back of the theatre—right in the middle of my song. I watched as they squeezed into their seats as others stood to make room. I was pretty upset. What happened to the new policy?

After the show, I hadn't forgotten about it. I was ready to start launching into a complaint when someone grabbed me and immediately said "Stephen, Joan Rivers is here! She came in a little late. She's coming backstage." Ah…I got it! I wasn't mad anymore.

We met Joan, who was very cordial and complimentary—and smaller and more soft-spoken than how she appeared on TV. She wore a beautiful black silk jacket with an incredibly long string of turquoise beads, looking as if she was attending a Broadway opening night.

As she posed for photos with Doug and me, she very kindly told me how impressed she was that I wrote the whole show and was starring in it myself. I remembered that she had done pretty much the exact same thing in her Broadway play, *Sally Marr…And Her Escorts* about a decade earlier. The next night, the late-seating policy was back.

We had several other notable visitors throughout the run at the York. I remember meeting and chatting with playwright Terrence McNally one night. Among his numerous credits were the librettos for the Kander & Ebb musicals *Kiss of the Spider Woman* and *The Rink*, which was one of my all-time favorites.

After a performance, famed songwriter Richard Sherman, who wrote the scores for movies such as *Mary Poppins* and *Chitty Chitty Bang Bang*, generously praised my score—a score that had lyrics like *"We could chloroform a rag, / and make him breathe the vapors"* and *"Wash the bloodstains off with kitchen soap!"* Those were certainly a long way from his "A Spoonful of Sugar."

Also attending performances were Tony Award-winner Anika Noni Rose from *Caroline or Change,* who would later be the voice of Tiana in Disney's *The Princess and the Frog*; the beloved actor Andre De Shields, who played the title role in the original production of *The Wiz*; and Broadway actress Meredith Patterson, who I had enjoyed seeing tap dance in *42nd Street*. All of them gave me very much appreciated compliments—and posed for pictures!

We were also honored by the attendance of several members of an organization that provided aide to parolees, not unlike the real Nathan Leopold. And one night there was an elderly man who was very excited to show me his pair of glasses. As he did, he revealed to me that they were from the same Chicago establishment where the real Nathan Leopold got his infamous pair!

The York also reached out to noted Leopold & Loeb author/historian Hal Higdon. And we were very lucky that he agreed to do a talkback after a performance one night. Mr. Higdon was very approving of my adaptation of the story—a story he certainly knew very well. He even pointed out that my plot point of Nathan dropping his glasses on purpose was not entirely farfetched.

* * *

After agreeing to two extensions, Doug decided to move on to do another show out of town. It was sad for me, but of course I only wanted the best for him. Closing the show was a very real possibility. I practically had to beg the York to reach out to a potential replacement, who I knew was now back in town.

Shonn Wiley had initially turned down the role of Richard so he could do *Ragtime*. He had told us it was a very difficult decision. Now that *Ragtime* was closed, we offered Shonn the chance to replace Doug.

He was interested. Mainly because, as he told us, he was always cast as "good guys," such as *42nd Street*'s hoofer Billy Lawlor, in the revival that was actually *on* 42nd Street, and heroic Jack Seward in Frank Wildhorn's *Dracula* on Broadway. Apparently, he liked the idea of finally playing against type. He came to see the show a few days after our casting director reached out to him.

In my self-deprecating mind, it wasn't just so he could get a feel for the show and his potential role, but it was so he could scrutinize my performance and see if he wanted to do the show with *me*. I was very nervous that he wouldn't think I was good enough or of a professional caliber to perform alongside. After all, he had starred on *Broadway*. Would he really want to be *my* co-star?

He must have liked what he saw—because he agreed. A few weeks later he was Richard to my Nathan. And now that I think about it, I might have raised the key of "Afraid" at *Shonn*'s request, not Doug's.

When Shonn took over, the biggest difference for me was that he was significantly taller than Doug. The blocking was originally conceived for two people of roughly the same height, so modifications were necessary. I had to crane my neck and practically stand on my toes when I needed to really get into his face. And the big kiss required a lot more maneuvering—luckily I didn't embarrass myself during our first time running through that moment.

Even some of the lighting was affected because of Shonn's height. But instead of the difficult process of refocusing the lights, some of Shonn's movements were just restaged. Instead of jumping up high on a piece of scenery during "Superior," well…he just didn't, or at least he didn't do it in the same spot where Doug previously had. One bonus was that when he blew the smoke at me during "Everybody Wants Richard" it went practically over my head.

Shonn's Richard was softer and cooler than Doug's. Less playful. More intense. But equally compelling. And, to be honest, I thought that Shonn and I together looked more like the real Leopold & Loeb. Especially as photographed for the new theatre marquee poster.

It was an adjustment, but I thought we worked very well together. When Shonn's first song began and he sang *"There's nothing like a warm, romantic fire,"* he immediately drew both me and audience in. And later, when he ordered me to *"Just lay low a few days longer, / and you'll see they have no case,"* I could tell that, as the character, he really believed it.

I was actually more relaxed at each performance with Shonn. Since I felt like I had "discovered" Doug (for *Thrill Me,* that is), I was nervous every time I went toe-to-toe with him on stage. It was like running a marathon every night—an ultimately fulfilling one. Once Shonn came in, I was more confident in my own abilities. And the marathon became a much easier sprint.

* * *

Shortly after I took over as Nathan, it was decided that the marketing materials would be redesigned. It was felt that the original logo just wasn't properly conveying the show as it actually ended up. Because of my initial contract for the production, I had various approval rights over things such as this.

Before a matinee one day, I was in my dressing room preparing to put my costume on. The stage manager, who also did some of the marketing and graphic artwork for the York, knocked on my door and asked if I could look at the new poster and postcard design. I said "I'm in my underwear, but it's okay."

So he came in and showed me the art. Then another member of the staff came in, soon followed by yet another, and we all stood and discussed this new campaign. I caught a glimpse of myself in the mirror and realized what an "only-in-the-theatre" experience it was to be having an impromptu marketing meeting while I was wearing nothing but skimpy black bikini briefs!

When that meeting was over I looked again at the new poster. Replacing the original generic sepia photo version was something much more direct. On a black background, it featured a list of hard-sell review quotes alongside a production photo of the new cast.

I realized that, along with Doug, I was now *literally* the face of *Thrill Me*. If only I had a time machine so I could go back to 1994 to tell myself that! But even *I* wouldn't have believed me.

I was also invited to *official* marketing meetings. I would often suggest that we do some sort of tie-in with the long-running Broadway musical *Chicago*—since both shows took place in similar time periods, in the same city, and involved murder. And as for historical accuracy, Beulah Annan and Belva Gaertner, the real-life inspirations for the *Chicago* characters, Roxie Hart and Velma Kelly, committed their murders that same spring of 1924 as Leopold & Loeb did. And all of them went on trial that same year.

The entire York staff was very much in favor of trying to make something happen. Finally, our press agent was able to get their press agent to agree to set up a photo op. Shonn (before he even had his first performance) and I were invited to come backstage at the Ambassador Theatre on Broadway, home of *Chicago*, in full costume so the "thrill killers" could meet the "merry murderesses." While traveling in a cab through the city in the summer heat, I was afraid that my waxed hair would melt.

We arrived at the end of a Wednesday matinee and were escorted to the basement wardrobe room and waited for the show to end. Then three photographers from various theatre websites arrived. A few of the women of the ensemble came downstairs, including Donna Marie Asbury who would later be put into the Guinness Book of World Records for her long run in the production. They posed with us for maybe twenty seconds, then left. Next, Luba Mason, the current star as Velma, posed with us for about ten seconds.

When the photos ran on the websites, it looked like we were all having a great time socializing about our two Chicago murder musicals. But it was all over in thirty seconds. And none of us ever said a word to each other. It didn't matter—it was great publicity!

Over the course of the run I found myself appearing on television and radio (including NPR) to promote the show. I was also interviewed for several magazines, newspapers, and websites. My thought at the time was that I had finally gotten my "fifteen minutes of fame." Well, more like three months of fame.

* * *

After three extensions, which spanned almost the entire summer, on Sunday, August 21, 2005, it was time for the final performance of the Off-Broadway production of *Thrill Me*. Of course, I wished it would have run for years. But since the initial six-week run ended up being more than doubled, with a huge amount of the performances unexpectedly starring *me*, how could I complain? Still, it was bittersweet.

I got to the theatre early so I would have plenty of time to savor the last moments. In my dressing room, as I started getting ready, it really hit me how lucky I had been. And, as a writer, how much I had learned from the experience of performing my own work.

I realized I had made certain things difficult for actors. Things I never really considered when it was all just on paper. I originally figured that since the show was only around ninety minutes, it wouldn't be too hard for someone to stay on stage for that relatively short amount of time. I was wrong. And I also learned that when singing high notes, it's much more difficult when the melody jumps suddenly from low to high, but easier when it gradually slides up.

Since I wrote them, I felt I knew *exactly* how certain moments should be interpreted. But once I was up there myself, I realized that sometimes my intentions were impossible to achieve due to various factors. In one of the final moments in *Thrill Me*, the Parole Board asks Older Nathan what he currently thinks of Richard, and he responds with the line "I think if he wasn't stabbed to death in the shower room so many years ago, I'd have probably…well…I don't suppose I should say that."

To Stephen the writer, the character is thinking "I'd have probably killed him myself." But for Stephen the actor, having taken the entire journey on stage, trying to make it feel real, it made more sense to play it as if the answer was "I'd probably still love him." All of this was knowledge I would try to always remember when writing my future projects. I wish every writer could have this same opportunity to both live in and learn from the world they've created.

While putting on my costume for the last time at the York, I thought back to the most difficult parts of the staging that I had to navigate. The singing of the rubato portion of "Everybody Wants Richard," while cigarette smoke was literally being blown in my face. Hitting the high notes in "The Plan," while facing the audience directly as Doug or Shonn's hand was creeping up my chest. And holding out the long final note of "A Written Contract" when Doug was poking at me with the knife. None of that was in my comfort zone. But I did my best. And I would miss all of it.

After the closing performance, we all went out to celebrate at a nearby restaurant. Michael Rupert wasn't able to join us that night. The next time I saw him was on Broadway when I went to see his acclaimed performance as the lecherous law school professor in the musical version of *Legally Blonde*.

We all said our goodbyes. I went back to my apartment and watched the sad, but moving, series finale of *Six Feet Under*—a show about death. It was not the right choice for that night.

* * *

The next day, or perhaps a few days later, the York began the process of tearing down the set and clearing out the theatre. I stopped by and picked up my prop typewriter. It was the same one I had purchased to use in the 2004 concert version.

I also was allowed to keep several other souvenirs from the show, including one of the small grey crates from the set, both of the prop candlestick telephones, the pocket watch, cigarette lighter, Nathan's eyeglasses in their blue case, and the bottle of acid that was actually the exact same bottle of vanilla extract that I had purchased for the Midtown Festival—this time dressed up with a new label.

I was also given many of my costume pieces including the blue striped shirt with French cuffs and its identical back-up duplicate, the silver cufflinks, several pairs of socks, and the beige prisoner cap (which smelled of my pomade). Most significantly, I got the pair of black wingtip shoes and the blue paisley bow tie. Now I could practice tying them forever.

* * *

But it wasn't quite the end for the everything related to the Off-Broadway version of *Thrill Me*. I was lucky enough to have adventures both planned and unplanned still in store. In fact, I would practically be busier after it closed than I was when it was running.

7

PUTTING *THRILL ME* ON THE RECORD

"But there's still your deal with me, Babe."

One of my biggest hopes while we were running at the York was that a major play publisher like Samuel French or Dramatists Play Service would make an offer to acquire *Thrill Me* for licensing and publishing. This would put the script into one of their prestigious catalogs, which would ensure that the script would be available for sale, and would practically guarantee that there would be many professional and amateur productions well into the future.

Dramatists Play Service seemed interested. Both the heads of the professional and non-professional licensing departments had come to the York and had recommended it to the president of the company. Ron conveyed to me that the president was unconvinced. Luckily, he finally booked a ticket to see the show when I was playing Nathan.

I was terrified that *my* performance would be partially responsible for the entire licensing future of *Thrill Me*. After the show, the president said to Ron that he thought I was great, but he was still slightly skeptical about the Leopold & Loeb story itself. Apparently he had "passed" on other plays on the subject. He told Ron that he would think about it. I was on pins and needles, seemingly for weeks.

Ultimately Ron got word that Dramatists Play Service indeed decided to acquire *Thrill Me*. I couldn't say "yes" fast enough. I breathed a huge sigh of relief. Another dream had come true.

It wasn't long before I was doing the last-minute fine-tuning of the script to get it ready for publication. In the dialogue, I altered a few lines and words that had always bothered me. For the purpose of clarity, I rewrote part of the lyric about Nathan being Richard's "lookout" in the introduction to the song "A Written Contract."

Next I had to be sure the piano score was as perfect as I could possibly make it. I had previously created the whole thing using industry-standard notation software. But now it was time to put all the embellishments and rewrites in. With a bit of guidance, I inserted every single note, rest, expression, tempo marking, cue, and lyric myself. Boy, was that tedious!

Then it was finally time to write my author's notes. I wasn't sure even where to begin. It was what I then thought would be my one and only chance to make my feelings and intentions known to all potential readers, producers, directors, designers and actors. So I just wrote what I felt would be the most helpful to all of them.

For the cover, Dramatists Play Service had a standard house style with columns of black stripes going down the left side, and across the bottom half. Every script looked exactly the same. All I got to choose was the color. I picked red. Red and black would eventually become the unofficial "*Thrill Me* colors" that I would always prefer.

I also was able to put in what is called a frontispiece photo, which is a fancy way of saying a photo at the beginning of the book. There was a certain production photo, taken by Jim Morgan, of Doug and me that I was crazy about. It depicted me, as Nathan, standing in the foreground, holding the birdwatching binoculars, with a foreboding expression on my face. Doug, as Richard, was standing in the background—wearing that boater hat—and watching me intently. He was ever-so-slightly out of focus.

The photo was full of mystery and drama. It perfectly encapsulated both the mood and the characters. I really wanted to use it. But there was a problem. Doug was quite far away from me in the shot. Thus, since the photo had so much emphasis on *me*, I knew I would be embarrassed to put it in the book. My name was already prominent on the cover, I was listed as member of the cast, and I feared choosing a photo like this could be seen as an ego trip.

When Shonn replaced Doug, a new photo shoot was called for. At that point I was already preparing the script for publication, although the contract wouldn't be finalized until two days after we closed. So I asked if we could recreate that exact photo, but this time with Shonn much closer behind me—and not out of focus.

I knew it would make me feel more comfortable if we were placed somewhat more equally. And indeed this photo was used in the published script (with the generous permission of Jim Morgan). Our positioning may not have been quite as true to the spirit of the show's blocking, but it made me feel better.

Soon I was editing the galley—which is the final proof of the eventual book. A few months later, in early 2006, I picked up my box of author's copies from the offices of Dramatists Play Service. I couldn't even wait for them to be mailed.

I held the first copy of the red-covered script in my hand and it was even more exciting than holding that first *Playbill*. I was now a published writer. Dramatists immediately started doing a marvelous job licensing productions and selling books.

I later was told that rival company Samuel French also had interest, but there was internal debate about it. By the time it was sorted out, *Thrill Me* was no longer available. But a few years later, Samuel French would come back into the picture.

* * *

Just a few days before we closed, the owner of a recording studio came to see the show. He was so impressed that he offered to give me studio time at a significantly reduced rate if I wanted to record a cast album.

I had to scramble a bit to put it together. But I was eventually able to take him up on his offer—though we wouldn't actually be able to start it for months.

The album was scheduled to be released in the Spring of 2006. Based on our different schedules, Doug and I had to get in front of the microphones at separate times.

In the first sessions, I laid down all my vocals, along with Eugene at the piano. And since we weren't sure if Eugene would be available when Doug was free, I sang along as he laid down all of Doug's music too.

I had previously decided that new endings would have to be created for almost every song because in the actual show there were no "buttons" or real endings. Everything just flowed into the next piece of underscoring—to help prevent that applause. So, at my direction, Eugene ad-libbed the new endings on the fly.

I hadn't thought about it before I started recording, but I suddenly remembered that in performance I took little liberties here and there with how I phrased the music and with how I would emphasize certain words based on my movements. So I wondered if I should try to recapture that on the recording, or if should I just sing the songs as perfectly as I possibly could, following every note and rest.

Since it was for posterity, and a tool for future productions, I decided to try to sing everything as written. I know it was the right decision but, sometimes when I listen to it, I miss some of the little character quirks that I did on stage. Those are now forever lost to time.

It was several weeks later when Doug came into the studio to lay down his vocals. At that time, we did record a few sections of the dialogue together. I had carefully reduced the lines from the script that came before and within the songs—so they would make better sense out of context.

I wanted the recording to be a full experience for the listener. So my idea was to make it *seem* like they were hearing practically the entire show, and thus be able to discern the plot—even though a lot of it would actually be missing.

For example, there was no trace of the Parole Board. And no radio voice either. Thus, I had to add some totally new short lines before one verse in "My Glasses/Just Lay Low"—so it would make sense.

Once Doug was finished recording, I did some retakes to better match some of his performances of our duets. Perhaps he sounded more energetic, perhaps he sounded more calm, perhaps he took a breath in a different spot than I did. Either way, it needed to be convincing that we were together in the same moment.

When the engineer and I started the processes of mixing and editing, I had to work very hard to try to be as objective as possible. This was because I always felt like my voice sounded inferior compared to Doug's. It was one thing to be singing the score on stage—when the viewer saw my entire performance—but it would be another when it was nothing but my voice in glorious stereo.

One of the things I've learned over the years is that sometimes when a singer is alone in a recording booth with huge headphones on and a microphone in their face, it's not unusual to push notes too hard or "oversing" in ways they would never do on stage.

That's why I wasn't nearly as confident while doing the recording as I was at the York. The engineer would never concede that there were any major issues with my vocals, and he was always very calming and reassuring to me. Sometimes that tactic worked.

Luckily, there are certain editing tricks that can be done to make notes longer, shorter, or more on pitch if they were just slightly off. Sung parts can be moved electronically if they need to come in a little sooner or later to better match the music.

There are also choices to be made as to which of several takes sound best. Sometimes I had to pick and choose small sections of different takes and have them spliced together to make one continuous verse.

It can be a nightmare wading through it all. The worst is listening to one's own voice totally raw, with no enhancement, and the music completely removed. But to make everything sound as good as possible, there are times when you've got no choice.

After doing a lot of editing and mixing, there was one single sung word in a duet section that just wasn't sounding right. I figured it was because I must have sung it slightly off pitch.

The engineer applied the "pitch doctor" software to that single note. First he turned the dial up a bit. Then down a bit. Was I flat? Was I sharp? More adjustments. Less adjustments. Finally, the engineer did every possible correction and it *still* wasn't sounding right. In fact, it kept getting worse. I was practically banging my head against a wall. This one word was taking hours.

The engineer suggested that we restore my track to the original way I had sung it, and try checking Doug's track instead. I literally laughed at him and said there was no way Doug was off. I was sure that the problem had to be me. He told me he had never recorded a single singer who didn't need at least one correction. So he asked me to just humor him.

When he checked the track, Doug in fact was ever-so-slightly off pitch—like a millimeter on the computer graph. That meant I was actually *on* pitch. I couldn't believe it! Had Doug been singing this note alone, it would have sounded fine. But as a part of a harmony section, there was a clash.

Of course that was a total fluke because Doug otherwise sounded perfect. There had to be a lot more tweaking of my voice than his. In fact, though we did pick and choose from his various takes and splice them together, I think this one note was the only actual correction we made on his tracks.

While I could have tinkered with it forever, all of the mixing, mastering, and last-minute editing was finally finished. By that point, I could barely listen to it anymore—it stopped sounding like music. But I took home the final version, and sent it off to the record manufacturing house.

Meanwhile, graphic artist Scott Fowler, a dear friend, created the beautiful artwork for the cover, disc, and booklet. Once again, that favorite photo of mine—the one with Doug a little too far behind me—came back into discussion.

I really wanted to use it as the cover art, but I still worried that it overemphasized me. Even though Nathan was the "me" in *Thrill Me*, I still felt awkward about it. Finally, I decided to compromise and use it on the *back* cover. Jim Morgan's marvelous photo deserved to be seen. While Scott was putting the layout together, I wrote the necessary liner notes and synopsis.

Within a few months, the *Thrill Me* cast album was released. And it even received its own set of rave reviews. Overall, I ended up being very satisfied with how it turned out, and I was confident that no one would ever be able to guess that Doug and I didn't record any of our songs together. It sounded totally seamless.

Though it took a while, I finally learned to appreciate my vocals. I felt that I actually ended up sounding pretty decent next to Doug. That vocal contrast was unquestionably a good thing to preserve for the ages.

* * *

Since *Thrill Me* had opened just days after the official cutoff date for the 2004-2005 Drama Desk and Outer Critics Circle Awards, I thought for sure we would be forgotten nearly a year later when the 2005-2006 award nominations were announced. I had tried to change our original production dates to avoid this situation, but to no avail.

On the night the Outer Critics nominations were announced via an online press release, I could barely believe my eyes when I saw that *Thrill Me* was nominated for Best Off-Broadway musical. It was never gonna beat *Grey Gardens*, but what an incredible honor. I was shocked.

Then, a few days later, the official press conference for the Drama Desk Award nominations took place at The Friars Club. The nominees were to be announced by *A Chorus Line*'s original star Donna McKechnie and composer Marvin Hamlisch.

With bated breath that morning, I clicked the link on *Playbill.com*. I was stunned to discover that *Thrill Me* was nominated for two Drama Desk Awards. One for Best Musical, the award for the producers, and the other for Best Music, which was for me personally!

Oh wow, that was such an exciting, whirlwind day. My friend Camille took me to lunch; my sister Lori took me to a fancy dinner. I received congratulations from friends, family, and colleagues.

I later shared the good news with two famous neighbors who lived in my building: Marilyn Cooper, who had won a Tony Award for her unforgettable performance in *Woman of the Year*, and celebrated actress Zoe Caldwell, who I was lucky enough to have gotten to see on

Broadway in *Master Class*. I happened upon them separately in the elevator and couldn't stop myself from gushing. Both of them seemed to be so happy for me. I was already basking in the excitement and it was only the beginning.

A few days later there was a cocktail party for the Drama Desk nominees at Arte Café on the Upper East Side where we all received our nomination certificates. While mingling, I was most excited to get to chat with Christine Ebersol, the triumphant star of *Grey Gardens*. It was odd feeling that, as current nominees, we were both on the same level that day.

Every nominee was asked to create a drawing that represented their show for both a temporary gallery display at the restaurant—and then I believe for an exhibition later in the lobby at the award show. I thought I drew a pretty decent interpretation of a typewriter.

The paper on its carriage read *"Thrill Me* by Stephen Dolginoff." Instead of the QWERTY layout, the arrangement of keys spelled out "The Leopold and Loeb Story musical," with "Relationships can be murder" written across the space bar. Hovering up at the top was a hand-drawn line of music. My scribbled signature finished it off. All of the drawings were supposed to eventually become part of the Drama Desk "art*kives" (get it?). I wonder where mine might be today.

The Drama Desk Awards combined both Broadway and Off-Broadway shows together, so I knew the competition against *Jersey Boys* and *The Drowsy Chaperone*, among others, would be very stiff. Had *Thrill Me* been nominated back in 2005, I would have really wanted to win and campaigned hard. But a year later, I sincerely felt like a winner just for being remembered. The old adage "it's an honor just to be nominated" was very true for me. I swear.

That said, we did mail copies of the newly released *Thrill Me* cast album CD to the voting members of both the Outer Critics Circle and Drama Desks. Just in case! Many of those voters personally thanked me for the gesture on the night of the Drama Desk Awards.

Among the musicals *not* nominated for the Drama Desk that year were *The Color Purple*, produced by Oprah Winfrey; *Lestat*, based on the vampire series by Anne Rice; *The Woman in White*, which was the latest big show to come in from London; and *Title of Show*, the cult phenomenon of the season. Neither Andrew Lloyd Webber nor Elton John were nominated for best music. I couldn't imagine how I made the cut ahead of those two.

As for the Outer Critics Circle Awards, the winners were announced via a press conference, or perhaps it was merely a press release. As I had assumed, *Grey Gardens* took the prize for Off-Broadway musical. There was a ceremony just for the winners several days later at Sardi's. I didn't care about not winning, but I sure would have loved to have gone to the party!

But for the Drama Desk Awards, there was still *a lot* in store. I was invited to a star-studded ceremony that would be broadcast nationally on PBS. I knew that there would be a selection of performances from some of the nominated shows, and I hoped *Thrill Me* would be invited to be one of them—and it was! But it almost didn't happen.

The producer of each nominated musical was obligated to provide the standard AFTRA union fees and payments to their performers since the show would be televised. There was understandable concern at the York about the budget for that. Finally, it was all worked out so that Doug and I could sing "Superior" on the broadcast alongside numbers from *Sweeney Todd, Jersey Boys, See What I Wanna See, Grey Gardens,* and *The Drowsy Chaperone.*

Early on the day of the awards, we rehearsed at Lincoln Center in the huge Concert Hall inside LaGuardia High School of Music & Art and Performing Arts, which was where the ceremony was being held. After that, I went home and got dressed. It was decided that instead of character costumes, Doug and I would wear black tuxes.

Jim Kierstead and I went to the Drama Desk's VIP reception at a swanky building on Fifth Avenue. A bus was provided to drive us uptown after the reception. Jim and I walked the red carpet into the lobby where another catered celebration awaited us.

Prior to our performance, production assistants came and got Doug and me from the audience. My seat was next to Cynthia Nixon of *Sex and the City*, who was a presenter that night. Doug was a few rows back. They took us straight to the make-up room.

We entered it to find Patti LuPone, who had her own private make-up artist, voicing a concern to actor Michael Cerveris about something or other. They were both nominated for the revival of *Sweeney Todd*. The stunning, soon-to-be-winner, Christine Ebersol, was looking in the mirror, and giving herself a final touch up.

The make-up people powdered my face to reduce the potential shine from the lights. In an homage to my original run in *Thrill Me*, I wore my slicked-back "Nathan hair"—so they didn't need to help with a comb or brush.

Doug and I were then brought backstage. We stood right next to the incredibly handsome Harry Connick, Jr of that year's revival of *The Pajama Game*. The sound people put on our microphones.

We only had a few moments to wait before we went on, and I was suddenly nervous. I was about to sing in front of a crowd that was probably ten times the size of those at the York. *And* it was full of celebrities. *And* it was being taped for television!

They had put the lyrics to "Superior" on a big teleprompter which loomed in the middle of the auditorium. I thought I would never need it, and didn't even glance at it during rehearsal. But now I was actually scared I might actually forget the words, so I was glad it was there.

Before I could get too freaked out, we were warmly introduced to the audience by host Harvey Fierstein. His *Torch Song Trilogy,* which he also starred in, was the first original non-musical play I ever saw on Broadway—what an inspiration! After his brief speech, onto the stage we went.

The pianist started the intro and once again Nathan and Richard asserted *"We're both Superior to all! / We've got more intelligence that anyone!"* I couldn't help but think back to a year earlier when we were singing the exact same song in "street clothes" for a small audience at Birdland. How far we had come!

The number went perfectly. I'll never forget that applause. After we got off stage, we were taken to the press room where we answered a few questions and posed for photographers. Then we went back to our seats and watched the rest of the show.

My first category came up. When presenter Deborah Gibson, the popular singer/songwriter and stage performer, announced that the winner for Best Music was *The Drowsy Chaperone*. I was just happy she pronounced my name correctly as a nominee. She later told me she had practiced it!

Best Musical was the last award of the evening, and none other than Angela Lansbury, Broadway's original *Mame*, *Sweeney Todd*'s first Mrs. Lovett, and star of TV's *Murder She Wrote*, came out to present it. When she read the list of nominees, it was a real kick to just hear her announce the title of my show, drawn out and dramatic as "Thrrrillll Meeee!" *The Drowsy Chaperone* won that one too.

After the ceremony, another bus took the nominees, winners, and other VIPs to the after party. It was at John's Pizzeria—the same place where, only three years earlier, I had agonized over Jim not being able to accept the Abingdon's offer for a full run of *Thrill Me*. And now here we were celebrating being recognized by the industry for our Off-Broadway production, alongside some of the biggest names in theatre. The juxtaposition was very poignant for me.

I gave my heartfelt thanks and said goodbye to Doug that night. About six months later, he made his Broadway debut in the first revival of *Les Misérables*. The next time I saw him, I was in the audience watching him perform on stage as Marius. He was where he belonged.

A week or so after the ceremony, I was able to watch the entire pre-recorded show on television. I was very pleased with how we looked and sounded. The clip of our performance would live online in perpetuity.

* * *

I felt a huge sense of accomplishment now that *Thrill Me* could be read, listened to, and seen in excerpts on the internet. People who never saw or would *ever* see a production could now enjoy it in the comfort of their own homes. And soon I would personally be enjoying a whole lot of *Thrill Me* as well.

8

THRILLED TO RE-ENACT THE CRIME

"It's the same old game, / with one new feature!"

Thrill Me was now published and handled by one of the top theatrical licensing and publishing houses in the world. The cast album was on sale and available at record stores (remember those?) and on websites everywhere. A collection of rave reviews was accessible for anyone to read online. More and more regional productions were being put into rehearsal, and I couldn't have been happier.

But there was very little time to relax and just bask in the satisfaction. Not only did I receive invitations to visit various productions and give talkbacks, but I was also asked to reprise the role of Nathan in a few theatres around the country. Though I knew it wouldn't be the same without Doug or Shonn, I just couldn't say no.

A few weeks after the Drama Desk Awards, I was back in the black wingtips and slicked-back hair for a short run as Nathan in Tampa Bay, Florida. It was a very small production in a very no-frills theatre. The very friendly and capable actor Johnathan Van Dyke played opposite me as Richard.

While in Florida, I had the pleasure of meeting an old friend of the real Nathan Leopold from his days living in Puerto Rico. He told me that they used to play cards together. It must have been difficult for him to see Leopold's crime-laden early years depicted on stage, but I thought it was very nice of the gentleman to have taken the time to see the show and talk to me.

* * *

Later in the year I traveled to Chicago to finally see *Thrill Me* in the place where it all really happened. This production, at the Bailiwick Repertory Theatre, was directed with a certain historical reverence. I found it to be a very appropriate take.

Unfortunately, once I got there, I discovered that they weren't working from the final published version of the script, since their license was granted in the period between Dramatists Play Service announcing the acquisition and then actually publishing it. That meant they had a pre-release manuscript which still included lines I later changed. I wish I had known this in advance so I could have sent them the revisions. But, in the end, it wasn't that big of a deal.

One of my favorite staging touches that the director put in was during "Nothing Like a Fire." The fire, it seemed, was meant to be blazing offstage left. As Richard sang, Nathan would keep turning his head toward it. Richard would grab Nathan by the chin to turn his face back to him. A small thing, but very effective.

After doing a talkback on stage, I met several people who had familial connections to both the Leopolds and the Loebs. I was always both thrilled and nervous to have those conversations. All in all, I had a very nice time, and I was treated very well by the cast and crew.

Once I was back home, the reviews started being published. I was very pleased that *Thrill Me* in Chicago was met with critical acclaim. It was definitely well-deserved.

A few months later, I flew to Orange County, California. In a theatre not far from Disneyland, I watched a production that was cleverly staged in front of a giant backdrop that depicted the typed ransom note. I do remember looking out of the corner of my eye to see the producer and director watching me watch the show. It was a little rattling. But the entire company was extremely warm and welcoming.

In January of 2007, I took a train to the Media Theatre, in a suburb of Philadelphia, to see their production of *Thrill Me*. It was performed on a set that that looked like a giant chess board. The audience was seated on all four sides around it in chairs that had been set up on the actual stage. The entire auditorium and regular seating weren't used at all. It was an ingenious idea. They essentially created a little theatre out of a large one.

I had previously been invited to observe their New York based auditions, so I already had a friendly rapport with the team. One of the things that still stands out in my mind about this production was when Richard actually put his head down and cried like a baby while Nathan sang *"Spare me the tears..."* at the end during "Life Plus Ninety-Nine Years." It was a chilling moment. Suddenly his bravado had disappeared, and he was reduced to a puddle. I had never seen it done that way before. It was an excellent interpretation of the moment.

Ron Gwiazda happened to be in the Philadelphia area that same day. He joined me at the show. I believe that was the only regional production of *Thrill Me* that Ron ever saw.

The artistic director had invited me to do a talkback, and it was publicized in the local newspapers. When I had first arrived in the beautiful lobby of the theatre, I was introduced to an elderly couple who knew the real Nathan Leopold in Puerto Rico after his parole. They specifically came to see me.

They were very excited to show me clippings and letters that he had written to them. I was afraid that they wouldn't approve of how I chose to interpret their old friend. They *knew* him. I didn't. But after the show, they were very gracious and truly enjoyed it—at least that's what they told me! A local journalist even interviewed them for a story which ran during the run. I'm sure it was great publicity for the production.

* * *

My commitment to play Nathan in a Seattle production began a month later. The artistic director of the theatre had seen my performance at the York. The only issue I had during negotiations was that I was reluctant to be away from my home in New York for the full five weeks or so that would encompass rehearsals and performances. Luckily, the theatre agreed to let me fly back home when there were a few dark days in our performance schedule.

For the poster art, the theatre licensed the first logo from the York. They even bought a quantity of the York's rectangular *Thrill Me* pin-back buttons that were used to promote the show back in 2005. A lot of time and care clearly went into preproduction, and there was plenty of advance publicity. I was even filmed for a fairly lengthy documentary-style interview, which was combined with scenes from our dress rehearsal. It was broadcast on a local TV station several times during the run.

Regrettably, working with the director was difficult. For the first (and only) time in my "acting career," I flat out refused to do a piece of blocking that I disagreed with. It was not one of my finer moments, and I'm not proud of it. But as the creator of the show, I had to stand my ground.

After "Roadster," the director wanted us to run in from opposite sides of the stage and then meet in the middle to sing "Superior." But, plotwise, literally seconds before the song, Nathan and Richard have just committed the murder and hidden the body. Together. How would it have made sense for them to arrive from two totally different places? I got my way, and we both ended up rushing on from the same side as I sang *"All of Chicago would go mad, / if they discovered what we did tonight!"*

The fairly large theatre had seating on three sides. The main section was in the center and there were two much smaller sections on each side. The stage left section was very far from the scenery and the stage right section was almost too close to it. The director seemed to take great pains to make sure the staging wouldn't disfavor the audience on the sides, which was admirable. But, in my opinion, it led to some very awkward blocking.

Major scenes were played to the extreme sides including parts of the telephone song and the climatic kiss. The problem was that there were some performances that had hardly anyone *in* the side seats. The center section was always full, and I felt sorry for all those people who had to watch our backs and profiles so much. Whenever I noticed that the side sections were sparse during a particular performance, I would try to "cheat out"—or turn a bit to the front—although then it was hard to stay in the light.

The desk and typewriter were located far downstage right. This meant that only a small corner of the audience really got to see the scenes that took place there, including the creating of the contract and the signing of it in blood. When Richard dictated to Nathan so he would type *"No matter what he wants, / I'll give him my best,"* I knew that "Stephen" was doing *his* best to make sure everyone was understanding what was happening, despite having to watch from a weird angle.

I think it ended up working out okay. And I was never less than proud when a few friends, who happened to be in Seattle at the time, came to see me in it. Though there was one performance that I wished *no one* saw.

Back when we added in the voice-over recording of the Parole Board, I was worried about the potential for a missed cue or a sound board issue. Luckily, I had never personally experienced any problems. That would all change one rainy night in Seattle.

I made my first entrance, stood next to a chair, and said my line "I suppose you'd like me to sit down?" I waited for the voice of the Parole Board to ring out from the speakers. Nothing. I started "acting" which was probably a mistake. I gave a forlorn look; I fiddled with my hands. Eventually I said something like "please, won't you talk to me?"

I looked up to the tech booth and saw our young stage manager. She was frantically scrambling at the audio player. I was mentally preparing to do the entire scene myself as a monologue, just like I originally conceived back in the late 1990s. But up in the booth, she reached for the microphone—which is usually used to speak to the actors or crew during a rehearsal. She now had that mic in one hand and the script right in front of her.

It was clear that she was going to start reading the lines herself as a last resort. There was nothing wrong with her voice, but it certainly wasn't going to sound like an authoritative 1920s Parole Board. I was afraid I wouldn't be able to keep a straight face. My monologue would be a *much* better option.

I literally tried to lock eyes with her from across the theatre so I could mentally will her to let go of that microphone. "Don't do it. Don't do it." Suddenly, she made one last push of a button and out came the Parole Board voice. All of this happened in a matter of seconds, but it felt like an eternity. And I still have never gotten to do that monologue.

After the show one night, I injured my shoulder. I had to perform the next day's matinee with my right arm severely impaired. I had to sort of hook it onto my vest by putting my thumb through a button hole, and then I tried to not move it at all. It basically looked like it was in a sling without the sling itself.

This made typing and holding the prop telephone nearly impossible. I had to use my left hand to put the props into my right hand. All of the fight choreography had to be cut.

My whole body was weak. At one point, during "My Glasses/Just Lay Low," I had no choice but to put the phone down on the stage and just sit on the floor next to it. Agony. But I kept going. After getting through the performance, the musical director commented, "Stephen, this has proved you can do this show with one arm tied around your back. Literally."

Once all was said and done, my favorite aspect of the Seattle production was the collection of gorgeous, high-quality publicity photographs that they commissioned. We looked fantastic in several carefully posed scenes from the show on the distinctive set, which was made up of varying platforms with a sky full of vintage-style windows frames hanging from above. Those windows were lit from the back to match the mood of each scene. The orange glow behind the glass panes during "Nothing Like a Fire" was stunning I still enjoy scrolling through those pictures.

* * *

Actor Joe Demerly wrote to me that he had always been a fan of the Leopold & Loeb story. He read reviews and publicity about *Thrill Me* and decided to travel from his home in Buffalo, New York, to see the show at the York on my opening night as Nathan. Afterward, he promised me that someday he would get a production up in Buffalo that he and I could star in together.

A couple years later, Joe kept his word. I signed on to do a production at The New Phoenix Theatre in September of 2007. Due to the weekend-based performance schedule, I was able to arrange to take the train home to New York City every Sunday once the show was up and running. I would then travel back to Buffalo on Wednesdays during the month-long run.

The production had a very distinct poster design, rendered in tones of yellow and orange on a black background. Its focal point was a piece of artwork created from a vintage photograph of the real Loeb leaning in to whisper into the ear of the real Leopold. The scenery was similar to the York version, though with a dustier more rundown look.

Rehearsals were a bit of a challenge since I had an unfair advantage. Obviously I was "off book" and knew every word and every song by heart. Plus, I had my character down pat from the moment we started. But Joe still had to learn all of his dialogue and music, and develop his Richard in the usual way.

I think it might have been frustrating for him, feeling like he was "behind" when he actually wasn't at all. In the end, he never should have worried. His performance as Richard was outstanding.

On our opening night I gave Joe and the rest of the company engraved silver pocket watches. Joe gave me a gorgeous engraved silver flask. It's still one of my most prized possessions.

Buffalo was experiencing a record heat wave that Fall. Annoyingly, there was no air-conditioning anywhere in the theatre, including the dressing rooms. On the opening weekend of *Thrill Me*, it felt like it was over one hundred degrees on the stage.

Because it was so hot under the lights, I started sweating through my costume the moment I walked on for my first scene. And, needless to say, my pomade instantly turned into a runny mess.

There were times when I thought I might faint. I don't know how I got through those first few performances. I added a red silk handkerchief to my costume so I could use it to wipe the sweat from my face. But I only used it in the second half after the murder. It was a desperate attempt to keep it in character—like Nathan himself was sweaty with guilt. *"If you want to see your son…"* dab, dab, dab *"…then you'll follow every rule…"* dab, dab, dab.

By the time our second weekend of performances came, the weather had cooled considerably. Well, there must have been something energizing about that earlier heat, because I found it was much harder to *"get my adrenaline going"* in the more comfortable air. Sweating added something to my performance that I was never quite able to recapture. But I still used the red handkerchief. I just didn't have to ring it out after the show.

There were other challenges in Buffalo. One night, after "Nothing Like a Fire," I crossed to the left corner of the stage where the next scene was to take place. But there was no light on me. For a moment I truly panicked, thinking I had made a mistake. I thought to myself "I know I'm supposed to be here. I know I'm supposed to be here." Finally, Joe joined me and I was confident we were in the right place—just in the dark.

After what seemed like an eternity, the orange "fire" lights which were focused all the way on the right side of the stage came on, which was just enough for us to be visible on the left. I figured that something must have had happened to the lighting board and the technical director was just turning on any lights possibly he could.

So we went on with the scene. And for the rest of the night we never knew what, if any, light would be on us. Some moments were almost totally played in darkness. *"Can't you understand this situation? / I think I understand, and clearly see!"* There were times when we could *barely* see.

After the show was over, we were told that indeed an entire dimmer panel had gone out. I wonder what the audience thought. They knew they were in for something "dark." But did they think it would actually be *that* dark?

At another performance a few weeks later, Joe had just finished singing *"You'll be safe inside my roadster…"* and then the pianist began the low bass notes on the keyboard, which would normally be played over and over again like a clock chiming midnight. On about the third note, the music stopped. And it didn't start again. We had run into the wings, as we were directed to do, and would usually have kept running straight back on to sing "Superior." But there was still no music.

Joe must have thought "the show must go on," because he was seconds away from continuing onto the stage. But I quickly grabbed him and held him back. After all of the earlier enduring of the heat, then the broken lights, and now the nonexistent music, I couldn't help but whisper to him that there was no way I was gonna do the rest of the show a cappella.

Just a few seconds later the music started again and on we went. Apparently, someone had somehow tripped on the very long chord that plugged in the electric keyboard, and it took the pianist a bit of time to get to the outlet to plug it back in. It was a bit embarrassing but at least a worse debacle had been avoided.

While it was great to perform with Joe that September, the whole production had been a series of obstacles. So I wasn't too sad when it was over. And I was very glad to have forged what I was sure would be a life-long friendship. *"We've got a bond, / we'll take it to the grave!"*

Many years later, Joe gifted me his cherished hand-signed copy of Nathan Leopold's autobiography. It was an overwhelmingly generous gesture. Even holding it now, knowing it was once in the hands of the real Nathan Leopold, gives me the shivers.

I also got the shivers in January of 2008 when I received a very surprising email. It was from a man who explained that he was a descendant of Richard Loeb's brother Tommy—the one whose name I changed way back in 1994.

He had previously seen my performance in *Thrill Me*. And he told me how pleased he was to see a version of the story that focused on the complicated relationship between the two characters.

He also wrote that family lore taught him that in comparison to his relative Richard, Nathan was far smarter—which totally tracked with my interpretation. I was very flattered to receive his message.

We continued to correspond for a bit, and he shared a few stories about his family. They were fascinating to read.

* * *

As insignificant as it seems, one of the biggest modifications I made to my performance after the Off-Broadway production was the addition of a pocket watch to my costume. It made a huge difference. In New York, such a watch was used only as a prop at the very beginning, and it was kept hidden in my pants pocket. But the costume design for the Seattle production included the watch chain visibly attached to my vest, and strung through a button loop. It was done a similar way in Buffalo.

During rehearsals, I slowly started to use the pocket watch more and more because it was just so present. In the first scene when Richard kisses Nathan, I played it like I was startled and dropped the watch, causing it to dangle from my vest and sway back and forth. I thought it made a nice visual.

In the scenes where I was waiting for Richard impatiently, I would keep opening the watch to check the time over and over again. Kind of like how I still checked my shoelaces before every performance. It was good way to fill those moments.

The prop also gave me an extra "Nathan quirk"—I would constantly be obsessed with making sure that the two sections of the chain were hanging on my vest perfectly evenly. In one of the lines at the end, when Nathan is to have his possessions returned to him, he mentions his "solid gold pocket watch." This tied it all together nicely because, by that point, the audience had become very much aware of that watch.

To feel more comfortable—and for good luck—in all three productions I was in after Off-Broadway, I wore my original eyeglasses, blue & white striped shirt, and (of course) the wingtip shoes. I also wore my original blue paisley bow tie in Tampa Bay and Seattle. But I decided to retire it after that, since it was starting to show wear. Still one of my favorite keepsakes, I now keep it tucked away in a safe place.

Even though I knew one would be provided, I bought myself a similar tie to use in Buffalo. This way I knew I would be pleased with how it looked. Maybe that's why the lights went out and the keyboard got unplugged—my tie must not have been similar *enough* to appease the theatre gods!

* * *

The only somewhat negative aspect of playing Nathan for a few years was my *hair*. I had to keep it consistently very long on top to achieve the 1920s slicked-back style. On stage, I loved how it looked. But in real life, it made me very self-conscious because it always seemed to be a mess. I could never find a way to tame it.

Despite that, I have to admit that wish I could have played the role forever. But by now I was pushing forty and it was a miracle I had still been able to pull off playing a teenager. Luckily, those stage lights were very forgiving.

So after the Buffalo run, it was ultimately time to cut my hair short again and permanently retire the pomade. Since I would no longer be an integral part of it, *Thrill Me* would now become something for me to "experience." And there would be experiences aplenty!

9

LIVING WITH *THRILL ME*

"They don't know your mind / the way that I do."

I was once again back to occasionally traveling to see productions around the country. When I did, I usually gave interviews to local journalists, and often participated in talkbacks. I was finally starting to get used to seeing versions that I had no actual input in. I always appreciated the invitations, and I never went into any theatre without an open mind.

But as I think anyone would understand, I was usually most critical of the actors playing Nathan. What can I say? As the author, I obviously approved of exactly how *I* had personally interpreted the role. It was difficult to see it done any other way.

I felt that Richard was a far more easy character to play. He could just be "evil" and it would work. Maybe not nuanced, but it would suffice. Nathan, I felt, needed so many various qualities to carry the show. So with a few exceptions, it was hard for practically anyone to meet my expectations. But there was nothing I could do but smile and be appreciative. Which I truly was.

* * *

Back home in New York, I got word one day that a student in South Dakota won a first place medal for "Dramatic Interpretation" at his state Speech & Debate competition with a cutting from *Thrill Me*. I used to do those competitions in High School so it really touched me. I reached out to the coach and sent my congratulations.

Later I was asked by another young actor if he could use a scene and song from *Thrill Me* as his audition for the prestigious Irene Ryan Acting Scholarship. I gave him permission, but I never heard how it turned out for him. I sure hope he made the right choice of material!

Another thrill was meeting the actor Farley Granger in 2008 at his book signing at The Drama Book Shop, a popular Midtown Manhattan spot for theatre people. Mr. Granger was the star of the Alfred Hitchcock film *Rope*. Thus he was the first actor to ever portray a character inspired by Nathan Leopold on film, albeit a highly fictionalized version. I couldn't help but notice that copies of the *Thrill Me* script were sitting on a nearby shelf.

I have to admit that *Rope* has perturbed me ever since the first few productions of *Thrill Me,* because many people would say things like "Oh is it like a musical version of *Rope?*" or "I know that story—I saw *Rope.*" It's not fair to either piece. Fans of *Rope* would likely be very disappointed by *Thrill Me* if they were expecting the same story but with songs.

Of course I acknowledge that *Rope* is a truly engaging, excellent movie, based on the Patrick Hamilton play. While it does feature two guys who appear to be in a relationship, a "thrill killing," and talk of Nietzsche, I contend that it is not the Leopold & Loeb *story.*

Here's the plot in a nutshell: Adult roommates, Brandon and Phillip, are discovered in their ritzy Manhattan penthouse apartment strangling their friend David to death with a long piece of rope. They hide the body in a large wooden chest. It all has to be done quickly because their housekeeper will soon be arriving, followed by a bunch of other friends who've been invited over for a dinner party.

The men decide to put a table cloth over the trunk and serve the buffet on top of it—on top of *David's body*. Everyone arrives and the party commences. Some of the friends start to wonder why David isn't there.

Eventually their old college professor, who was also invited, deduces exactly what happened. Both the murderous plan and David's body are at last uncovered.

The entire thing happens in about an hour and twenty minutes of real linear time. Does that sound anything like *Thrill Me?* Not to me anyway.

At least *Rope* is able to be enjoyed by just about anyone, anywhere, at any time. I had hoped there could be some sort of filmed version of *Thrill Me* itself.

Around the time of the Off-Broadway production back in 2005, I pitched it to the newly formed Here TV, an LGBT-focused premium cable network that had recently launched with much fanfare. They responded quickly, and asked for more information about the show. But nothing ever came of it.

* * *

A few years later, when the 2008 Los Angeles production was getting ready to open right in the middle of Hollywood, I sent another e-mail to the director of development at Here TV. Within a few weeks I heard back. He was interested in further information so I sent the script, the CD, and some press clippings.

When the show got a rave review in *The Hollywood Reporter,* I forwarded it to him immediately. He wrote back within five minutes. Clearly the notice in a well-read trade publication gave *Thrill Me* the legitimacy that he needed! He asked me to arrange tickets to the show for him. Since I was flying to California to see it myself, we decided he would attend on a night when I was also there.

The theatre was located on Hollywood Theatre Row, in a building that housed three different stages and a café. A huge *Thrill Me* poster hung outside. It was essentially a life-sized photograph of a shirtless Nathan, standing behind a formal-suited Richard, with his arms wrapped around him. The title of the show was displayed in red letters with little blood splatters all around it. I thought it was an image that worked very well and definitely set the right expectations.

For the most part, I enjoyed the show. It was set on a very wide stage. The focal point was a collection of platforms that were covered in a tarp that looked like a giant version of something used to cover a body. Above hung several light fixtures that appeared to be straight out of a 1920s police interrogation room.

After the performance, the executive from Here TV met with me in the lobby. He told me that he loved the show and would pitch it to the network. The idea was to possibly tape the production for broadcast as part of a new program which he said was to be called *Here Onstage*.

Normally, this news would have sent me over the moon. But the problem was that I didn't feel that what was on stage was the best possible representation of my vision of *Thrill Me*.

The production was certainly of very high quality, and everyone involved was extremely talented. But, in my opinion, there were too many liberties taken with the material. They added much of Older Nathan's dialogue to the Parole Board recording, apparently so that the actor himself could move set pieces and props around. Thus many of those scenes were played *entirely* in voice-over.

There was extra stage business that I felt hurt the flow of the story. Applause breaks were either added in specifically or were just allowed to happen, despite the very clear instructions in the script and score. The actor playing Richard was absolutely perfect for the role, and his acting was great. But, due to vocal limitations, he needed to "talk-sing" many of the songs.

Clearly most critics and audiences had no problem with any of it, and all of this was fine for the stage performances. But if Here TV recorded and broadcast the production, it was likely to become the "definitive version." It could potentially be seen by more people in one night than would ever see the play. Should a version with talk-singing have that distinction?

Obviously, the deal wouldn't have just involved me. Agreements would also have to be put in place with everyone in the Los Angeles production. They were all elated by the prospect. I gingerly had to start a conversation about the adjustments they would have to make in order for me to allow it all to happen.

I feared that broaching this may have offended them because, in their eyes, the show was clearly a hit. But they seemed to understand

and agreed to try to implement my requests if the deal went any further. Still, I wasn't convinced that a few changes here and there would ultimately make me happy.

If only we could have gone back in time so the opportunity could have happened in New York! But the network was based in Los Angeles, and they evidently had none of the concerns that I had. I struggled with all of this for several weeks. I knew that I was in no position in my career to turn down a television deal, but I secretly hoped that it wouldn't come to pass.

More executives from Here TV went to the show. Initial discussions were made between the network and Ron, but nothing concrete. And I'm sure representatives also talked to the production team in Los Angeles. The network must have been happy to find out that the run of *Thrill Me* was extended, which would give them more time for the possible taping.

Finally, with the clock ticking before the production closed, Here TV decided not to move forward. They promised to consider *Thrill Me* for a future endeavor—which never happened! At least I could sleep again.

I kept in touch with that executive over the years, always sending clippings, news, etc. I honestly don't know if there ever was a *Here Onstage*. Finally, he moved on to a new job, and that was the end of my contact with the network.

After the Los Angeles production closed its successful run, it would later be nominated for an Ovation Award for Best Production of a Musical in an Intimate Theatre. The actors won a Garland Award for Best Ensemble Performance, and I received a Garland Honorable mention for my score. I was thrilled!

* * *

By now there had been twenty or so productions. Aside from the pre-recorded Older Nathan dialogue in Los Angeles, they were assumedly performed exactly as written. But I now started getting requests from producers and directors for various changes. Since the licensing agreement, not to mention copyright law, unequivocally requires my permission for any alterations, I'm at least glad they asked.

One theatre wanted to add nudity. I'm no prude—after all, naked Richard was part of my very first idea for the prologue. But as the script now stood, I just didn't think it was called for. Besides, there's hardly any time for the characters to get their clothes off, much less back on. So I refused to allow it.

Another production requested a different "Prelude." I never got to the bottom of what they actually felt they needed or what was lacking. But I didn't have an alternate one to give them, and I wasn't going to create one.

A few theatres inquired if the keys to several of the individual songs could be changed. This wouldn't be an unusual or unreasonable question for most musicals. But the *Thrill Me* score was created as a whole, and I believed that changing any of the keys—especially raising them, which was the usual ask—would totally destroy the dark mood that I worked so hard to create.

And since the underscore flowed in and out of the songs, it could be very awkward and jarring to hear any unintended modulations. Back when "Way Too Far" was lowered for me, and "Afraid" was raised for one of the Richards, the underscore was painstakingly reworked around them. So the answer to these requests was always "no."

I was once asked if there was any cut material that I wanted to put back in. I would have thought it was obvious that if something was cut, it was cut for a reason. But instead of explaining that, it was easier to just reject the "opportunity."

There was also a director who wanted to know if there was anything I wanted to "rewrite" especially for his production. That was certainly a loaded question. I politely declined. At least I hope it was politely.

Fortunately, every producer and director in question was generally very understanding when I turned them down—even though perhaps some of my responses were curt. I knew that they were only trying to make their production the best possible and in no way intended to offend me.

But if I'm not always firm in insisting that the script must be performed exactly as written, then what did I work so hard for? I did my best and I wrote what I wrote. Perhaps nudity, a different "Prelude," new song keys, or the addition of cut material would be all it would take to turn *Thrill Me* from what is generally considered a well-written piece, or at least a piece that I can stand behind, into something less successful?

No one would expect a published novel to be rewritten to suit one person's individual tastes. Or a movie to be re-edited based on someone's own ideas for improving it. I believe that plays and musicals should be treated no differently.

* * *

Much to my surprise, there was suddenly a production that didn't want to change the *script*—but wanted to change the *casting*. Without even realizing it, I was asked to allow a female production of *Thrill Me* at a university. I accidentally let it happen because I misunderstood their initial application.

It was totally my fault and, once I discovered the situation, I had no choice but to let them proceed. They didn't necessarily play the characters as female. They were simply neutral, with both dressed in slacks and white shirts. It was performed just for their acting class.

I would then get *many* more inquires for female productions from other theatre groups. But it wasn't a door I really wanted to keep open. Turning the requests down was difficult, and was sometimes met with great disappointment. But Leopold & Loeb were real people. And thus it was hard to wrap my mind around the idea of not casting male actors.

One of the biggest obstacles to overcome would be regarding the vocals. Specifically, how to translate the dark, low, baritone sound into something equivalent for female voices. It would still need to sound like the dialogue blended seamlessly into song. The size of male and female vocal ranges isn't usually the same, so it wouldn't be just an issue of changing the octave or the key signature. I'm not sure how the student production dealt with it, and I probably don't *want* to know.

While it would be a challenge for me to reconfigure the score, it probably wouldn't be impossible. And I would consider it under the right circumstances. But until that choice is made by me, the casting for the show still requires two males.

* * *

For the most part, the early years in the licensing life of *Thrill Me* were a total joy. I would usually start my mornings by checking the Dramatists Play Service website. It had a listing of all upcoming productions. This was usually the first place I would find out about where *Thrill Me* was scheduled to play.

There was a production in Richmond, Virginia that I was invited to see. I took a train and arrived at the tiny theatre with very low expectations. But it was positively marvelous. I loved how they just kept it as simple as possible so the young actors could shine.

I didn't get to Texas to see a production in Dallas, so they sent me a set of photos. They revealed a very distinctive take on the show. The whole thing seemed to unfold in Older Nathan's prison cell, which was very elaborately designed.

When I read that there was about to be a production in Sioux City, Iowa, I reached out to Russ Wooley, the artistic director of the Lamb Theatre, where it was to take place. I sent him my thanks and offered to answer any questions that might arise. That led to a cherished friendship that has lasted ever since.

The staging he created in a small black box theatre—with a set that was primarily comprised of steamer trunks—was extremely unique. I wish I had gotten to see it in person. Russ, along with his wife Diana (the executive director of the Lamb), would go on to present the world premieres of my next three musicals.

I did get to see a production in New Jersey that was staged by a director named Linda Wielkotz. It was actually in the back room of a bar. And it sure was dark!

Linda did an impressive job in such an unusual, minuscule space. Her set design looked like an attic full of junk—from which the various props would be pulled. Linda also become a good friend, and later went on to direct more of my work.

I also went to see a double-cast college production that had the non-performing actors backstage on microphones as the Parole Board. That way all four guys could be a part of every performance. Their poster was very striking. It was a photograph shot from a low angle looking upward. It seemed like the *viewer* was the victim, who was "looking up," as Nathan and Richard were looking down—just about to cover the "victim's eyes" with a white sheet. I loved it.

A significant production opened in Athens, Greece. Their main publicity photo used a rather daring image of the two men holding a teddy bear that was wearing glasses. The actor playing Nathan was pointing his finger to its head, like a gun. I'd never seen anything like that before. Or since!

* * *

It was truly an exciting couple of years for me and the show. I found it hard to imagine what could possibly come next. I had achieved just about every goal I ever had—and then some. But very soon, I would be reaping the benefits of an unexpected lucky break that would transform the life of *Thrill Me* forever.

10

THREE OVERSEAS THRILL RIDES

"You want the details?"

In early March of 2009, I was sitting in the business class section of a Korean Airlines Jet—drinking champagne—while on my way to Seoul, South Korea with a couple of loved ones in tow. It would be only the second overseas trip I'd taken in my lifetime. I was pretty nervous because I'd never really loved to travel. Sitting on *any* plane was actually quite rare for me.

But I couldn't pass up the experience to see the opening of the third year of *Thrill Me* performances in a brand-new theatre. The show had become a bona fide hit in Seoul since its opening in early 2007, and I was finally going to be able to see it for myself. I was also scheduled to speak to the press, give a talkback, and even perform for the South Korean fans. *Fans?*

Yes, *Thrill Me* had developed a huge fan base. Because South Korean bookstores carried the Dramatists Play Service script, and the cast album had been available at the *Thrill Me* merchandise stand once the production first started, even *I* had genuine fans. I received effusive emails galore through the *Thrill Me* website.

As I was waiting to take off, with my heart beating quickly, I thought back to how it all started. Sometime in late 2005 or in early 2006, Ron told me that we got a licensing request from a producer in Seoul named Michael Park of Musical Heaven Productions (which would later be renamed DAL, and eventually MP & Company).

My understanding was that, at Ron's suggestion, Michael had seen the show at the York toward the end of the run, during one of my performances as Nathan. Apparently, he was trying to get the rights to stage a popular musical called *The 21ˢᵗ Annual Putnam County Spelling Bee*, which Ron also represented.

But those rights either weren't available or there was a lot of competition for them. So Ron pushed *Thrill Me,* and Michael bit. Thank "musical heaven" that he did!

It was another occasion that proved it was a good thing I had taken the risk and stepped into the role of Nathan. Otherwise, there would have been no show for him to see, and if this piece of good fortune didn't happen, my career would be very different now. Though, at the time, I had no idea what the scope of the production would be. I just thought it was a normal license—even though it would be for a run of several months.

After the contract was signed, Michael Park visited New York in the Fall of 2006. I met him in Ron's office, with my suitcase at hand. After the meeting I would be boarding a sleeper car on an Amtrak train to Chicago to see that production of *Thrill Me* at the Bailiwick.

We discussed the translation. It was important to both Michael and me that the show be as appealing as possible to his intended audience which, statistically speaking, would mainly be females in their twenties. Michael explained that very often mainstream western musicals would be translated as close as possible to the original text, even if the context might not make sense to South Korean theatregoers.

So I agreed that the script wouldn't have to be a word for word translation. Instead, I let them adapt it however they felt it would best be received. And Michael put together a great team to do it.

There was one translator for the dialogue, and another for the lyrics. Things like humor, metaphors, and figures of speech were changed the most. "Nothing Like a Fire," for example, was eventually translated as "You're Playing with Fire."

There was also a conversation about adding more instruments to go along with the piano. I gave permission for that to be explored. But ultimately Michael realized that it wasn't necessary, and his production of *Thrill Me* retained the single piano.

Instead of requiring the Asian actors to pretend to be Caucasian young men in Chicago with western names, there was talk of setting *Thrill Me* in Seoul in the 1970s. Michael told me that era would feel similar to Chicago in the 1920s. But eventually a decision was made to just keep everything vague and abstract. Similar to one of my early discarded ideas!

So there was no reference to time, place, or even character names. It wasn't in Chicago, nor was it in Seoul. It had 1920s touches, such as the candlestick telephones, but the costumes and hairstyles seemed more modern. Nathan became "I" and Richard became "He." They never referred to each other by their actual names. Consequently "Everybody Wants Richard" became something like "Everybody Wants You," for example.

I'm confident that my allowing all of this was a key reason for the production's major success. It didn't feel like an imported American musical, but more like a musical relevant to South Koreans. They instantly embraced it.

I did require one thing from Musical Heaven. They needed to explain, in the printed programs (which are called "brochures" over there), that the story the audience would be seeing was based on the true story of Leopold & Loeb, and that it happened in 1920s Chicago. They agreed—and then some!

I literally only meant that it needed to be a sentence or two. But their gorgeous brochures, which were sold at the merchandise stand, included an extensive multi-page historical write-up that they specially created. There was also an extensive array of vintage photos of Leopold, Loeb, Bobby Franks, the crime scene, and the evidence. Many of the photos I had never even seen myself!

So they watched "I" and "He" on stage, but the rapidly growing base of young female Korean fans knew they were watching Leopold & Loeb. A musical and an American history lesson!

When I started getting photographs and video clips, it was clear that Musical Heaven's production had the size, budget, and quality of a Broadway show. It was even nominated for Best Foreign Musical and

Best Original Score at the "Korea Musical Awards," their equivalent of the Tonys. I could hardly believe it.

The fans apparently loved to watch the portrayal of a relationship between two men, and they really seemed to enjoy watching the guys kiss. In fact, an extra embrace and smooch was added at the end of the curtain call, which was met with enthusiastic cheers. It didn't hurt that the show was, and continues to be, cast with very good-looking performers.

There were two separate casts who would alternate during the standard eight-show week. This was very different than single-cast New York productions. I was told that it was the common practice in South Korea. No cast was considered more important than the other.

After the first season in 2007, Michael extended the show and moved to another theatre. Soon after, we agreed to a deal for 2008— and then for 2009. And in that third contract, my visit was included.

* * *

I landed in Seoul, was met by members of Michael's staff, and taken straight to a huge theatre to watch another one of Musical Heaven's productions. It was an excellent show based on a popular South Korean movie.

Afterward, while we were being escorted out a back door, I was suddenly mobbed by a group of fans who recognized me and started asking for autographs. I kept thinking they must be mistaking me for someone else. They couldn't possibly know who *I* was out of context.

But they giddily kept saying "thrill me! thrill me!" I was completely overwhelmed. Actually, "in shock" was more like it. While I had certainly signed a few Playbills after the show at the York, and many CDs and scripts over the years, nothing even close to this reception had ever happened to me. It was like I had entered the bizzarro world. What a welcome!

The next day I gave some press interviews, watched one of the cast's dress rehearsal, and posed for photographs with them on stage. Then I finally got a chance to meet my "internet friend" from South

Korea, Haemin Lee, in person. For the past few years she had been sending me information about the production, translated articles and reviews for me, and also passed along questions from the fans for me to answer.

The following day I did more press. One interview after the next. It seemed like it would never end—but I loved every minute of it. Every journalist was so well versed in all things *Thrill Me*. They would ask very specific questions about the motivations of the characters, and they would be delighted anytime my answer coincided with their personal interpretations.

Finally, it was time for me to attended the first "year three" performance of the show, which was a preview matinee. I was met by a group of fans on the way in, and I was happy to sign autographs for all of them. Once I was sitting in the theatre, which was named The Stage, it almost felt like a dream. I couldn't believe that I was really there.

When the lights dimmed, a series of chimes played. I believe this was a ceremonial, cultural, custom. The audience sat so still and quiet that it almost felt like I was there alone until the thunderous applause at the end.

The scenic design utilized detailed platforms up against dark grey brick walls to represent each character's bedroom. At the back of the stage was a huge, heavy-looking "garage door" that would open with a deafening sound to reveal the headlights of Richard's roadster behind it. A group of single-bulb lamps hung overhead.

There were also some very fun special effects. When the "Prelude" began, a projected moving image of a lit match flickered near the pianist. During "Roadster," there was a creepy illuminated walking footprint effect, straight out of an "invisible man" movie. It was projected onto the stage floor to represent the steps of the victim walking toward Richard. At one point they would even turn and walk the other way, until finally following him off the stage. During the telephone song, there was a projected film of storm clouds swirling across the top of the stage to symbolize both the ominous mood and the passage of time.

One of my favorite little touches that the translators made was the addition of the loud squawk of a bird at Richard's first entrance. When he came behind Nathan to scare him with the line "Quit watching the stupid birds," it added an extra jolt. This exact sound was repeated at the end when Older Nathan was remembering Richard, who then appears as if in his mind.

For this version he said "Babe" as written in the English language script, but then he repeated "Quit watching the stupid birds" (in Korean) to make it clear that *this* was the moment Nathan was remembering. It was extremely effective, and I wished I had thought of it myself.

Seeing this also made me regret not tying Older Nathan's line at the end about "a picture of Richard" to the first scene. Instead of using binoculars to watch birds, Nathan could have been taking photographs of them. During "Everybody Wants Richard," he could have snapped a photo of Richard—and then the picture he references at the end would have been assumedly this one taken in 1924 in Jackson Park.

But thinking about it further, this would have meant an authentic looking early 1920s camera would be required. Those things were *big*! And it would probably need one of those huge flash-apparatus-things.

When the show was over, I was mobbed for autographs again. I gladly signed for every single person who wanted one, and posed for lots of photos. I didn't care about how I looked, or the angle of my head, or if I was being shot from my best side. I was so appreciative of the fact that total strangers wanted a picture with me—so all my usual vanity disappeared.

Once the crowd was gone, I posed for press photos with the extremely friendly and talented director of the show, Jong-Seok Lee. They snapped pictures of us on the set and around the theatre. Then we were taken to a lovely restaurant which was located way up high in an extremely tall building.

We sat on gorgeous purple crushed velvet tufted seats and did an interview for a theatre-related magazine called *The Musical.* I was very excited about this because Haemin had previously sent me copies of the thick attractive publication. I practically felt like I was going to be in *Vogue*!

The interview was set up as a discussion between Jong-Seok and myself. A few months later, a copy was sent to me at home—and I thought it turned out great. I sure looked *very* happy in the photos.

The next night was the official opening of the show. Afterward, I did an onstage talkback and discussion with Jong-Seok and one of the translators of the script. This was followed by an official autograph session. They set up a table for me in the lobby with a series of pens and markers at my side. The line was long—practically the entire audience had stayed.

I signed programs, CDs, scripts—you name it! I did my best to take the time to talk with every single person that approached the table—some of them quite nervously. Their smiling faces meant the world to me. To say I was moved would be quite the understatement. No one had ever treated me like a celebrity before. I wondered if I deserved it. But, regardless, I was totally in heaven.

Many fans that night presented me with thoughtful little keepsakes, which I greatly appreciated. I also received a cheesecake and a banana. I ate the cheesecake (delicious) and banana (healthy) later that night. But *all* of the other gifts are still in my drawer to this day, reminding me of the immense generosity and hospitality I received in Seoul.

After the autograph session, Michael took the entire company to a Korean barbecue restaurant for an opening night party. Well, I guess they just call it "barbecue" there.

The following night I got to watch the other cast perform the show, and I was struck by how different they were. I had just assumed that both casts would be directed to play everything the same way. Boy was I wrong.

In the first cast, the actor playing Nathan was spry, nervous, and he moved around lot; Richard was slow and careful. The second cast was almost the exact opposite. Nathan was sullen and still, carrying the weight of the world on his shoulders; Richard was animated and excited by just about every little thing.

All four of them had valid and unique interpretations of their roles. And all four of them seemed to have separate fan clubs who would apparently provide meals for them before every show.

Early the next day, I gave an interview to a magazine called *Movie Week,* which was the Korean equivalent of *Entertainment Weekly.* They took photos of me all over the *Thrill Me* set. When I was back in New York City, I got a copy of the magazine in Koreatown. It wasn't far from the same Macy's store that I was on my way to, years earlier, when I first thought of the title of the show.

Later that night in Seoul, instead of a regular performance, a special ticketed event was held at the theatre. I was on stage to represent *Thrill Me* alongside the director and the cast. It was a complete sell-out.

As part of the occasion, the production team had previously requested that I create a twenty-minute speech which included stories about writing and performing in *Thrill Me.* I needed to write it in advance so the translator would be prepared to translate me live on stage. This meant that I would say a sentence or two, then I would pause as she would speak my words in Korean.

They also asked me to sit at the piano to play and sing a few songs from the show. Let's just say that playing the piano *in public* has never been one of my favorite things to do. I'm honestly not that good of a pianist, though I can fake it reasonably well. But I decided to face my fears and just *do* it. Within the telling of my stories I played and sang bits of "My Glasses/Just Lay Low," "Why," "Way Too Far," and "Life Plus Ninety-Nine Years."

A question and answer session then followed with myself and other members of the company. Next there were performances from the casts of *Thrill Me* and another musical. After that came a drawing for a giveaway contest.

At the end, everyone else left the stage and the evening concluded with me alone up there at the piano singing a section of the *Thrill Me* title song. During the whole thing, I wore one of those microphones that wrap around your face—like a rock star. And that's actually what I felt like...for one night only!

In trying to avoid the mob, the staff brought me out using a different door than usual. But the fans were still there waiting. I signed more autographs, posed for more photos, and gave out all of pages of the sheet music I had used during the night's performance to a few lucky fans.

* * *

While I was in Seoul, I met with another theatre producer who ran his own company. He was interested in buying the South Korean film rights to *Thrill Me*. That was certainly an exciting prospect. He started our meeting by presenting me with a beautiful ornate metal letter opener. After his pitch, I was very enthusiastic.

In May of that year—just a few months after I came home—he negotiated with Ron, culminating in a signed deal. I believed, at that time, that he was very serious about putting the movie into production quickly, and I was very excited. But as of early 2024, the movie has never been made.

Unfortunately, the way the contract was worded, the rights would never revert back to me. And over the years, I've gotten various different offers for South Korean film versions. I've tried to get the rights back, even if I had to buy them. I've talked to lawyers in the hope of finding a loophole. But it was all to no avail.

None of this was the producer's fault. A deal is a deal, and I willingly agreed. Luckily the only thing in that contract was the right for him to make a single South Korean language feature film. I retained the motion picture rights for the entire rest of the world—in every other language. I also kept all television rights.

The film contract also contained language mentioning things that are now nearly obsolete, like DVDs and soundtrack CDs. So if he ever started to make the movie, we would need to renegotiate to account for modern necessities, like streaming and downloads.

The producer has proudly mentioned his owning of the *Thrill Me* film rights in the press from time to time. So it's possible that I could wake up tomorrow…or the next day…to news of a start date.

* * *

On the day I left South Korea, the staff at Musical Heaven presented me with a beautiful gift of miniature wooden theatre masks. Then I was taken down a street in the theatre district that they wanted to be sure that I saw in the daylight. When we got to that certain block, I was told to look up at the lampposts.

All of them were displaying vertical *Thrill Me* banner ads as far as the eye could see. They were swaying in the wind. It was as if that multitude of *Thrill Me* flags were waving goodbye to me. It took my breath away. What a fitting way to leave South Korea. It had been the trip of a lifetime. Michael Park had made sure that I was treated like a king.

* * *

The Seoul production of *Thrill Me* quickly established itself in the South Korean entertainment industry and became a long-running popular hit. It's been in production for close to twenty years now with no signs of stopping.

As is the custom in the country, shows run seasonally. So it may play for six months one year, then take several months off and reopen in a new theatre for two separate three-month runs the following year, and other scenarios like those. It's also toured to the cities of Busan and Mokpo.

As the years would go on, sometimes there would be as many as *five* separate casts in a season. Occasionally they would even trade partners to create new pairings for special performances. It's a great benefit to the production because many fans want to see every "team," as they are called.

So instead of buying one ticket, they buy several. I've seen photos of fans displaying their collections of advance tickets in their hands like…fans—the kind you use to cool off with!

Since *Thrill Me* was never branded with a single specific or official logo, it allowed the marketing department in South Korea to create a series of distinctive designs over the years. The original poster was long and thin with half of each actor's face shown, and half cut off. Between them they held a lit match.

A later version had a dramatic black and white image that focused on two male hands—one grasping the other. Another poster featured a photo of the upper half of a vintage typewriter at the bottom with the text of the contract above it.

One year they commissioned a stunning Manhwa illustration (a style similar to Manga or Anime) drawn by the famous artist Hee-Jung Park, which I would describe as depicting Nathan reaching for Richard against a dark, stormy sky. I was sent photos of that particular poster enlarged and displayed on huge columns in Seoul subway stations. It must have been seen by tens of thousands of commuters.

The scenery and effects would also change over the years. One season there was a "jury box" on one side where the audience could be seated up close to the actors. Another year, the set had vivid projected backgrounds.

For one version, instead of the footprints, a child's swing made of rope and a wooden seat flew down from above. It looked like it was hanging from a tree. When Richard approached, it magically started swinging as if Bobby Franks was on it. On cue it would stop, symbolizing Bobby following Richard to his doom.

Due to receiving many requests, Michael eventually made a special arrangement with Ron and myself to start licensing amateur and school productions of *Thrill Me* all throughout South Korea. His office also would license professional concert performances of songs from the show, which became a frequent occurrence.

And the South Korean *Thrill Me* wasn't just confined to the stage. There was a two-part dramatic radio adaptation which was broadcast by a company called "Studio Musical." It featured narration, songs, dialogue, and a general discussion of the show. I even gave permission for a comic book adaptation to be published, which turned out simply gorgeous.

Michael Park truly changed my life with his production. I sometimes wonder if even he could have predicted the magnitude of success that his *Thrill Me* would achieve. There were times I practically had to pinch myself to prove it was all really happening. I couldn't have been happier—or more surprised!

* * *

By the time *Thrill Me* entered its second decade of performances in 2010, the show was being performed all around the world. There were productions as far away as Sydney, Australia in a version that featured a pianist dressed to evoke Bobby Franks; and as close as my old stomping ground of Kansas City, where a myriad of images were projected onto the stage floor.

Surprisingly, a publicity photo from that Kansas City production depicted the two characters sharing a hot dog, while covered in blood. I guess after the director did his research, he *really* wanted to get that moment in somehow, somewhere. Perhaps if I looked further, I may have discovered additional photos with the root beer and the tennis racket! Regardless, I wasn't able to see that version, but I was very happy that many hometown friends and family members did. And my dad kindly mailed me one of the posters.

One day, totally out of the blue, another goal was achieved when I received a major offer. It was for a production of *Thrill Me* in London. Finally!

Back in the late 1990s, Martin Charnin had planned to open the show in London, and now it was really going to happen at last. I hoped that since it played so well in New York, it would also be popular "across the pond." After all, I knew they loved their thrillers over there!

The English producer told me he was interested because he had seen the Los Angeles production—the same one that Here TV almost televised. So that version ended up leading to an exciting opportunity after all! He entered contract negotiations with Ron. A trip to London so I could attend the opening, which would be the following Spring, was included in the deal.

The show was booked to play the small Tristan Bates Theatre (which was later rebranded as the Seven Dials Playhouse). It was located right in the heart of the West End theatre district. I was told that casting would get underway soon. The producer and I had a discussion about trying to get celebrity voices for the Parole Board and Radio. We both agreed to brainstorm, but I already knew that I didn't have a list of British celebrity friends.

* * *

Around the time the contract was being finalized in October of that year, I went to a horror-themed convention known as the Chiller Theatre Expo. It was held in a big hotel, not far from Manhattan. There was a showroom full of collectibles for sale, alongside other rooms filled with celebrities from today and yesteryear at autograph tables. Over the weekend I would meet TV stars like Barbara Eden from *I Dream of Jeannie,* Larry Hagman from *Dallas,* John Astin from *The Addams Family,* and movie stars such as Leslie Anne Warren from *Clue,* and Patty Duke from *The Miracle Worker.*

Also at a table was British actress Patricia Quinn, who had been immortalized as the original Magenta in *The Rocky Horror Show* on stage, and *The Rocky Horror Picture Show* on screen. I had come of age watching *Rocky Horror* as a teenager. While I was a bit on the young side then, I was still part of that first generation of fans that turned the movie into a cult classic. It was very exciting to finally get to meet a member of the cast.

The line at Pat's table was usually very long—but when I got to the front, there was a very rare lull behind me. So I thought it would be fun to mention *Thrill Me.* She was a celebrity. She had a voice. She lived in London (I assumed).

What was the harm in taking a chance? I used the Tristan Bates Theatre as my opening. "Ms. Quinn, I have a small show opening in London early next year. Have you ever heard of the Tristan Bates Theatre?"

Had she! She knew that the theatre had been named after the late son of actor Alan Bates, who had helped found and fund the theatre. He was a friend of hers. Pat then wanted to hear more about the show, so I told her about the upcoming production. She was so lovely and attentive.

We even had drinks together at the hotel bar after convention hours and continued the chat. I've found that performers always seem to be flattered when a potential role is dangled in front of them. So as I sipped my drink—probably a white wine, I just casually mentioned "you know, there's a Parole Board in the show.. " If this book were a screenplay, the next thing I would write would be "Cut to:"

...The Spring of 2011 and I'm in London. At the Tristan Bates Theatre. Sitting next to me is Patricia Quinn—holding my hand tightly as we watch the first performance of *Thrill Me*. She then leads a rare-for-London standing ovation at the end, and gives me a great big hug.

Pat had indeed recorded one of the Parole Board voices, along with musical theatre star Lee Mead as the other. Popular actor-comedian Les Dennis was the voice of the Radio Newscaster. It meant the world to me that Pat became part of *Thrill Me*—all because I was brave enough to strike up that conversation at her table. And luckily, I chose the right way to open!

* * *

While in London, before seeing *Thrill Me*, I had the chance to check out some of the hit shows playing on the West End, visit with a few friends, and do some press for the show by recording a radio interview for the BBC in an office above the theatre. I was on the *BBC*! That alone was worth the trip.

When I arrived at the Tristan Bates, the first thing I saw was the fittingly classy brown-toned *Thrill Me* poster in a glass case near the front door. It featured one young man hugging another one from behind as a trail of cigarette smoke billowed upward. This early version used generic male models, but it was later replaced with a similar photo using the actual performers—the fantastic duo of Jye Frasca and George Maguire.

The production used a conceptual grid design at the back of the stage that I thought resembled a large prison cell, or perhaps a cage.

It had props stowed within its various sections. Along the sides of the stage were movable pieces of furniture. The pianist was visible behind the grid. When the audience entered, they saw a single, lonely chair spotlighted stage center.

Director Guy Retallack created what I considered to be a highly professional, and very literal-minded, staging. He applied a lot of logic, even going so far as making sure that Older Nathan wore his own pair of glasses, which were different from the ones worn by teenaged Nathan. A very smart touch.

After watching the first performance, I had two minor quibbles. For the first, I was used to seeing Nathan and Richard drag their fingers across the freshly typed contract, as if signing their names in blood once their fingers were pricked with Richard's knife. But in this version, they signed their names using a pen and then each added a blood spot.

It was well executed and was probably more believable being done that way. But I worried that it took a little too much time for the actors to deal with the knife, the pen, the signature, *and* the blood. At least there was plenty of underscore, and I'm sure the audience didn't know the difference.

My second concern was the realistic concept that was applied to "My Glasses/Just Lay Low." In most productions at that point, the song was staged with the actors holding prop candlestick telephones that weren't actually attached to anything. So as the song progressed and reflected the passage of time, they were free to move all around the stage.

But here in London, one phone was placed all the way stage left, and the other all the way stage right. They were each attached to the wall with a cord. This certainly made it more "real," but it meant the entire long song was performed without much movement, since they were tethered to their spots. While there was plenty of emotion and urgency in the vocals, I wondered if this staging was the right choice.

Since that first performance was actually a preview, my feedback was requested. And I did mention those two issues. But Guy was a very smart director and knew exactly what he was doing. He changed nothing. The show became a sell-out hit, and many rave reviews quickly started coming in. By the time I got back to New York City, a transfer to a larger West End theatre was soon being offered. I couldn't argue with success. Just like Nathan would sing, *"We're together, it's a truce!"*

There was a bit of confusion over whether or not my existing contract with the producer granted rights for such a transfer. We weren't sure if a brand new contract was needed. After he had some back and forth with Ron, it was eventually worked out.

At this point, Jim Kierstead came on board to join the expanded producing team for the run at the newly-christened Charing Cross Theatre, which was not far from Trafalgar Square. Both actors agreed to move with the show, which was a relief. This time there would be no need for an emergency replacement!

During the run at the Charing Cross, Patricia Quinn did a talkback that I really wish I could have seen or been a part of. But a second trip to London just wasn't practical. Although, I *was* generously invited and offered a plane ticket by the head of the Charing Cross.

I was ecstatic to learn that fans from South Korea were flying to London. Apparently, they were eager for the chance to see the show performed in English. They even dutifully recounted the experience by comparing and contrasting the casts from both countries on their personal blogs.

Award nominations were soon announced. I was personally nominated for an Off-West End Theatre Award ("Offie") for Best New Musical, and the show itself received seven nods in total. For the Whatsonstage Awards, *Thrill Me* was nominated for Best Off-West End Production. Although the Charing Cross was considered a West End theatre, it was not a member of the Society of London Theatre (SOLT) and thus not eligible to be considered for the Olivier Awards.

"Brought you into this ordeal, Babe. / I don't want to let you go…" proved to be a prophetic lyric because after the London production closed its

limited run later in the year, the producers brought it back several times with new cast members. There were runs in 2014, 2015, 2017, and 2018. It played the Edinburgh Festival Fringe and other London theatres such as The Bridge House, The Arcola, and The Other Palace—which was owned by Andrew Lloyd Webber at the time.

It also went on tours throughout England and Ireland. It even played South Korea at the Busan International Performing Arts Festival, which was the English language premiere there. The Korean fans flocked to it, proving to the short-sighted festival presenters that they hadn't scheduled nearly enough performances. I couldn't help but gloat—I'm only human.

After the last engagement, I predicted that the production would return to the UK yet again someday. It would only be a matter of when. I was even informed that the scenery was put into storage, just waiting to be reassembled when the time was right.

* * *

Dramatists Play Service had acquired the North American rights to *Thrill Me* back in 2005, which meant the United Kingdom rights were still controlled by me (through Ron's office). Since the London run was such a success, we decided to ask Dramatists Play Service if they would now be interested in acquiring those UK rights.

Well, they were. They were more than happy to take over control of the territory, which would give them a cut of my royalties. The only problem was that they didn't want to pay me any advance whatsoever, which would have been standard.

Luckily, Ron had invited representatives from the London branch of Samuel French to see the show. When the transfer to the Charing Cross was announced, we approached Dramatists Play Service again to see if they might be willing to pay an advance. Same answer.

But we rather quickly got word that Samuel French was interested. They wanted the licensing rights for the United Kingdom (technically for the British Isles) and would publish their own paperback "acting edition" of the script. Needless to say, they offered a very nice advance.

Wanting to be loyal, I asked Ron to go back to Dramatists Play Service one last time to see if they wanted to match Samuel French's offer. They told us that they "wished Samuel French good luck." Ouch. I was a bit taken aback because they had made already a quite decent amount of money from *Thrill Me*, and it was obvious there would be future interest in the show in the UK. But they clearly had their reasons, and I had no choice but to respect them.

Samuel French didn't need any luck. They quickly earned back the advance they paid me and went well "into the black" due to licensing various UK productions. This paved the way for my next two musicals to be published by Samuel French instead of Dramatists Play Service.

All in all, I guess I ended up having the best of both worlds by being published by the top two theatrical licensing and publishing companies in the world. On the cover of the Samuel French published edition was that favorite photo of mine.

It hadn't magically transformed itself. I was still prominent and Doug was still slightly out of focus. But by that time, I had stopped worrying about what people might think.

* * *

Later in 2011, Michael Park decided to expand *Thrill Me* further into the Asian market by producing the show in Tokyo. He partnered with Horipro, a major entertainment company in Japan.

They hired Tamiya Kuriyama, a very respected, award-winning opera and theatre director to stage what they called a "workshop" to test the waters. This was really a complete production, just on a small scale. After two successful runs, the first in late 2011 and the second in the Spring of 2012, it was decided that a large full-scale production would open in the Summer of 2012.

Michael kindly invited me to Tokyo to see it. I was far more adventurous then than I would be now, but even still, I wasn't sure I wanted to take another long trip. But I'm glad that I did.

Visiting Tokyo was an adventure of a lifetime. What a wonderful city. And what a wonderful production. If I hadn't seen it with my own eyes, I never would have believed it, and I would have been deprived of the joy of seeing my little baby *very* grown up.

The first tangible thing related to the production that I saw was the artwork. While the title was presented straightforwardly in white letters against a blue background, the logo itself was probably the most unusual one that I had ever seen. I can best describe it as a branch on which hung two shadowy reddish berries, each surrounded by a cage-like skeletal husk.

It was eventually explained to me that this was the fruit of the Hozuki plant, which was in the same family as deadly nightshade, meaning it was poisonous. I suppose this was meant to symbolize "forbidden fruit." Or perhaps a more literal visual cue was the intention—with the berries "imprisoned" within the cage. Whatever the meaning, this was a very unique choice of logo.

Sunday, July 15, 2012, was the opening night at the Galaxy Theatre in Tokyo. It was decided that I should come in a few days later. This way the production team would be able to open the show without having to worry about me and my schedule, and the casts would have gotten a chance to settle in a bit. I arrived on the following Saturday.

It's usually very hot in Japan during July, and this summer was no exception. In fact, I don't think I've ever been so hot outdoors in my entire life. Japan was still recovering from a massive earthquake that hit the year before, knocking out a major power plant.

It was explained to me that energy was still being conserved, and thus air conditioners weren't running at full strength. Anywhere. When the characters, also known as "I" and "He" in this version, sang *"Feel the heat intensify,"* they really meant it!

My hotel was actually attached to the theatre complex. In addition to the hotel and theatre, there were restaurants and shops on the premises. One such restaurant had been renamed "The *Thrill Me* Café" for the run of the show.

I went in. Sat down. And ordered from a *Thrill Me* branded menu—while on a huge video screen next to me played the *Thrill Me* trailer on a loop. It was the best meal I ever had!

When I entered the theatre lobby for the first time, I went straight to the considerably large merchandise booth where there were more *Thrill Me* goodies than I ever thought could exist. Posters, programs, keychains, tote bags, photo sets, chocolates in branded containers, opera glasses designed to evoke Nathan's binoculars, and of course *Thrill Me* Off-Broadway cast album CDs and English language scripts. Across from the booth was a bar which offered an array of *Thrill Me*-themed cocktails, but I was too overwhelmed to decide on what to drink.

I turned around to notice that a mob scene was slowly forming around me. I had been recognized! It was time for autographs. This was totally unexpected and unplanned for by the production and it caused quite a bottleneck, with a line in front of me snaking through the entire lobby. A member of the staff had to adjust where we stood, so we wouldn't block the entrance.

I wanted to give everyone the attention they deserved, but it was difficult because there was very little time before curtain. The staff was making it clear that there would be no delay. And I certainly wasn't gonna miss one second of the show!

This happened before *every* performance I attended. Similar to Seoul, the audience was mostly women, but there were definitely more males and more older people attending the show in Tokyo. It seemed like *all* of them had something they wanted signed, and if they didn't, they took a quick trip to the merchandise booth to buy something.

Since I was signing so many autographs as fast as I could, I had no choice but to shift into rote-mode. Because it was so unusual for me to even hold a pen instead of a keyboard, I looked down at one program to discover that I had written "For Deposit Only." My brain had just gone to the endorsing of a check, which was the rare time when I actually signed my name in "real life!" I disguised it with musical notes and flowers. That lucky person got quite a piece of original art!

Seeing the pleased looks on the faces of everyone who wanted to meet me was enough to have made the entire trip worth it. They probably couldn't imagine how pleased and excited I was to meet all of *them*. While I could have kept signing and greeting forever, finally it was showtime.

The interior of Galaxy Theatre was huge. It had three seating levels. When I walked inside, I was greeted with scenery that looked like they were gonna do a giant show like *Ragtime*. It was a striking two-story design.

On the floor level was a large platform, the center portion of which could be moved backward for a strategic effect toward the end—dramatically whisking Nathan backward like in a push in/pull out shot from a movie. The platform could also mechanically split open, leaving a gap in the center, which allowed both actors to sit down inside it to represent separate prison cells and the police van at the end of the show.

On the sides were the various pieces of furniture and props. In the center was a metal staircase that led to a walkway above, with a dramatically lit open doorway at the top of the stairs. The piano was located on the walkway in the stage left corner.

The show was magnificent. One of the things I really liked was when Nathan became "Older Nathan." Each time it happened he clasped his hands tightly in front of himself. It was so simple, yet so effective. Like in South Korea, the audience hardly made a sound until the applause at the end.

As part of a cultural exchange, the most famous cast from South Korea traveled to Tokyo to perform in the show alongside the three alternating Japanese casts. So not only did I get to see the show in Japanese, but also in Korean. For those performances, translated Japanese supertitles were projected on the sides of the proscenium.

The South Korean actors were extremely popular and had become very famous in theatre and on television, but they weren't in the show when I was in Seoul in 2009. So it was a very fortunate opportunity to get to see them alongside the original Japanese "teams." All of the actors were marvelous beyond belief. And, like I discovered in Seoul, all of the teams were very different from each other.

* * *

148

I had been asked to do what they called a "mini concert" after the evening performance of the show on my last night in Tokyo. They planned for me to come onto the set to accompany the actors on the piano as they sang "Nothing Like a Fire." I made it very clear to them that the music wasn't going to sound the same—since I didn't have that third hand!

It was one thing in Seoul when I was accompanying *myself*, but it was a different story to actually play for the actors. But I promised that I would make it sound passable with a much simpler arrangement. After they sang in Japanese, I was to play and personally sing Nathan's song "Why" in English.

I was brought on stage with a microphone in hand and a translator at my side. I greeted and thanked the audience. Then, to get to the piano, I had to climb up the metal stairs to the platform where the grand piano sat. Those stairs were steep! And it was very tight up there. I was afraid I might actually fall off. We had a rehearsal earlier that afternoon and I'm pretty sure that I tripped going down them. I crossed my fingers that it wouldn't happen again in performance. And it either didn't or I blocked it out.

After the songs were done, I carefully climbed back down onto the stage. The actors presented me with a beautiful bouquet of flowers, and a "production staff only" *Thrill Me* t-shirt, which was black with blue decorations. I appreciated them both.

Before I left Tokyo, I got a chance to meet up with my friend Miki Goto. She had been providing me with all the latest Japanese *Thrill Me* gossip, and had translated news about the show for me. I would have been lost without her help.

* = *

The run was a very big success. And, just like in Seoul, there would be demand for *Thrill Me* to return for more seasons in Tokyo. Though there might be more than a year with no performances scheduled, *Thrill Me* has never been gone from Japan for long.

Nowadays, it's usually performed in Tokyo theatres that are smaller than the Galaxy. But it also goes on tour to cities such as Osaka, Hakata, Nagoya, and Takasaki—where it still plays in huge theatres.

The Japanese merchandise booth would also get huge. There were always new items like buttons, mugs, t-shirts, sweatshirts, and calendars. Sets of little flat Lucite dolls of the actors standing on miniature versions of the *Thrill Me* set were among the more unusual pieces. I've got way too many of those!

After the run in 2012, the staging and scenery of the Japanese production was adopted for use in South Korean production for many seasons. Both versions matched for a while until they started experimenting with new ideas and designs in Seoul. But in Japan, it never changed.

* * *

So I was privileged to be given three overseas trips, and each one turned out to be momentous and unforgettable. I was extremely appreciative of the producers, the tour guides, and the interpreters that were assigned to help me. Seeing each production—and in some cases, *performing*—so far away from home, was an incredibly emotional experience for me.

But perhaps the most important thing of all was that I got to meet fans from all over the world and discover that while I may not have been well-known in New York, in Asia I was kind of a big deal. In theatre circles, at least! And *Thrill Me* itself was growing into an even bigger deal.

11

THRILL ME KEEPS KILLING IT

"There is no need to be nervous. / There's no way we're gonna lose."

As the decade went on, I received many invitations to visit productions of *Thrill Me*, which I always appreciated. But of course, I couldn't accept all of them. This was mainly because I never wanted to draw resources or attention from a production. I preferred that they focus all attention on their opening night, and not worry about picking me up from an airport or train station—or be concerned with my opinions.

I would also find that it was much easier to just promote as many productions as I possibly could on my social media channels. To my friends and followers I became "famous" for posting pictures of myself holding a production's poster art or publicity photo with a big smile on my face. That said, there were a few productions nearby on the East Coast that I simply couldn't resist attending.

There was a notable version in Connecticut late one Fall. I was very pleased to be invited to their opening night gala. It was a fairly short train ride, and I was put up in a lovely nearby hotel.

The logo for the show had the usual black and white background with red letters. The main art depicted the bars of a prison cell with the hands of a prisoner reaching out from them. The set had metal fencing and crates used as chairs and tables, similar to the Off-Broadway version. It also had a clock projected onto the ground when the audience entered. I suppose this was to suggest Older Nathan mentally going back in time.

For opening night, drinks and hors d'oeuvres were served in the lobby. In the theatre, there was tiered seating which surrounded three sides of the stage. Votive candles had been placed on short tables between some of the seats.

Toward the end of the performance, the stage lights suddenly went out unexpectedly. Something had gone wrong. As you can imagine, I immediately thought back to Buffalo!

The actor playing Richard, while in the middle of singing a verse, calmly walked up to the front of the audience, grabbed a couple of lit candles, and brought them back with him onto the set, creating enough light for them to finish the show. Disaster averted! It proved that *"There's nothing like the glow of sizzling embers, / to brighten your face."* It was the talk of the after party.

A few years later, in the Summer of 2015, I took a train to the Ritz Theatre in Haddon Township, New Jersey, which is a suburb of Philadelphia. There must be something about producers in that area, because just like the version at the nearby Media Theatre eight years earlier, a small theatre was created out of a large one. The audience was seated directly on the stage and not in the auditorium.

The artwork featured sexy photos of the two actors. The scenery had lots of slatted wooden crates—I think I sat on one of them during my talkback. The piano was cleverly placed behind a stack of pallets.

In the early Fall of that same year, I was asked to do a talkback after a performance at the Wellfleet Harbor Actor's Theatre/Julie Harris Stage in Cape Cod, which is near Provincetown, Massachusetts. I couldn't resist the generous invitation to visit the beautiful area. This version, directed by the very welcoming Jeffry George, featured the first married couple to star opposite each other in *Thrill Me*, Ben Berry and Adam Berry.

Apparently, putting on a production after the summer was an experiment since most of Provincetown would be closed down for the season. But the theatre was curious to find out if they could still draw enough of a crowd for one more show. I was, well, thrilled that *Thrill Me* was chosen for that slot.

The poster featured a gorgeous picture of the two Berrys, taken by photographer Susan Karchmer. She actually won a photography award for the image—which was well deserved. When I arrived at the theatre, Susan presented me with a signed, matted, poster-sized print. I was overwhelmed by her generosity. Once I got home I had it framed and added it to my ever-growing collection.

The set at the Wellfleet was very large. There were multiple platforms at varying levels, a ramp that led up to one of them, a section that almost looked like a dock adorned with rope, and a back wall made up of aged wooden slats. That wall looked fantastic when an array of various colored lights would seep through the gaps from behind. The piano was on stage as usual.

Jeffry told me there was one slight challenge. Due to everyone's schedules, they had to rehearse a lot of it in various home living rooms. As a result, many of the individual scenes were performed in small sections of the set—the big wide stage wasn't fully taken advantage of. But in the end, it didn't matter.

The show was positively splendid. The reviews were fantastic. And I truly enjoyed doing the talkback with the cast. Though to be honest, after so many years, it was starting to become little tedious to be answering the same questions again and again. "How did you get the idea?"…"Why is it so popular in Asia?"

But how could I complain? It had already been over twenty years since I first started writing *Thrill Me*, and there were times when I feared it would be stuck in a drawer forever. So I was very grateful that anyone, anywhere, still wanted to hear me talk about it. And of course, *they* were all hearing my answers for the *first* time.

Finally, at the end of 2015, I was asked to do a press interview in advance of production of *Thrill Me* at Luna Stage in West Orange, New Jersey—not far from New York City. I was happy to do it because this would be a very special production, from my point of view. My dear friend from college, Cheryl Katz, was the artistic director of the theatre and would also be directing the show.

Cheryl had directed the first two musicals I ever wrote. And eighteen years earlier she had superbly directed the important staged reading of *Thrill Me* for the Dramatists Guild Musical Theatre

Program. I'd always hoped she would get the chance to stage it for real someday. So here we were at last!

A few months earlier, Cheryl invited me to sit in on her auditions that were held in New York City at the Actor's Equity Building, not far from my apartment. Come to think of it, *a lot* of the places in New York that I've written about are pretty close to my apartment. That's the benefit of living in Midtown, I guess.

I felt that Cheryl made some very unusual, but ultimately inspired, casting choices. She basically turned the characters on their heads. As Nathan, she cast the dreamy Joe Bigelow. He had movie star good looks and deep brown eyes. Joe was the type of guy that I imagined could easily inspire a song about "everybody wanting" him.

Then, to play Richard, Cheryl chose the intense, striking, Dean Linnard. With his curly hair put into a 1920s style, and when the light hit him a certain way, he cut a compelling yet disturbing figure. His intelligent acting choices made him seem more like the most antisocial guy in school, instead of the most popular.

To put it another way, typical directors, in my opinion, would have instead cast Joe as Richard and Dean as Nathan. Before I saw it, I frankly just couldn't imagine how it could possibly work. Well, I found out on opening night.

It was fascinating to watch a drop-dead gorgeous Nathan pining after such a different type of Richard. This time it was *Nathan* who ended up in a sleeveless tank as Richard ogled him.

I felt that Cheryl and her actors created an intriguing challenge to the audience's perception of who usually "goes after" who, and what type of person is the one in control of a relationship. It highlighted the unlikely attraction between the two men, but in the reverse. And it added a lot of tension.

Dean's "Roadster" was purely mesmerizing. Joe's "Way Too Far" was simple and effective. These two were *so* in sync on stage—their chemistry off-the-charts. What, ahem, happened between them "in the dark" was very easy to imagine. It made me wish that Cheryl's exact rehearsal process could somehow be replicated everywhere.

Scenic designer Brian Dudkiewicz provided another touch of genius. He set the show on a narrow runway-style stage, with audience sections on each of the two long sides. This forced one half of the crowd to face the other—like voyeurs watching voyeurs watching the actors.

An elevated platform was center stage, featuring a trap door from which props could be hidden or retrieved. At one far end was an expertly constructed wall with a large dusty window. At the other end was what I would call a partially-destructed wall of a prison, featuring two built-in perch-style seats. In a dramatic moment, when the actors were upon these seats, they evoked caged birds.

The pianist was seated behind a set of prison bars that were embedded into the wall. Hanging above the entire expanse of the theatre was a distressed beamed ceiling grid.

After predominantly rave reviews, the show was a sell-out smash. Performances were added to the run to help fulfill the demand. I went back to see it a second time. It was even better. As a matter of fact, I wish I could see it again today.

By casting the roles against the usual type, Cheryl pulled off one of the best English language productions I had ever seen. As a director, she really plumbed the depths of the actors' souls. Now I wouldn't recommend that other productions cast it like this—unless they have Cheryl onboard to direct it, at least.

During the run, my friend Joe Barros, the artistic director of New York Theatre Barn (NYTB)—a theatre company that he founded—invited the Luna cast and myself to perform at NYTB's annual Christmas show. It was held downstairs at the Daryl Roth Theatre Off-Broadway. It was a nice way for me to actually get to know the actors a little bit.

I talked about the show and specifically the Luna production, then I introduced Joe and Dean. They performed "Superior," just as Doug and I had done years back at Birdland and at the Drama Desk Awards. We all had a lot of fun that night. And it was the beginning of a rewarding professional relationship with Joe Barros.

* * *

The German premiere of *Thrill Me* was at the Katielli Theatre, under the leadership of Bernd Arends, who was also the translator of the script and lyrics. As the production was coming together, Bernd asked me if he could add a cello to go along with the piano.

Since by then I'd already been down the road of considering extra instruments, I told him that I really didn't think it was needed. The show was proven to work all around the world, in theatres of all sizes, with just the piano.

But I believe he had a colleague who was a cellist, and he really wanted me to consider it. So we created an agreement in which he would have test recordings made of two songs with piano and cello. If I approved them, a cello part could then be written for the entire show.

I know that a lot of hard work went into the making of these recordings. The cellist was extremely talented. But when I heard the samples, in my opinion, the cello was just too "busy" and it interfered with the piano part. Since the cello was being added to the existing piano arrangement, there really wasn't "room" for it.

The writing of a brand-new piano part to allow space for the cello was off the table. I suggested that the cello just double the bass line of the piano, but Bernd told me that the cellist didn't want to do that because it wouldn't be a creative enough experience. I understood completely. So once again, no additional musician joined the pianist at *Thrill Me*.

Bernd's production was quite successful. Moritz Staemmler, a representative from Felix Bloch Erben (FBE)—which was the major German theatrical licensing and management company—went to see it. Bernd and I hoped that he would be interested in acquiring licensing rights to *Thrill Me*, which would be beneficial for both of us, since Bernd's translation would be a part of the deal.

Moritz was very complimentary of the show, but I do recall that he wasn't sure of its viability outside of a small niche market. He promised to think about it. I prepared myself for bad news. But, to my delight, he decided to offer me a contract, and I signed with FBE for the German Language rights. Now *Thrill Me* was handled by three major licensing companies around the world.

Moritz had just one concern. The title. Bernd's production didn't use a translated title. It was simply the two words in English. Moritz told me was that, when the words "thrill me" were spoken phonetically in German, they sounded like a type or brand of bird seed! He was afraid it wouldn't be taken seriously.

Well, I didn't want the show to essentially be known as *Bird Seed: The Musical*, so I agreed that the title could be changed. I told Moritz that he and Bernd could come up with suggestions for alternatives. But Moritz changed his mind, though I'm not sure why, and *Thrill Me* remained *Thrill Me*. Many productions would follow in Germany—and I believe it has far eclipsed the niche market.

I keep track of it all thanks to my dear friend Petra Knickmeyer. As a true fan, she can always be relied upon to travel to see it anywhere in the country. She kindly reports back to me with production details and sends me candid photos with the actors. She's even mailed me posters and programs that she's collected from all around Germany so I can add them to my collection. I'm just pleased that she always enjoys the show.

* * *

The Canadian premiere of *Thrill Me* in Toronto contained a special added bonus. Though I was pretty sure that my days performing in *Thrill Me* were long since over, I was actually *in* this production. Well, sort of. I was asked to be the voice of the Radio Newscaster. I was very flattered.

This meant that I got to be featured in one of my favorite songs, "My Glasses/Just Lay Low," without even having to sing! Using the *Garage Band* program on my Mac, I actually recorded the lines in my apartment. And I was very proud of myself for figuring out how to overlay the sound-effect of static over my voice.

Come to think of it, maybe I should have held out for the larger role of one of the Parole Board voices! Anyway, I unfortunately didn't get a chance to go to Toronto to see the show. Hmm...I wonder how I was...

* * *

There had been close to one hundred productions of *Thrill Me* globally by the time the Spanish version opened. It was produced by Alejandro de los Santos, who also starred as Nathan. It played engagements in Madrid and Barcelona, then toured all throughout Spain—winning multiple awards along the way.

Their online video trailer was appropriately moody. It featured quick cuts of various props and the actor's faces serving dramatic looks. A child's toy "top" was left spinning at the end as the music faded. The scenery was simple but effective in tones of brown, and there was meticulously sculpted lighting. Alejandro's production was extremely popular and I would have loved to have gone to see it, but I never got the chance.

I did get to see photos and videos of the show, and I *also* saw the very sexy artwork which featured a shirtless photo of both Alejandro and his co-star David Tortosa. It was used on banners, ads, and posters large and small. I can only imagine that image must have sold a *ton* of tickets. My original Midtown Festival poster might have been a bit provocative, but this one was next level—in the best possible way.

I did get to meet both of the guys separately in New York when they came here on vacations. It was a real thrill to visit with them and talk about the show. The "selfies" that we took together were very popular on my social media, especially since they were placed next to a photo of that hot poster!

* * *

The first production of *Thrill Me* in the Czech Republic was staged in Prague—on a *boat*! Or maybe it was more of a barge. But when translated, it was called the Mystery Boat Theatre. Talk about a challenge! I'm assuming the boat stayed docked, but I really don't know. So far this was the only production that wasn't done on dry land.

The show was directed by the notable Lumír Olšovský. It was practically on a bare stage with just a bench, a ladder, and a few other abstract pieces on a wooden floor made up of long vertical planks. The pianist was off to one side.

The poster designs used photos of the actors on a vivid red background. Nathan was dressed in a white shirt and suspenders, looking more or less like the character usually does. But Richard had on a black leather motorcycle jacket with a black hoodie underneath.

It was a striking dichotomy, and it was indeed how they were costumed for the actual show. The first biker jacket in *Thrill Me*! I can only wonder if the audience had life jackets under their seats.

* * *

A different director in Germany contacted us with an offer to do a lengthy run at the English Theatre of Hamburg. It was an extremely lucrative proposal. Though it would be a German production it would be handled by Ron, instead of FBE, since it wouldn't be performed in the German language, but in English.

It sounded great, but there was just one catch. I had to allow them to put in an intermission. I supposed that the selling of drinks and snacks was a key part of how they budgeted their shows, and there could be no exceptions.

I understood, but it was a tough decision to make. I could have easily said no—but it was such a great contract otherwise. Frankly, I was glad they asked in advance because they could have just sneaked it in without telling me.

I decided to agree. But I still worried that the entire flow and momentum of the show might be ruined if it was interrupted. After the audience got a break, could that momentum be regained? And where would the intermission go? After "Way Too Far"…after "Superior" perhaps? They let me decide. I ended up thinking that it made the most sense to end the first half with "Roadster."

The production was cast out of London and was a very big success. So much of a success that it was remounted *in* London early the following year at the Jermyn Street Theatre, which was one of the places Martin Charnin had scouted for his potential *Thrill Me* way back in the late 1990s. The strictly limited run was completely sold-out. And that time there was *no* intermission.

* * *

When *Thrill Me* was first presented in Seoul, it was considered unique. Small dark musicals were nothing new in the West at that time. But in Asia they were a very new and unusual concept. So once the show was a hit, *copycats* started to emerge. There was suddenly a slew of small dark musicals, often based on true crime stories—usually featuring handsome men.

Those shows had every right to be staged, and I was actually flattered by them. The drawback was that they started to slightly cut into the audience for *Thrill Me*. After all, there were only so many nights of the week that a fan could attend the theatre. And the hiring pool of actors wasn't unlimited.

Suddenly there was competition for producers to get their desired performers under contract, book theatres, and line up their production schedules. Thinking that *Thrill Me* could actually be in jeopardy, I started to worry—which got me nowhere. I decided I needed to be proactive and actually *do* something about the situation.

At this point, I hadn't had a moment to write anything since *Thrill Me* went into production back in 2003. But I got an idea. I figured the best person to write a "*Thrill Me* copycat" was the actual writer of *Thrill Me*. So I decided to write a new musical, in English of course, but with the goal of having it open in Seoul and play alongside *Thrill Me*—perhaps during the off season. Brilliant, right?

I thought about the most popular elements of *Thrill Me* in South Korea—a handsome pair of men, with a least the hint of a relationship between them, a design that suggests darkness, and at least one kiss between the guys. Then I factored in the fact that the audience was mostly young females. Because of that I thought it would be a good idea to add a strong, young female character.

The most popular song from the show seemed to be "Nothing Like a Fire." I thought evoking that somehow would also be a good idea. So after just a few months, my musical *Flames* was born. The plot is described thusly:

> One year ago, Edmond died in a horrible fire. He took with him the dreams of his fiancée, Meredith; the trust of his best friend, Eric; and the answers to the burning questions that still linger about his death and the terrible crime he committed.
>
> But on a stormy night, at the cemetery where he rests, the secrets from his past will finally refuse to stay buried, and those he left behind will finally refuse to stay silent. In this original, suspense-filled, musical thriller, there are enough twists, turns, and surprises to keep audiences guessing up until the final shocking moments.

Since it was an original story, set in the present day, it was not so much a "copycat" of *Thrill Me*, but more like a "cousin." Of course, since my music has a fairly recognizable style, the score had a similar sound. I couldn't wait to give it to Michael Park

I sent it to him and was anxious for his feedback, thinking a contract would soon be offered. Michael, it turned out, had zero interest in producing a "copycat." He told me that since he had "the original" that was enough. So much for my brilliant idea!

Luckily, my old friend Russ Wooley at the Lamb Theatre in Sioux City was more than happy to stage the world premiere. He did a fantastic job with it—and I know he really had fun decorating that cemetery.

Then Samuel French picked it up for worldwide English language publishing and licensing rights. Shortly after that, Moritz Staemmler at FBE decided to pick up the German language rights. Bernd Arends was back on board to do the translation.

Soon there would be a small production in London, from which came an excellent cast album. There were other stagings in the United

States; a gorgeous version in Germany, which was costumed and designed to look like a black and white film noir movie; and even Michael Park eventually produced a staged concert version as part of a theatre festival in Seoul.

A few years later, when a Chinese company wasn't able to get the rights to *Thrill Me*, they decided to produce *Flames* instead. Their dazzling production, which was staged on a huge revolving cemetery set, opened in Shanghai and then toured China. The company followed this by producing a concurrent "small immersive version" in a specially created black box theatre, where it settled in for a long open run of several years.

The "copycat" truly started having a life of its own outside the shadow of *Thrill Me*. And it turned out that I had no need to be concerned. *Thrill Me* in Seoul quickly stabilized itself among the competition. It remained as popular as ever.

* * *

I was extremely pleased—or perhaps the word should be "stunned"— that by now there was never a moment that a production of *Thrill Me* wasn't either on stage, in rehearsal, or in the planning stages somewhere in the world. In fact, there was only one significant place it hadn't yet been. And that place had never truly even been a goal for me. But fate decided that it was time to at least try.

12

THRILLING OPPORTUNITIES

"How many times must I address your doubts?"

While I was contending with various *Thrill Me* deals both national and international, I got an unexpected offer out of the blue one day. A Broadway producer, with whom I was familiar, approached me about optioning *Thrill Me*. For Broadway. Yes, *Broadway*!

He took me to Sardi's to make his pitch. I was extremely flattered. And while I obviously knew that having the show on Broadway would be a major coup, and a goal for any playwright or composer, I wasn't initially sold on the idea.

At a seminar for playwrights that I attended around this time, one of the speakers was the executive director of the Dramatists Guild. He lamented to the enrapt crowd that it was impossible for anyone to make a living as a theatre writer without having had a show on Broadway. Even an unsuccessful one, he said, would still bring in licensing revenue just for the fact that it came from Broadway.

Well, he was wrong. I'd already proved that it was *not* impossible. The constant *Thrill Me* productions all over the world meant that I was in fact able to make my living as a theatre writer—and I didn't have to worry about or "need" Broadway.

So for the very first time I was apprehensive about a major offer. The problem was that I was worried about what could happen if, theoretically, the Broadway version was less successful than the Off-Broadway one? Could it tarnish the show from there on out? I really had to wrestle with this for a while.

Finally, I decided to at least entertain the prospect and let Ron start negotiating a contract to see if we could make it work. But there was substantial issue almost immediately. The producer insisted on having a full "Broadway sized" orchestration of the score created.

This was now approximately the fifth time that the concept of adding instruments to *Thrill Me* had come up. And I was pretty tired of it! The producer told me personally that he felt there was no way the show could be done on Broadway with just a piano.

I pointed out that it was currently working on the "Broadway" of both Seoul and Tokyo. And it was considered fine for the small West End production. But there was no convincing him. While we continued discussions, my heart wasn't really in it. So, ultimately, the whole thing just didn't pan out.

* * *

Jim Kierstead told me that he had been informed about these discussions and suggested that he himself option *Thrill Me* for Broadway instead. By this time, Jim had built an impressive list of Broadway producing credits. While I was still apprehensive, I knew I could fully trust Jim. *Thrill Me* would be in more than capable hands.

So after some back and forth, I took Jim up on his offer. Ron began negotiating with Jim's lawyer—which took months! It was shocking just how intricate a Broadway contract had to be. But this was big business, and every little clause was necessary.

Right up front there was one thing we had to agree on—the music. While Jim didn't have the same reservations about the single piano as the previous producer, musician's union minimums were a reality on Broadway. Each theatre on Broadway, based on its size, had a required number of players that had to be hired. However, the union could be asked to grant a waiver to allow the single piano. The show's worldwide history would probably make a compelling case, but there was no guarantee.

It was likely that if the production were to happen, *Thrill Me* would be put in one of the smaller Broadway theatres that had the lowest minimum of only three required musicians. So I agreed that, if pressed, it could be done with a conductor (who I believed would be considered a musician) and *two* pianos.

My idea was that there would be a "Nathan piano" on which a pianist would play Nathan's solos, and a "Richard piano" with the other pianist playing Richard's solos. For the duets, both pianos would be played using, what would hopefully be, intricate arrangements. Sort of like the popular bluegrass hit "Dueling Banjos"—but in a theatrical style.

It was possible that these pianos and pianists would be seen on stage, perhaps even costumed in parallel with the actors. Or they could have been offstage, with each having some kind of unique sound to distinguish them from each other. Jim seemed to love this whole concept.

Once all other concerns were ironed out, we both finally signed the option agreement—as well as a later extension. This meant that from January 1, 2015, through March 15, 2017, Jim had the exclusive rights to produce *Thrill Me* on Broadway. But I knew full well that, even with an option agreement in place, there was no guarantee the show would ever actually land there.

The agreement had a very standard clause that restricted *all* production rights to the show, professional or non-professional, within one hundred and fifty miles of New York City. Thus Jim had to grant a special waiver for a particular staging that fell within that parameter. He seemed more than happy to do it because it gave him the chance to invite potential investors and producing partners to see a very well-done version of *Thrill Me* nearby.

* * *

From my understanding, Jim's main job as the lead producer was to assemble a cast, a director, a design team, and create a budget. Then he or his representative would present the full plan for the show to one of the Broadway theatre owners.

At that time there were three major ones: Shubert, Nederlander, and Jujamcyn; along with the independently owned Circle in the

Square. There were also non-profit theatre companies operating on Broadway who held long-term theatre leases. In theory, a producer could partner with one of them for a production or rent their theatre during a break in their season.

Suffice it to say, there were always far more shows vying for theatres than there could ever possibly be theatres to house them. Thus the owners could afford to be extremely choosy—and they were.

In order to get a theatre, a producer would generally need big name stars in the cast. Short of that, a big-name Broadway director would be required. And if neither of those were the case, pretty much the only other chances were for a show to be based on an extremely well-known movie, have a triumphant run at a major regional theatre, or be a hit production coming in directly from London.

It was exasperating for me because among the things not on that list were: a great script, a great score, or a worldwide reputation going back over a decade. It was only my opinion, but I thought that no one cared about *Thrill Me* itself—other than Jim of course. Everyone else only wanted to know what big name Broadway director was attached and what Hollywood stars had been signed.

I felt like Jim might as well have optioned a "blank notebook." I really had to work hard to brush away those negative thoughts practically every day. But, looking back, I think I was being hard on myself. Perhaps everyone automatically assumed that *Thrill Me* must be worthy of a Broadway production and its quality was just "a given."

Jim had a well-liked Broadway director in mind to helm the show. I was told that, unfortunately, the director was so busy at the time with other projects that he didn't have a chance to read the script. And by the time he did, and expressed interest, it was already too late.

Jim reached out to other potential directors, and I personally met with a few of them. One was a Broadway choreographer who was looking to get his first Broadway directing gig. He actually asked if the script was going to be "redeveloped for Broadway." That essentially meant "rewritten under the guidance of the director." Was I offended? Yes.

I couldn't blame him personally. I had observed over the years that it was a common practice in the Broadway industry that writers usually would be forced to endure endless readings, workshops, or developmental labs. And practically everyone would give feedback that the writer would be expected to implement or at least seriously consider. That's certainly not how it works for fine artists, or sculptors, or fiction authors. Not by a long shot.

I'd even heard horror stories about directors who also tried to claim co-authorship due to their "contributions." It's as if everyone in the business automatically thinks that it's impossible that the script might actually been good enough in the first place. Not to put *Thrill Me* in the same league, but I would openly point out that shows like *Guys & Dolls*, *My Fair Lady*, *Cabaret*, *Hello Dolly*, and so many others somehow managed to become classics and staples of musical theatre without all those extra steps.

Those shows simply went into rehearsal, perhaps after a few "backers auditions," which were done only for the purpose of raising money. Then they usually opened in an out-of-town venue. Rewrites were done based on actual audience response. Finally, the show would come to Broadway and face the critics. I wonder what the fates of those famous musicals might have been if they were first produced during the Broadway of today.

I could only guess what this potential choreographer-turned-director thought was lacking. Did it need an added dancing chorus? Did he *really* think that the script wasn't good enough after the approximately one hundred and twenty-five productions that had taken place by that point?

Since I didn't fit into the typical box of "desperate writer who would do literally anything to have a show on the Great White Way," he probably thought I was crazy for not wanting his expertise. Luckily, the experienced Broadway director Jim eventually did hire had no such issues with the script, and approached the show respectfully.

* * *

Casting for Broadway proved to be extremely difficult. To me, there just weren't that many "stars" who were the right ages—or who could at least create the illusion of being the right ages. I felt that anyone who was already famous for playing a "grown up" on TV, or in the movies, was out because audiences would probably have a hard time imagining them as a teenager again.

Jim told me that he wanted to approach Neil Patrick Harris and his husband David Burtka. I honestly thought that they were both way too old at that point. Though I must agree that Jim was right that they certainly would have been a draw.

The casting director that Jim hired sent formal offers to Matt Bomer, Chris Colfer, Darren Criss, Johnathan Groff, Adam Lambert, Joseph Gordon Levitt, and Justin Timberlake. All of them turned us down. Of course, I have no idea if each "pass" came due to the opinions of the actors themselves—or only their gatekeeping agents.

We reached out to the representatives of Zac Efron, Freddie Highmore, Nick Jonas, Robert Pattinson, Evan Peters, Daniel Radcliffe, and Finn Wittrock, but the casting director was told that there was no interest from any of them. We weren't quite sure if it meant they either didn't want to be in *Thrill Me* itself or in *any* Broadway show at that time. An offer was intended to be sent to future Tony-winner Aaron Tveit, whose agent said he might be interested, but I'm not sure if that offer ever went out.

The casting director also provided a dossier of statistics on actors such as Skylar Astin, Penn Badgley, Ansel Elgort, Andrew Garfield, Grant Gustin, Jeremy Jordan, Liam Hemsworth, Kevin McHale, Hunter Parrish, Eddie Redmayne, Wesley Taylor, Michael Urie, and Elijah Wood—among others.

In my opinion, many of these guys were real longshots. Some of them didn't even seem to be the right age or type. And I felt that several were not truly big enough stars to fit the requirement. None of them were ever pursued.

* * *

With no "celebrity cast," the prospect of actually getting the show on Broadway now seemed like it was gonna be practically impossible. In the second year of the option, Jim changed course and we started *really* thinking outside the box. If we couldn't find the right actors, maybe we could instead get a "celebrity *director*" to hopefully satisfy the needs of the theatre owners and investors. This would mean letting go of the one whom Jim had already engaged.

I suggested Tim Burton, who had helmed *Beetlejuice, Edward Scissorhands, Sweeney Todd,* and a multitude of other hit movies. And if he was also willing to design the scenery and costumes in his famous signature style—we'd be the talk of the town. It was a *gigantic* longshot—I had no idea if Mr. Burton had any interest at all in directing for stage. But maybe…just maybe he'd find the material of interest. Jim thought it was an inspired idea. Sadly, it was just a pipe dream and it never went anywhere. I'm not sure if Jim was ever able to get even *close* to Burton or his people.

I know Jim did his absolute best and worked very hard on the project. But it just never seemed to catch fire. And when our agreement expired, I was actually a bit relieved from the stress of it all.

A short time later, Jim briefly considered trying for a new *Off-Broadway* run instead. And I warmed up to the idea. We were both enthusiastic about a certain theatre that had an effective, seedy, atmosphere.

We even discussed bringing in director Cheryl Katz to do a recreation of her earlier production. Unfortunately (for us) the then current tenant at the theatre kept extending their limited run over and over again. By the time they closed, Jim and I had both moved on.

* * *

Around this same time, Michael Park decided that after so much success in South Korea and Japan, it was time to produce the show in China—which was obviously a gigantic market. When he asked to acquire the rights, I agreed immediately. The production would start with a modest workshop in Shanghai.

169

In China, the government owns the theatres. Certain content must be censored, and scripts must be approved by the government itself. No exception would be made for *Thrill Me*, and I knew this very clearly up front.

One aspect that wouldn't even be up for discussion was that the actors couldn't kiss each other on stage. In my opinion, if the kissing in *Thrill Me* was what made it a success, then I must not have done a very good job overall. So, due to the circumstances, I had no problem with those moments being removed. And I understood that the relationship between Nathan and Richard, or "I and He," as they would be called, would be toned down. That's just how it had to be done. It wasn't personal.

The script was eventually approved by the government, and a large theatre was secured in Shanghai for the premiere engagement the following year. The advance plan was to split the first year of the production into two different seasons, one in July and one in November. After that, there were plans to tour the show to Beijing and other cities. Then hopefully there would be many return engagements in Shanghai, similar to the pattern in Seoul and Tokyo.

The staging and scenery were based on the now-standard Japanese version. At the time, this would unify the three major Asian productions. The logo was based on one of the early South Korean designs featuring the hands of two men.

The July run began, and just as had happened in South Korea and Japan, *Thrill Me* was an instant success. Though I was invited, I chose not to travel to China. But I got plenty of reports and lots of information from fans on social media. Of course the producers also sent me production photos and videos. The July run ended on a high note.

The November performances began, this time in a different theatre. Ironically this theatre usually housed children's theatre productions. I noticed something particularly noteworthy from several online photos. In the lobby of the theatre there was a set of long wide steps that led from the lobby into the auditorium. These steps were decorated to look like a giant typewriter. Imagine that you were walking on the keys starting with the spacebar at the bottom step, all the way up the ribbon at the top. It was so cool!

Unfortunately, "something happened" during this second run. And though I've never been told the exact chain of events, I believe I eventually pieced it together. Apparently, feeling very confident with the success of the show, at least one pair of the several casts of actors started adding the kissing back in—much to the delight of most of the female audience, I would assume. But not to the delight of the government.

There must have been complaints because the show was instantly under scrutiny and changes had to be made in order for the run to continue as planned. My understanding is that government representatives had to monitor the show. This must have created a very dicey situation. But in my opinion, since rules were established and agreed to, they should have been respected.

All I know is, when the second run ended, all further plans were canceled. I was afraid that might be the end of *Thrill Me* in China forever. Goodbye gigantic market. Michael's contract expired. But I had an inkling that if there was strong enough demand from the fans, *Thrill Me* just might get a second chance in Shanghai under the right circumstances.

* * *

With the Chinese production closed, and the Broadway prospect over, it was back to dealing with all the other typical daily aspects of *Thrill Me* that I had gotten used to by that point. One morning, out of nowhere, I received an email from a TV producer at the Discovery Channel's sister channel: Investigation Discovery. The producer worked on a series called *A Crime to Remember,* in which a group of experts would go on camera to describe and narrate the story of a famous crime, interspersed with actors recreating key moments.

The third episode of their fifth season would be about Leopold & Loeb. She wanted to know if I was interested in talking about possibly being one of the expert narrators. I told her that I certainly was, and a phone interview was soon arranged.

A few days after the interview, I was invited to do the show. It would be filmed at a television studio in New York, not far from my apartment (as usual). I was given a list of questions in advance and my answers would essentially be the talking points for my segments of the episode.

It was decided that I would start being featured about ten or so minutes into the episode, which would be after the murder had been committed. I was to pick up the story from there and focus on what happened personally between Leopold & Loeb, while other narrators would concentrate on the actual crime, the police investigation, etc. My billing on screen would read "Stephen Dolginoff-Writer & Composer, *Thrill Me: The Leopold & Loeb Story*." What a great plug for the musical!

I went to the studio in February of 2017. They brought me into the hair and make-up room, where my skin tone was evened up a bit. I then went to the catering area where I waited to go on camera. Soon I was escorted into a very dark studio, which was dressed to look sort of like a police interrogation room, with a bare hanging lightbulb and fogged out windows.

I sat on a stool with a huge camera right in front of my face, and another seemingly inches away on my right. At least that's my best side! The control room was in a different part of the studio, so I never saw who was in there. The sound person attached a small microphone to my dark blue blazer. Dark blue because they wouldn't let me wear my preferred black.

They started rolling the cameras. The producer sat in front of me and asked those predetermined questions, which I answered as best I could. After we were done with the questions I was asked to record a whole series of potential transitions for the purposes of editing such as "Then Nathan…" "Then Richard…" "And then they…" "But Nathan…" "Next they…" and the list went on and on.

The episode aired a year later in February of 2018 with the title "Hearts of Darkness." I was very satisfied with how it turned out. I sounded cogent, confident, and personally engrossed in the story. I now was immortalized on screen and on streaming as a genuine expert on Leopold & Loeb. And with this credit, I got an IMDB page!

* * *

Around the middle of *Thrill Me*'s second decade of performances, Ron's associate agent, Amy Wagner (who had been working with him for years), started taking over most of the day-to-day handling of the general *Thrill Me* business. Amy had always been in the loop, and I was in excellent hands working with her. It seemed like not a week would ever go by without us having to discuss something *Thrill Me*-related. And soon would come several major doozies that we had to deal with in ways that we never could have anticipated.

13

THRILL ME'S WORLDWIDE INDICTMENTS

"Binding contract, no excuse."

Thrill Me operated very efficiently business-wise. One of the licensing companies would secure a production, or Ron (and later Amy) would negotiate an international version. Then an agreement would be signed. The payment would be made. The show would open. The contract would be honored. And that would be that. It was like a well-oiled machine. Except when it wasn't.

My very first taste of this was actually relatively early on. There was a fairly high profile production that I heard great things about. I even had several wonderful conversations with both the director of the show and the artistic director of the theatre. While checking online one day during the run, I came across a very well-produced video trailer. But to my shock, I discovered that they had rewritten the first verse of "A Written Contract."

The verse was supposed to be *"You're not fit to pour me bathtub booze. / You don't deserve me. / You're not fit to lick my wingtip shoes. / You just unnerve me!"* But they changed it to *"You're not fit to pour me bathtub gin. / You don't deserve me. / You're not fit to lick these shoes I'm in. / You just unnerve me!"* For all I knew they had rewritten even more.

Right after I saw the video, I personally tried to contact someone at the theatre just to find out if, for some strange reason, the actor just sang it wrong while they were recording. But that was highly unlikely, given that it rhymed and he looked quite confident while singing it.

I was told that the artistic director was out of town. When no one else called me back, I reached out to my contact at the licensing

174

company. He promised to get it taken care of ASAP. The clincher was they had invited me to *see* this production. Didn't they think I would have noticed the change? I guess they didn't care because, of all possible scenes from the show, they posted *that* one on the internet. They had to have known I would see it.

When it all shook out, they apologized, restored the correct lyrics, and explained that they made the change to accommodate the fact they couldn't find "wingtip shoes" as mentioned in the verse. Whatever the reason, it didn't matter. And regardless, it was hard to believe that they thought the lyrics were meant to be taken literally. I wouldn't have cared if the actor was barefoot while singing it, as long as it was sung correctly.

* * *

A few years later, the notion of *Thrill Me* being done correctly was also lost on a certain non-professional theatre (which isn't a form of judgement, just a licensing classification). While their production was up and running, I received a Google alert with a link to a *public* blog post written by a member of the production team. I opened it to read that this person was dissatisfied with the prologue scene, calling it both "lackluster" and "not particularly compelling." Yikes!

I was absolutely devastated. I couldn't believe that something like this was written and posted publicly. I can deal with critics. I can handle audience opinions. But this was a member of the team. *A member of the team.* Wasn't it obvious that I would read it? In my opinion, anyone affiliated with a production is supposed to defend, not disparage, the script. Otherwise why take the job?

According to the post, they apparently decided to create a brand-new prologue to start the show. It was described as a stylized choreographed depiction of the murder of Bobby Franks, prominently featuring Richard, who would then be present on stage for the entire first Parole Board scene that would now come after.

Just the idea of putting dancing or even stylized movement into *Thrill Me* seemed very strange and unnecessary to me. And I seriously don't have any theory how all of that was intended to work. All I know is that it made me profoundly upset.

But I dried my tears and contacted the licensing company to try to get the production shut down—even though they were already over halfway through their run. I had never attempted to close a production before, though I definitely had the power to pull the rights if they were indeed making changes of any kind. There was no doubt in my mind that the addition of a choreographed wordless scene, and the inserting of Richard into the prologue, most certainly were changes.

I'd come to learn over the years that sometimes theatres or directors think that—as long as they don't change or add any actual "lines"—they can make any other adjustments or embellishments that they want.

It just doesn't work like that. Imagine what kind of Pandora's box that could potentially open. But it happens all the time.

The theatre did essentially apologize for what was written in the blog, and understood my displeasure. But they attested that the free-lance team member's blog had no affiliation with the theatre itself. They also confirmed that since the show had already opened, the person was no longer in their employ and there was nothing they could do. However, the post was immediately removed.

All of that was very nice, but they also refused to admit that what I read on the blog was *true*. They wrote that it was just this person's "explanation of the personal creative process," a musing of some kind. They swore that it was not at all what was actually staged, and there was no new scene before the prologue being performed.

In my opinion, that was very hard to swallow. Why would the team member write about this choreographed piece (going so far as to describe how and why it was being done), then post it after the show had opened—for all to read—if it was just some sort of musing?

A representative of the theatre also wrote that since they had no record that I myself or anyone from the licensing company had actually seen the production, we "couldn't prove it." It was my perception that they were being very defensive, which I found to be a tell-tale sign. And, for all they knew, I could have been on a plane the next day with a ticket purchased under an assumed name—or sent a friend to see it.

Despite their assurances, I was never convinced that the actors *didn't* perform that interpretive dance version of the murder at the start of the show. In at least one review, there seemed to be an allusion to it, but it wasn't totally clear. An online video clip seemed to depict it, but it *might* have been from a later moment in the show. Or it could have just been promotional material. Thus, I can never be sure what happened on that stage.

Perhaps they truly thought they were making the show better. They at least admitted that they had changed the Parole Board prologue so that Richard was indeed there on stage with Older Nathan. The character was dead. Was he supposed to be a ghost? Because "Ghost Richard" would have been a new character.

I'll never know what they intended. I just know that I wrote a very specific entrance for Richard, and this wasn't it. The licensing company told me that they felt this was too small of a change to shut them down. I strongly disagreed.

My contract promised that there would be "no changes, additions or alterations in the title, book, music or lyrics of the Play without the Author's consent." It didn't distinguish between a small change or a large one.

So now I was not only disappointed with the theatre, but also with the ultimate decision of the licensing company. For the first time I felt unsupported. But I suppose they were trying to look at the big picture. I believe that the theatre had already remitted their fees, so canceling would have meant returning a substantial royalty payment. They probably felt that they were doing me a favor.

All of this made me long for the early days of the Midtown Festival and the York—back when I was at every rehearsal and *nothing* could be changed without my consent. To be honest, at this point, I would sometimes feel guilty for "complaining" because I was sure there were many other writers and composers who never had their show produced anywhere, and would have gladly traded places with me no matter what the circumstances.

But I hope *no* playwright ever lets themself be taken advantage of, and never just brushes unauthorized changes under the rug. I may have lost this round, but at least I put up a fight. It was hard to imagine it then, but an even worse situation would happen a few years later.

* * *

"And I hope the contract is the answer / to finally keeping you in line!" That's what Nathan and Richard sing to each other after they've signed their contract in blood. Well, I signed an agreement for an international production in a major city that would make *me* practically wanna draw blood myself.

I was told that the director, who was the one who discovered the show and lobbied for it, began translating the script right away—in partnership with one of the actors. Apparently, they found *Thrill Me* to be deficient. I wish they had simply decided that writing *their own* original Leopold & Loeb musical would be their best course of action. That way a lot of resentment, legal threats, and production issues would have never happened.

It all started when I first saw their posed publicity photos online. I really enjoyed their concept, which featured the actors in modern dress. The only problem was that there were *three* actors instead of two. I contacted the producer immediately and it was explained to me that the role of Nathan was double cast and they wanted to show off all three actors. That sounded reasonable enough.

When I started seeing production photos, it was clear that they had created some striking visuals and clever scenery. It featured movable Lucite panels that could be written on with colored markers. For example, during "The Plan," Richard could scribble arrows and directions. Unfortunately, I could see that there was also a *separate older actor* as "Older Nathan."

Then, upon reading a press interview, I found out that they had added a huge new scene featuring the voice-over of an actor impersonating lawyer Clarence Darrow giving his famous lengthy closing argument. It was a speech written by Clarence Darrow, not Stephen Dolginoff. There was also an added voice of a Judge to pronounce the verdict.

Oh, and if anyone was ever upset that I nixed my original idea for the prologue years before, a naked shower scene was in *Thrill Me* at last! This time with both of them being doused with "water" behind those Lucite panels. And it was oddly wedged in as a silent scene between "Afraid" and "Life Plus Ninety-Nine Years," while Darrow's speech was played in voice-over. Just thinking about it now makes my blood boil.

Needless to say, none of this was legally allowed. I had the *right* to cancel their production immediately. With all the evidence I had, there was no licensing company in the world that would get in the way this time. I suppose they thought it would be better to ask for forgiveness rather than permission.

We contacted them and told them in no uncertain terms to remove the older actor, Darrow's speech, the judge, and the shower scene, or they would need to close immediately. The first thing they did was admit their mistakes and apologize profusely. They were directed to take a look at the very unambiguous clause in their contract (it's in *every* theatrical contract) which prohibited all of this. They had signed it. No one forced them.

Months before, they had sent me their translated script. Anytime a translation is made, it's the responsibility of the producer. I personally have no scripts in languages other than English to license. While some writers contractually require a "backwards" translation to be created so it can be compared against the original, I never do. Thus, this script wasn't sent for approval, just for my archives.

I don't think I had even opened it previously, but now I felt compelled to take a look. By using a translation app, I could see that Darrow and the judge were indeed listed in the voice-over section. But it didn't matter. I was under no obligation to ever even open that script, so they couldn't make any claim that I had given some kind of tacit agreement. Plus, there was absolutely no mention of using a separate actor as Older Nathan.

The director and producer begged us to not pull the rights, *and* to allow the changes to remain. They felt they were important to the integrity of their translation. They clearly didn't care about the integrity of *Thrill Me* itself.

I was extremely hurt by this. I lost sleep, playing it all over and over again in my mind. To me, it seemed like they felt that, as the author, I somehow had no rights to my own property. The contract meant nothing to them. *I* meant nothing to them. The hurt turned into anger and then the anger turned back into hurt.

The show was either up and running or just about to start performances. A lot of tickets had been sold. Because of this I did something against my better judgement that I still regret to this day. I ultimately just didn't have the heart to cancel the production. I allowed it to continue, contingent on an immediate extra royalty payment and a new contract addendum detailing every unauthorized change.

Further, I made them agree to print a disclaimer, written by me, to be displayed on house boards at the theatre, and printed in their programs or on handbills that would be placed on all seats in advance. It also had to be distributed to the press and posted on all of their social media accounts. This disclaimer explained, among other things, that what they were presenting was *not* actually the world-renowned *Thrill Me*.

They were willing to do all of this. They felt their changes to my work were so important they were willing to pay extra and jump through hoops. My disclaimer basically shamed them, and I'm not sorry—because that was exactly the idea. It meant that every unauthorized thing they did was made public. If only I had just pulled the plug on the show once and for all, it may have been sad for all involved, but it would have resulted in a more desirable, cleaner, break.

More complications happened when they wanted to extend the production after their contract expired. I let them know that I would be more than happy to give them a new contract to perform *Thrill Me* as written, with all of their changes and additions removed. But that was apparently too big of an ask. So no extension.

A couple of years later, due to audience demand, they even proposed remounting it without the separate Older Nathan. But they just weren't willing to give up Clarence Darrow's voice-over speech. Since I didn't write the speech, I felt I had no power to license it. For all I knew it was under copyright and not in the public domain. And it wasn't my job to find out.

We couldn't work out the details for a remounting, and I wasn't unhappy. To me, this production of *Thrill Me* was best left in the past. But that said, those stunning onstage Lucite panels looked fabulous.

A year or so later, a different producer in the same city contacted us with a request to mount his own all-new production. He wanted to use this same translation, albeit *without* the separate Older Nathan, the Darrow speech, or the shower scene. I considered it, but ultimately declined.

I had no idea what else had been "improved" in the translation. And I just didn't want it ever to be performed again. Perhaps this producer will be willing to create his own translation someday, and back to the bargaining table we will go.

From this point on I made sure that every international contract under my control had an extra clause to specifically forbid adding voices, adding actors, adding wordless scenes, and so on. I have no idea if even *that* would have protected me from this particular situation. But at least no one could ever claim ignorance again.

* * *

A well-received international production had a successful run and was brought back the following year. After that second run also proved to be quite popular, the producer requested a new contract for an extension. I couldn't have been happier about it. Production artwork, photos, and videos looked great.

I was hopeful that it would have a long future. But it all came to a crashing halt after the producer asked me to sign a document to be forwarded to that country's music society. It was their version of the ASCAP, the United States company that collects music royalties (usually from radio or internet airplay), and distributes them to composers, lyricists, and publishers. ASCAP has agreements with their various international counterparts, so my payments from all countries are routed through ASCAP itself. I usually receive them on a quarterly basis.

This request for the document confused me. I'm still not exactly sure that I understand it to this day. What the producer seemed to be conveying to me was that the music society wanted to charge him royalties, to be distributed to me, for the live public performances of the *Thrill Me* score. He told me that he would need a document to prove that he had a separate contract with me and was already paying royalties. Thus, the society wouldn't need to collect them.

I had never heard of such a thing. ASCAP doesn't work that way—they never collect royalties for live stage performances. I also pointed out that he didn't ask for such a document during the first run. And I never received any royalties from a performance in that country via ASCAP.

He still wanted me to sign it and he sent me a sample version of the document. It required my signature and passport number. That was an absolute "no." I wasn't going to provide my passport number to anyone, and certainly not an international organization that was supposed to have sent me royalties for the previous run, yet hadn't. I told him that he had a signed contract proving he had the rights and that would have to be sufficient.

A few days later I got an email from ASCAP informing me they had received a notification that I had waived the rights for them to collect *Thrill Me* royalties on my behalf from that production. They attached a supporting document which they wanted me to confirm was correct.

Just glancing at this made me think that the producer must have solved the issue by providing the original contract and everything had been taken care of. That would have been great. I was actually surprised that ASCAP had contacted me so quickly. Then I opened the attachment. Oh, boy!

"But you'll never be my equal / if you don't promise me you'll sign!" sings Richard to Nathan. What would he have done if Nathan refused to sign? Maybe what this producer did.

The document had a list of the songs from *Thrill Me* and a statement which basically read: "I, Stephen David Dolginoff, carrier of American ISBN number 0822221020, as the author of the list of musical works, and responsible for their respective copyrights, declare that I discharge from collecting the copyright royalties…blah blah blah." And underneath was a line that had *my signature* on it. Red alert!

I immediately replied to ASCAP. Instead of confirming the information was correct, I explained that I never signed the document and absolutely under no circumstances did I agree to it. ASCAP promised to investigate.

Because I knew for a fact that I didn't sign it, I can only assume that the producer had taken my signature from his *Thrill Me* licensing contract, and either traced it or photoshopped it onto the document. But since this was never put to the test in a court of law, I should state that at this point, in my opinion, all of this meant that the producer *allegedly* committed forgery.

Instead of using a passport number, he must have decided to take a risk and instead use the *Thrill Me* script's ISBN, which is a commercial book identification number used by publishers. The number had literally nothing to do with me personally, and certainly didn't prove my identity.

It was a risk that at first paid off for him because the music society accepted it and thus passed it on to ASCAP for my approval. And sadly, had he suggested trying to get the document through without my personal passport number, I probably would have agreed. But here I was, staring at a document that I never signed. He had literally attempted to take the control of my royalties away from me.

I contacted him immediately and provided him with the email from ASCAP, along with a copy of the document with my "signature." He apologized profusely. I explained that, in the United States, this would be considered a crime—though I have no idea if that was the case in his country. In my opinion, he was so desperate to not have to pay those additional royalties—which would have been nominal— that he took matters into his own hands, assuming he would not be caught.

Since the contract for his extension hadn't been signed yet, I explained that I would never be able to trust him again. After a bit of back and forth between Amy and one of his producing partners, his extension was canceled—despite the fact it was already being advertised, and the entire company was planning on having the employment.

Sadly, his actions led to severe consequences. And even though ASCAP told the other society that I *didn't* waive the royalties, I never received *any* payments from them. Not one thin dime. Whether or not the production paid them, I have no idea.

* * *

In some countries, people—especially young people—aren't so well-versed in how copyright law works. They are often unaware of the fact that *everyone* needs to get permission to perform a play or musical that isn't in the public domain. I learned this the hard way.

It was discovered that a group of students at a college in a big city were performing an unauthorized, unpaid for, production of *Thrill Me*. A few years earlier, at this same college, a properly licensed and sanctioned production had taken place, so it seemed hard to believe that the staff of the school would think they could just let their students present it without permission this time.

The company that handled licensing requests for these types of productions didn't want this to go unchallenged. So they asked me to join in a lawsuit against the college and the students. They also asked me to register a copyright in their country, which they felt would help bolster their case.

Once I got all of the details, I realized why the company was so concerned. Not only did this production take place *after* they warned the students involved to either pay the standard royalty fee or cancel the show, but the students then actually worked to *hide* it. They performed it "secretly" with social media hashtags such as "forbidden." In other words, the students *knew* they were in the wrong, yet nevertheless chose to continue anyway. They took away my control!

In light of this, I considered the company's request. But *Thrill Me*, like any dramatic or written work, is automatically protected by international copyright treaties. Because of that, there are no legal requirements for it to have a separate copyright in any country other than the one where it was created. So I was advised by Ron and Amy not to do it because it could potentially set a bad precedent.

I also wasn't interested in being a party to the lawsuit, even without the separate copyright registration. Although I was being denied proper royalty payments, and while I hated to disappoint the company, I didn't want my name to be brought into the legal system in a place where I didn't even live. Instead, I offered to write a personal letter to the school expressing my outrage. I hoped it would at least embarrass them.

That meant the company could only sue for fact that the school had interfered in their rights to license *Thrill Me*. If that was the road they wanted to go down, I gave them my full support. While I don't believe that the production company ever actually pulled the trigger on the lawsuit, from then on they made it clear—in a very public way—that there would be much tighter oversight over school productions. No group would be allowed to get away with an unlicensed production ever again without serious consequences.

I don't think it's been a problem since then, and many more such productions have been staged. Whenever I see one mentioned on social media, usually by a student theatre club, I confirm that they indeed have a contract. Sometimes the first request from a student comes to *me* via my website, and from there I pass it along.

* * *

I was very optimistic when a producer wanted to put on a significant new professional production of *Thrill Me* in a major city. Due to the nature and scale of the proposal, the licensing agreement we submitted had more safeguards than usual.

For example, I wanted to be guaranteed that the score would be played on a real piano and not a synthesizer. I also wanted to be sure I got box office royalties commensurate with my previous contracts, and my usual percentage of merchandise sales. Finally, if I was personally in the city where and when the production was taking place, I wanted to be able to attend any performance of my choice. It didn't matter if I was in a seat, standing in the back, or even watching from the wings.

I wasn't prepared for the response we got back from the management company that the producer had hired to secure the agreement. They essentially complained that my requests were somehow outrageous. They literally complained that I "had no right to ask for those things." Excuse me? Like any writer, I had every right to *ask* for whatever I wanted. And they had every right to refuse—but complaining was uncalled for.

Friendly compromise and further negotiation was what would have generally been expected. But, in my opinion, they were quite hostile right off the bat. I personally found their counter offer to be insulting. In it, they suggested an advance payment that was less than what I would have usually received for a small-scale *amateur* production!

As a writer who wasn't a "big name," I felt that I was basically being told to stay in my place and accept whatever crumbs were being thrown my way. Luckily, I didn't matter to me whether this production happened or not. *Thrill Me* was going as strong as ever both nationally and internationally.

So I didn't accept the crumbs. It's actually my sincerest wish that no writer *ever* does. In this case, I had to assert myself and protect my rights. After all, it was *my* property they wanted to license, yet they chose to treat me with blatant disrespect. How could they think I (or any writer) deserved that?

I know the producer himself didn't want me to feel bad, but I had no choice but to reveal to him how hurt I was. Though not hurt enough to cave. He told me that he asked his management company to continue negotiating. They literally *refused*.

I suppose, from their point of view, they had protected their client, the producer, from having to rent a real piano, pay standard royalties, and promise that the author could see his own show. I hope they were proud of their work on his behalf. I wonder what they charged him.

* * *

While there might have been a handful of challenges, there were also many wonderful productions all around the world during the second decade in the life *Thrill Me*. It was difficult to keep track of them all.

If I couldn't see a particular staging, I at least wanted to have a sense of the artwork, the set designs, and the reviews. I was able to have occasional chats with several directors and actors from various productions—and they made sure I got as much material as possible.

A Brazilian production had a set consisting of prison bars and brick walls, and a daring series of posters and ads which depicted both actors with blood splattered faces and clothing. A production in Budapest had advertisements with the familiar image of yellow crime scene tape running across it diagonally under the title.

Then there was a Belgian tour; productions in Mexico, Austria, Vienna; and of course multiple versions in Germany. A notable staging was done in Buenos Aires with striking artwork created by graphic designer Mati Gordon. English language versions continued to be produced in the United Kingdom, Australia, and all throughout the United States.

* * *

After a few years, it was time for *Thrill Me* and its cousin *Flames* to welcome a new "member of the family." I decided I was ready to musically tell another true story—which ended up as *three* true stories in one musical.

For inspiration, I thought back to the very first play I ever saw, *Arsenic and Old Lace*. It included a comedically frightening character who is described as looking just like classic horror movie icon, Boris Karloff. So for nostalgia's sake, I knew exactly what my starting point would be. And I also knew that I would need an old *Thrill Me* friend to help me bring my new "monster" to life.

14

THE THRILL KILLERS RETURN TO NEW YORK

"I'm one perfect accomplice, / who'd never betray you, / if you thrill me."

Having last worked with Doug Kreeger nearly a decade earlier at the Drama Desk Award show, I was extremely excited when he agreed to record a couple of songs for the album of my new horror movie themed musical. One of those songs would even be a duet with me!

The recording sessions happened to coincide with a period when he would be back in New York City from his new home in California. On the recording, Doug would portray master horror movie make-up artist Jack Pierce, and I would be the person in his make-up chair—none other than Boris Karloff himself!

While I toyed with a few different titles including *Horror Fan*, I ended up naming the show *Monster Makers*. It was first performed in New York in a concert version at the Daryl Roth Theatre produced by Joe Barros' NYTB. Then it was later staged at the venerable cabaret/supper club 54 Below, which is downstairs at the famous Studio 54 (I hate to say it, but it's also practically next door to my apartment). As had happened with *Flames*, Samuel French picked up the worldwide English language licensing and publishing rights; FBE acquired the German language rights.

On the back of the published script I described *Monster Makers* with this synopsis:

> A musical triple-feature inspired by three monstrously true behind-the-scenes tales of the most famous monster movies in cinema history!

In 1920s Germany, director F.W. Murnau fears he may lose a lawsuit brought by the estate of Bram Stoker over his silent vampire film *Nosferatu,* which is suspiciously similar to *Dracula.* Will all of the prints be destroyed?

In 1930s Hollywood, make-up man Jack Pierce works to create the defining look for Frankenstein's monster while trying to appease the demands of the studio. Will he get the credit he deserves?

In 1970s England, actor Peter Cushing hopes to be able to finish the final British sequels to *Frankenstein* and *Dracula* before outside forces threaten to get in the way. Will his horror fans be disappointed?

Will all of these men triumph when they fight for their art against the various demons they must face? As these famous monster makers each discover— sometimes real life can be even more frightening than the movies!

After the recording was made, there were productions of the show around the United States, in the UK, and Canada—each got rave reviews. But, in my mind, I will always hear Doug and me duetting as a couple of "monster makers."

It was fabulous working with Doug again, however briefly. His talent had beautifully matured and developed over the years. I felt that he and I still had a unique chemistry and an amusing contrast when acting opposite each other. Even just on a recording.

I could only wish that we'd get the chance to do something else together. One day, not too long after the recording was finished, I got a very unexpected surprise.

* * *

On January 27, 2017, I was signing *Thrill Me, Flames,* and *Monster Makers* scripts and CDs at BroadwayCon, the theatre-related fan convention.

It was held that year at the huge Javits Center on the West Side of New York City. This would be my second year in a row as a guest at The Drama Bookshop's booth. I was on a schedule alongside Charles Strouse, the composer of such musicals as *Applause* and *Golden Boy*, who was promoting his biography, and the respected author of so many books about Broadway, Steven Suskin.

BroadwayCon was very busy. Not only was I signing, but I was also posing for pictures and talking up my work to those who weren't familiar with it. I even got the chance to tell playwright/performer Charles Busch, perhaps best known for his *Psycho Beach Party,* all about *Thrill Me* when he visited the booth during my time slot.

While standing at the table, I suddenly received a text from Doug. He asked if I had ever considered a *Thrill Me* reunion or anniversary concert, because he was game for one. It was one of those "mic drop" moments for me.

Just the thought of getting to go on stage with Doug one more time was unbelievably exciting. That year would be the twelfth anniversary of our Off-Broadway production. The twelfth seemed like an unusual milestone to celebrate. But we had missed the tenth, the fifteenth was still years off, and there was no time like the present!

Doug had explained that he was going to be in New York City for an extended period. He told me that he was eager to make as many plans as he could. Obviously he wanted as much visibility as possible for his temporary return.

I was extremely flattered that he wanted to perform with me again. It was like a dream come true. I had always secretly wished that if I could just get to play Nathan "one more time," with all of the knowledge and experience I had gained over the years, it would probably satisfy me for the rest of my life. I immediately said "yes," and we started talking about various scenarios.

Would it be one night only? Would it be a just concert of the songs? Would there be "celebrity guests" to sing some of them alongside us? Would we do the dialogue? Would we produce it ourselves? Would we do it at 54 Below? At the York?

Many possibilities were discussed. At that point, Doug was only scheduled to be in town through July of that year. But a few months later, he shared with me that a musical he himself had co-written was chosen to be featured in the prestigious annual New York Musical Theatre Festival—which was a showcase of new works. I was so excited for him. This meant he would be in town through August, giving us more time to plan.

It was finally decided that Joe Barros would be our director and we would perform at NYTB's new center of operation: The Cell, a small theatre on 23rd Street in the neighborhood of Chelsea (farther from my apartment than usual). What could be more perfect than Nathan and Richard in "The Cell?"

The show would be a fundraiser for NYTB. Working with Joe and his theatre company would make this event much easier for Doug and me. We would have access to resources that we never would have had otherwise.

It was decided that we would create a fully, though modestly, staged version of the entire show on the small stage. We would be costumed, and have lighting. To lower expectations we would still bill it as a "concert," but it was truly shaping up to be a full-fledged one-night-only *revival*. The date was set for August 17, which gave us just a few months to get ready.

Posters and advertisements were created by Mati Gordon, the graphic artist of the Buenos Aires production. The main feature of the new artwork was a red-tinted, shoulders up, publicity photo from 2005 of Doug being embraced by me from behind. Below us, the title was presented in white. The slogan "Coming Back for You" was displayed at the top against a black background.

After our initial press release went out and tickets went on sale, we sold out the entire theatre very quickly. Joe suggested that we add an additional performance on the same night—a late show.

I was pleased that the demand was there, but I truthfully didn't know if I would have the stamina to take the emotional roller coaster a second time if it was merely an hour or so after the first. And renting the theatre on a consecutive night would have been cost prohibitive. So the reunion remained a "one performance only" event.

* * *

Soon, reality set in. I was forty-nine years old! Would I still be able to pull it off and not embarrass myself? Sure, it was a one-night reunion, but I didn't want to look like a fool up there. Then again, I was already way too old the first time, so what difference would it make now? At least I was still the same size I was back in 2005.

But by now I had a full beard, as did Doug, and neither of us wanted to shave them off. Mine was peppered with grey just like the hair at my temples. We decided that we would just present ourselves exactly as we were and not try to pretend we were any younger. The goal was to at least recreate the spirit of what we had done Off-Broadway twelve years earlier.

Interestingly, many international translated versions of the show would be performed with actors who appeared to be much older than teenagers. So there was a least some precedent. My assumption was that they "translated out" the references to characters specific ages.

The decision of how we should actually be costumed fell to me. I thought it would be best if we wore black, white, and grey tones. Doug sported a black suit with a white shirt and a grey tie. I wore a charcoal grey vest and slacks. This would be the first time I didn't wear my original shirt, opting for a light grey one with white cuffs instead.

And though I tried a few different options, I thought that a bow tie looked silly on me at that point. Maybe it was because I was older. Maybe it was something about how it looked under my beard. I can't quite put my finger on it. But I wore a regular necktie that was black with silver flecks.

I did, however, wear the original cufflinks and my original pair of glasses from Off-Broadway. I also had my red handkerchief from Buffalo. And I used a new gold-toned pocket watch to hang from my vest so I could nervously play with it, just as I had done in those regional theatres.

As for the footwear, I bought myself a brand-new pair of gorgeous black and white wingtips. But these were *slip on* shoes. There would be no worrying about tying those laces tight enough!

And there was *no way* I was gonna grow out my hair. This time, Nathan's hair would look uncannily like Stephen's hair. No pomade needed!

Our musical director and pianist was Zac Orts, who had previously worked with me on both *Flames* and *Monster Makers*. Zac certainly had no trouble playing the score. Forget needing a third hand, Zac seemed to play the piano with his entire body. But, considering that I hadn't done the role in so many years—and wanted to feel as secure as possible, I broke my own rule about key changes.

We lowered the keys of my solos "Why," "Everybody Wants Richard," "Thrill Me" and "Way Too Far." It wasn't that I couldn't necessarily hit the high notes anymore, but I didn't want to have to worry about them. I also felt that it would save my voice enough so that I could keep the original keys of the duets and harmony sections with Doug intact, such as "Nothing Like a Fire," "Superior," "My Glasses/Just Lay Low," and "Keep Your Deal with Me."

I never told Doug this outright, but "Life Plus Ninety-Nine Years" was taken down a step—since I sang the lion's share of it. And the key change in "The Plan" (which came right before the high harmony) was raised by only a half step—instead of the whole step as written. Sorry, Doug! I knew *he* could sing them in any key, but we would *both* sound better if I was more comfortable.

Since Zac and I could work together on smoothing out the transitions in and out of underscore, it was all able to be finessed so that nothing sounded jolting or odd. But that doesn't mean those keys would be right for a standard production. So, please, no one get any ideas!

* * *

When we started our brief rehearsal period, it hit me that *Thrill Me* wasn't a daily part of Doug's life as it was mine, so I wasn't sure what his Richard would be like this time. Did he remember how he had played the role years back? Would he want to try something new? I think it ended up being a combination of both.

My Nathan would be the same, but different as well. For one thing, I was slower! But I was far more self-assured than I ever was back then. I think I was a smarter Nathan. And of course, by that point, I was practically the age that the real Nathan Leopold was when he was paroled. So I guess my energy was more of an older person looking back than a younger person channeling an older one.

On one hand, I had nothing to prove. But on the other hand, I had a *lot* to prove. I wanted it to be the best performance I could possibly give since it was probably my last chance to do it before I would be *laughably* too old.

When Joe Barros started blocking the scenes, he created a truly brilliant "instant show." In fact, it was one of the most innovative and effective stagings of *Thrill Me* that I had ever experienced. It was performed entirely on a small rectangular platform with two black wooden chairs.

This made it seem as if the whole show was taking place in the Parole Board room, which would be filled with Older Nathan's memories and imagination. Logically, the Parole Board room really *is* where *Thrill Me* is taking place—it's where Older Nathan is actually telling the story. So it worked very well.

Though we had full costumes and lighting, we had no props. The hand props that were considered necessary (gas can, book, typewriter, knife, bag of stolen goods, ignition key, and telephones) were mimed. But mimed in an unusual way.

There was no concern for logic. Joe suggested that we imagine that a prop would just appear in our character's hands when needed and disappear when finished. It was genius.

When I sat down as Nathan in front on the typewriter, it was as if it was just suddenly there in front of me. I mimed typing on it, and when the scene was over I just stood up and walked right through where it had supposedly been.

When we were singing to each other over the telephone, we mimed holding the earpiece with one hand, but didn't worry about indicating a mouthpiece. To indicate hanging up the phones, we just dropped our hands. There was no miming of picking anything up or putting anything down. It was just like magic.

Other smaller props were completely ignored, such as the binoculars (Nathan just used his eyes), cigarette (Richard didn't pull it out since Nathan had no lighter), stolen items (they weren't pulled out of the mimed bag), murder weapons (at their first appearance Richard referred to them as if they were already laid out in front of him, after the murder he referred to them as if they were back in the car), and the ransom note (it stayed in the mimed typewriter).

Exceptions were made for costume pieces including Nathan's glasses, which came from my pocket, the blood red handkerchief, and, of course, the gold pocket watch on the chain attached to my vest, for that nervous fiddling. Richard had a handkerchief as well.

Joe's staging was so creative that I almost wished that there were never props or scenery in any production of *Thrill Me*. They suddenly seemed superfluous to the flow of the story.

As we rehearsed, it became clear that I could do the show totally off book. In other words, I didn't *need* to hold my script. But scripts would be expected to be held in a concert version. The more I thought about it, the more I *really* wanted to perform without it.

Joe, Doug, and I talked about it. We all decided that, since I was the author, it would make sense to the audience that I had everything memorized. Doug would still carry his script—which was as unobtrusive as possible, in a small black binder.

Joe suggested, and I agreed, that I should at least walk on with the script at the beginning to establish it. Then I would confidently put it down after my first few lines to the Parole Board, which for the first time would be performed by only one voice instead of two. After that, it would be hidden away for the rest of the show.

Joe also felt it would be important for Doug to have a big moment without the script. So a section of "Nothing Like a Fire" was chosen for him to hand me his script while he performed an entire verse without it.

Truth be told, though the script was in his hand, Doug only glanced at it when absolutely necessary. He knew his lines. It almost just looked like Richard was carrying around his "Nietzsche book." And if it had really bothered Doug, I would have carried my script too.

While I felt much more confident this time, I was nevertheless nervous to do the show with Doug. He was still that "superior" actor that he had been twelve years earlier—actually even more so, since he had now played major roles everywhere from New York to Los Angeles.

I had personally gone to see him perform on stage alongside Tony-Award winning Broadway stars like Chita Rivera, John Cullum, and George Hearn, whose combined credits practically represented the entire history of the modern musical. But now, it was gonna be *me* up there with him again! Just like every night Off-Broadway, for this performance I knew I would have to summon up every ounce of determination to hold my own. So once more, it was marathon time.

Just as I had done in my living room twelve years earlier, each morning before rehearsal I would walk through all of the blocking in the courtyard of the gym where I was a member. This time a couple of bright orange lounge chairs became my "set." I did the entire show over and over again. I was determined to be perfect.

* * *

A few days later, it was time for the show. The Cell was set up so that there was a walkway high above the stage. Behind it was our dressing room. We got ourselves ready, then "places" was called. Doug and I wished each other luck, and I positioned myself for my entrance.

When I heard the first notes on the piano before my entrance, which required a walk down a stage left staircase, I almost threw up. Just like in 2005! I couldn't believe it was really happening.

But I descended that staircase as the music of the "Prelude" played. From there I walked onto the small stage platform. I said my first line, and from there on it was ninety minutes of pure magic. Doug and I still had that stage chemistry. *"Watch the sparks begin to fly!"* seemed quite true when sung that night.

When it was over, I was more satisfied than I ever thought I could be. I proved to myself that I could still do it—and frankly I was even better than before. Doug was predictably flawless. I was so happy that the show got to be seen by not just my friends who were there the first time, but by many new friends who had never gotten the chance before.

There were even some fans who flew in from Asia. One was a journalist from Japan who interviewed me briefly after the show. Much to our surprise, critic Peter Filichia—one of the first to review the original *Thrill Me* fifteen years earlier, had agreed to attend. When his review was broadcast on *Broadway Radio* a couple of weeks later, he once again gave *Thrill Me* a rave. It was the perfect, validating ending for such an unforgettable experience.

* * *

With the decade almost over, I decided to remedy something that had been gnawing at me for years. I needed to make amends with Christopher Totten. It had always bothered me that I never looked him in the eye and told him why he wasn't cast in the Off-Broadway production. Twice.

I doubt he had given it a second thought after such a long time. But I always worried he might have mistakenly thought that *I* was the one who didn't want him. Especially since he knew that I ended up playing the part myself.

So I took Chris out for a drink and told him the whole story of what had happened. How I fought for him, but to no avail. But even still, I apologized for not trying even harder. He held absolutely no grudge, and was totally cool and understanding. I was very relieved. And I had another reason for the meeting—an acting role for Chris.

Joe Barros wanted a follow up to *Thrill Me* for NYTB since it was such a success. So it was decided that my musical *Panic* would be performed at The Cell almost exactly a year after the *Thrill Me* reunion. Once again it would be expertly directed by Joe himself.

Doug and I were already set to star in it. And I desperately wanted Chris to appear alongside us. With the three of us in it, it would essentially be a *Thrill Me* reunion of a different kind. I was ecstatic when Chris accepted the offer.

Panic was the show that I started writing after I put *Thrill Me* in the drawer many years earlier. It was the behind-the-scenes-story of the 1930s *War of the Worlds* radio broadcast. There had been a few productions by this point, but I was never completely pleased with the script. So I heavily rewrote it for the production at The Cell and then further revised it afterward. Eventually, the final version would be described like this:

> When *Panic* begins, one full year has passed since the fateful night of the historic Halloween broadcast. The now-famous actor/director Orson Welles has gathered his Mercury Theatre Company back together at the CBS Radio Studio to present a brand new 'live radio musical' which cleverly dramatizes how the broadcast was originally devised, performed, and received.
>
> As Welles hosts, the Mercury players re-enact the incredible series of events which reveal how none of them could stop Welles from creating what he was sure would be his ticket to fame in Hollywood. But, in the process, he also created panic, pandemonium, and outrage.
>
> Since many listening Americans mistakenly believed that the radio drama was a *news report* declaring a real invasion from Mars, the company was in big trouble—until Welles found a way out of it. Was it an accident, or was it Welles' plan all along? Either way, Welles became a star overnight, and the entire media industry would never be the same.

It was a total blast that the three of us "*Thrill Me* veterans" got to work together, playing a trio of sparring showbiz types. Chris was the sweet young writer, Doug was the harried but patient producer, and I was the egotistical control-freak actor. Typecasting? I'll never tell.

This time we did two performances on consecutive nights, and both were completely sold out. Another great review from *Broadway Radio* followed. With the new script, *Panic* would go on to have stagings all over world. But there was no version more special to me than this one at The Cell. Getting to share the stage with both Chris and Doug was a dream come true. I hoped they'd be game to join me again someday.

* * *

The second decade of *Thrill Me* would come to a close after more and more productions were staged. There was an all-new London production at the Hope Theatre, another UK tour of the *original* London version, a new Australian production, and a second staging in Belgium. Seoul and Tokyo continued. The United States got productions in Denver, New Orleans, Boca Raton, and even fairly conservative Ogden, Utah.

Thrill Me had never slowed down. In fact, it was quite the opposite. I could hardly believe it was already the end of 2019. Now it was time for *Thrill Me*, my 1920s musical, to move into the 2020s. I wondered what the new decade would bring. But I wasn't prepared for the shocking answer.

15

THRILL ME IN THE '20s

"There's no choice, you must be stronger. /
Don't you fall inside their trap."

Now in its third decade of performances, *Thrill Me* started 2020 with a professional production in East Lansing, Michigan. I was invited to their New York auditions and was very pleased with how the casting turned out. Before the actors went out of town, I was invited to dinner with both of them and the director so we could all discuss the game plan for what I was sure would be "a great *Thrill Me*."

The Michigan staging was soon followed by a return engagement of a previous production in Wuppertal, Germany. Then there was another round of performances of the original Belgian tour. Productions were already scheduled for later in the year, others were in the midst of being licensed and negotiated. Everything was running full steam ahead.

* * *

Then the world changed.

* * *

I was very lucky that *Thrill Me* wasn't playing in New York City or London at the time, or it would have been closed down like all other shows. Fortunately, productions in Europe and Asia were able to continue. It meant there had to be a bit of rescheduling, certain requirements had to be put in place, and theatre capacity had to be reduced. But when all was said and done, between all the various overseas productions of *Thrill Me* and the Shanghai production of *Flames*, I was fortunately able to remain financially secure during those difficult first few years of the decade.

* * *

Fairly early in those dark days of 2020, an independent Polish producer/director pitched a production of *Thrill Me* that would play Warsaw as part of a prestigious theatre's programming later that year. I was very enthusiastic about the ideas he shared with me. A deal with the theatre was soon made.

This was a version like no other. It utilized boxed video screens that encircled the actors on the stage floor—they could be stood on and sat upon like a bench. A tiered wall of those same video screens loomed behind them. The screens would be used to project near-constant moving images, both realistic and metaphorical.

This time the Parole Board voice was actually a mature actor who filmed the part. I gave special permission for this. The script, in any language, goes out of its way to state that it must be a voice only. But this filmed concept intrigued me. Though he was shot mostly in shadows, he was definitely visible, and uniquely projected during his various scenes. On one screen might be his face, on another his mouth, and one more might show the cigarette in his hand with its billowing smoke.

There were plenty of ominous black birds flying across the screens for Nathan to watch at the beginning. As to be expected, there were onscreen flames at "Nothing Like a Fire." During the title song, pictures of over-sized flickering lightbulbs were projected. As Nathan desperately sang to get Richard's attention, a preoccupied Richard just went around hitting the tops of the screens to make the lightbulbs stop flickering.

A grand piano was inside the circle of screens, and most of the action took place around it. When it was time for Nathan to type the contract, he traded places with the pianist, and used the piano itself symbolically as the typewriter. He actually played the accompaniment of the song himself.

Projected during "Superior" was Nietzsche symbolism and film clips that simulated the point of view of the characters running through the woods. When Richard sang "Afraid," the image of a giant rope seemed to be tightening across the entire stage. Sometimes the screens simply displayed a vivid wash of color. All of it was simply breathtaking.

The poster art was created by the famous Polish artist Andrzej Pągowski. It was a vivid painting of Nathan and Richard rendered as a single head with two faces in fiery red hues, against a blue background. Definitely a unique interpretation.

When the show opened in late 2020, travelling to Poland was not even an option. So I was able to experience this fantastic production thanks to a video that I requested as part of our agreement. For their first run of performances, they were allowed by the government to have a well-spaced audience at 25% capacity. I was sent a photo of the "sold-out" crowd—fifty people spread out in a theatre that sat two hundred. It was an unusual situation, but the show went on.

And it would continue to be part of the theatre's regular repertory, with several return engagements, as the decade went on. It would also travel to be performed at various theatre festivals around Poland. Eventually, it was able to have the 100% capacity, truly sold-out performances that it deserved.

I was so taken with this production that I wanted to commission a full scale, multi-camera, filmed version of it—to hopefully license to a streaming service such as Amazon Prime, Broadway HD, or Broadway on Demand. I was willing to produce and finance the entire thing, but it would have needed to be put together by the team in Poland since I couldn't be there.

The one catch, of course, would be that the actors would be required to perform it in English. They both could speak it, but it would take a while to learn the text and be comfortable with it. I didn't care about their natural accents. I actually loved the idea of it being a "European version," so I wanted no effort made for them to sound like they were from Chicago. The actors and the director—who had almost all of his previous experience in film—were very receptive to my plan.

Discussions began with the theatre, and they also seemed very interested. Budgets were drawn up, schedules were looked into, and preparations were slowly starting to be made. An issue arose when the well-intentioned theatre wanted to put up part of the budget so that there could also be a separate Polish language version filmed at the same time.

Unfortunately, this opened a can of worms that was too hard to close. I was firm in my desire to fund the whole thing so that I could unambiguously own and control it all. But the theatre very much wanted to be a partner.

And while talks would occasionally start up again a few times, the cameras never rolled. I do still hold on to the possibility that one day we'll be able to make it happen in Poland. If so, I hope it will be viewed by everyone, everywhere. It deserves it.

* * *

Just because I was interested in a filmed version of one particular production, didn't mean that I was fully onboard with the concept of online theatre as a whole. But in the first few years of the decade, due to there being so many dark theatres around the world, I started getting requests to allow videos of captured performances to be streamed for home audiences.

The Polish version that I had hoped to film would have been re-conceived specifically for home viewing. But putting on just a standard video of a stage production was an idea that I didn't love.

I truly felt then, as I do now, that no matter what the circumstances, if a show is staged for the theatre, then it should be experienced live. Not watched on a TV, computer screen, or smartphone. But these were difficult times. So I temporarily changed my mind.

The first request came from The English Theatre of Hamburg in early 2020. I tried to work something out with them, but we had trouble agreeing on an acceptable deal. I had to ultimately turn them down—it wasn't easy.

Then I got a compelling request from the exceptional Czech Republic production. The Czech producers had previously gotten my permission to record a high-quality archival video. I found their staging to be very innovative. It was performed on a set comprised of a textured grey wall and a black floor. A metal prison-style cot was center stage as the main focal point.

When it was time for the typewriter, there was no prop on stage. Instead, illuminated behind them, was a huge black and white photo of the actual one that belonged to the real Leopold. In a truly stunning effect, instead of typing, Nathan held a white sheet of paper in front of himself. From a projector, the words were "typed" directly onto the page. Then those words were enlarged on the wall behind him.

There were other clever projections utilizing real-life evidence photos from the crime scene. During "My Glasses/Just Lay Low," photos of Bobby Franks and Leopold's real eyeglasses flashed by. For the Parole Board scenes, specially filmed clips were used.

The metal cot was tipped over onto its headboard so that Richard could sing "Afraid" while climbing it. Eventually he sat perched high up on its footboard. For "Life Plus Ninety-Nine Years," it was turned onto its side, creating the claustrophobic interior of the police van.

Since it was such a great production, I decided to allow the video to be streamed. We negotiated a simple agreement. For one night only in May of 2020, *Thrill Me* had its "video premiere."

Next came a request from Bernd Arends, who had produced a second production of *Thrill Me* at his theatre a few years earlier. There was no previous archival video this time, so he wanted to reconstruct the set and bring his cast back into the empty theatre to film the show without an audience.

Since Bernd had been the first person to discover *Thrill Me* for the German market and had done the translation, I felt that I owed this to him. I made a new agreement with FBE so that they could negotiate the deal on my behalf. In the end, it would be streamed on three separate dates during the late Spring of 2021.

When I received my copy of the video, I was glad I agreed to let it happen. It was another great version of the show. One that deserved to be experienced by more people.

The set was comprised of haphazardly tilted metal trussing beams, a shelf at the back full of props, and various projections on the back wall. Real smoke appeared on stage during "Nothing Like a Fire." The scene also featured a huge hand-drawn image of a warehouse projected behind the actors. It was the first time I had ever seen any *literal* depiction of a warehouse.

Other projections included a noose during "Afraid," and a wire fence during "Life Plus Ninety-Nine Years." There was also a stunning image of a silhouetted Bobby Franks at the very end as Nathan sang his final *"Thrill me."*

There were meant to be three actual *live* streams of the Japanese production. Each was to originate from a different tour city in May of 2021—each with a different cast. But due to various mandated theatre closures, they instead streamed pre-recorded three-camera archival videos which had initially been created as backups.

Also in 2021, the Seoul production created gorgeous 4K archival videos of each of their three casts. By this time, the production had stopped recreating the Japanese scenery and staging. It reverted back to the original designs from 2007. I agreed to allow these three videos to be used for a total of twelve streams in the Spring of 2022. This would help offset losses from the previous year's occasional theatre closures and capacity reductions.

Unfortunately, it was my understanding that one of the actors didn't consent to the deal that was offered for the usage of the archival video. That meant that the four streams of the recording of him and his onstage partner were canceled. I personally felt bad for the partner who lost out due to no fault of his own. This left a grand total of eight streams.

Luckily, all of the streams in each country were extraordinarily successful—with viewership numbers that exceeded my wildest expectations. It pleased me that so many fans got to enjoy *Thrill Me* from home during those troubling times. While it was a tough call at first, I know I ultimately made the right decision to allow them all.

* * *

Due to the issues with the government, the Shanghai production had been off the boards for about three years. But in the year before the shutdown, I suddenly started receiving requests from several different producing organizations in China to bring it back—just as I had hoped. I have no idea why these offers all converged at the same time. It was almost like some kind of statute of limitations expired, but I doubt that was the case. I was getting pitch decks, taking meetings, and reading proposals. It was all very exciting.

As flattering as all these proposals were, I didn't have the heart to cut Michael Park out of the picture. So I asked Amy to inform him of the offer that we were on the verge of accepting. This at least would give him the chance to match it. Much to my delight, he did.

So Shanghai would once again see Michael's production—though at first it had to deal with capacity reductions and other restrictions. It would still be based on the original Japanese version, with the same scenic designs and overall concept. Michael chose a local company as his Chinese producing partner. The only major difference this time was that the characters would now be known as "Nathan and Richard," rather than "I and He."

As usual, several teams of actors were hired for the production. New posters were created, and many gorgeous photo shoots took place. There was one with each actor in front of a chess board, expressing differing attitudes, and another with the actors posed lounging throughout a stylish mansion.

All new merchandise was created, including a series of enamel pins and a pair of resin dolls based on the characters. Each one of these dolls came in an orange box with dialogue and lyrics from the show in

English printed on all four sides. A sticker on the bottom noted which doll was a Nathan, dressed in blue with a painted-on watch chain, and which doll was a Richard, dressed in beige. Since I thought that they were so incredibly cool, I requested and received an entire box of them.

Small immersive theatre productions were starting to become popular in Shanghai around this time. The producers of my musical *Flames* had already created such a version to run alongside the large-scale production. Michael Park and his partners decided that the same would be done for *Thrill Me*.

A small theatre was secured. This one would let the audience be practically on stage with Nathan and Richard, or at least very close. Now there were *two* productions in Shanghai. The small one would be an "open run," and the large one would run seasonally. There would, however, be times when both were playing at the exact same time.

The small immersive production played a standard weekly schedule for over a year. But it had to take a few months off when all Shanghai theatres were unexpectedly closed again temporarily as an emergency measure—just when we had all thought the worst was over. This version was quite successful, though I was told that early on there was an issue with the lights shining too brightly in the audience's faces. This was likely because of how they had to be angled in the very small space. I believe it was eventually corrected.

The large version would play four separate seasons in Shanghai through early 2023. It had to withstand yet another kissing scandal, further monitoring by the government, and renewed concerns of being shut down due to content. I wasn't there to witness any of this, so I know precious few details.

By mid-2023, the agreement for the Chinese rights expired. Once again, a couple of companies made offers, but Michael Park decided to renew his contract for a production in 2024. This would be a different version, not based on the Japanese staging. There would be all-new scenery and all-new artwork. Hopefully, there would also be *no* kissing. And no surprise theatre closures.

* * *

In New York, it seemed like the theatres were going to be closed forever. In reality, it was about eighteen months. And when they reopened, the very first show I went to see was a small production of *Thrill Me*. It was produced by Little Red Light Theatre Company at the NuBox Theatre, which was located just about a block away from my apartment—the closest to me yet!

It was among the earliest shows to open after the long period of uncertainty. Since it was in New York City, I had to grant special permission as part of their agreement with the licensing company. Generally speaking, any proposed licensed production in New York, Los Angeles, or London includes a requirement that the author, or author's estate, sign off on it.

I was invited to their casting session. A few *Thrill Me* alumni even showed up to audition. I appreciated that my input was welcomed. Once the cast was in place, rehearsals began under Actor's Equity's necessary and understandable new rules. There were so many strings, conditions, restrictions, and obstacles that I'm shocked they were able to pull the whole thing off.

I also went to their first table read, which was the first time in years that I had heard the script in English. It was like being reunited with an old friend.

Walking into the NuBox on opening night made me feel very circumspect. The last time I had been in a theatre was at a matinee performance of a Broadway play the day before the closure, which now seemed like a lifetime ago. And now for my first time back, I would be seeing *my own* show. It was very gratifying that it ended up working out that way.

A QR code for a digital program was displayed in the lobby since none were distributed. In the theatre, the scenery for the show looked like a gable-roofed attic made of wooden beams and slats. Furniture covered in tarps would be revealed as needed for the various scenes. The piano was located off stage.

Both Jim Kierstead and Joe Barros were among those joining me to watch the performance. I couldn't have imagined a better way to put an end to such a tough year and a half for all of us.

* * *

Things were finally getting back to normal around the world. The Hope Theatre's popular version of *Thrill Me* re-opened in London's West End at the Jermyn Street. It would be the first theatre to have hosted two completely different productions of the show. Once again, it proved to be quite a hit, and even won an Offie Award.

This version looked like it took place in a police station. There was a window with vertical metal blinds which could reveal lighting effects from behind; a "murder board," which displayed newspaper clippings and crime scene photos connected with zigzags of red string; shelves displaying the props as "evidence," complete with tags; and a few wooden crates, which the actors would move around as needed for the various scenes. I would have loved to have seen it in person but I wasn't ready to get back on an airplane yet.

Soon there would be an English Language version in Hong Kong, staged completely in the round, featuring actors who were originally from the United Kingdom. Members of the production couldn't wait to tell me that neither the actors, the crew, nor the theatre staff were prepared for the onslaught of fans who flew in from all across China and other parts of Asia, many bearing gifts. I was told that it was chaos in the lobby after each performance as fans clamored to meet the actors. A small table for after-show autograph sessions had to be quickly set up.

Later, there was a version in Florida that was directed by a previous Nathan from a production that had taken place over a decade earlier. I received more than one much-appreciated invitation to see it, but I had to decline. That ended up being a good thing, as there probably wouldn't have been room for me. The entire five-week run was completely sold-out.

* * *

Actors who hadn't even been born when I started writing the script were now triumphing in productions all around the world. Directors who were still in school when the show premiered Off- Broadway were now helming their own versions. *Thrill Me*, thankfully, never seemed to slow down. As Richard sings, *"Blood's a lifetime guarantee, Babe!"*

But as the early years of the 2020s proved, nothing is ever really guaranteed. If *Thrill Me* was going to continue to thrive, I felt that changes had to be made to help ensure its future. Although I had always sworn—both to myself and others—that I had finished writing *Thrill Me* long before, every rule has its exceptions.

16

ALL-NEW *THRILL ME*

"And don't act like you're holding something back."

Every now and then, I made some small but significant tweaks to the text and lyrics of *Thrill Me*. And I ultimately decided that all of them made the show better in one way or another. So I needed to find a way to make them a permanent part of the already well-established script. The first thing I had to do was organize them all.

The earliest of these tweaks, and the only "official one," had come when it was time to publish the Samuel French UK edition. I rewrote a line in "My Glasses/Just Lay Low." *"If we wait a few days longer, / I don't know if I could cope"* became *"If we wait a few days longer, / and get caught— then there's no hope."* The reason was simply because I came to feel that "cope" didn't sound like a word that a teenager of the 1920s—even a smart one—would use. But the Dramatists Play Service script remained unchanged.

For the English Theatre of Hamburg a few years later, I provided a change to a line in "Superior" in which Richard was referring to the victim as *"a twelve-year-old whose time was ripe."* In real life, Bobby Franks was fourteen years old at the time of the crime—and I was really tired of being asked why I "changed his age." That's *not* what I did.

While it might not have been a good idea to mention *any* age in the lyric, in my mind I felt that Richard, the character, was merely estimating Bobby's age. He didn't know for sure, and it's not as if he would have asked—it was just casual speculation that was mentioned in passing during the song. He wasn't writing a biographical treatise. Neither was I.

But after so many years, I was tired of defending it. Actual press releases from productions would even seem go out of their way to mention "fourteen-year-old Bobby Franks" as if to taunt me. So I changed the line to *"a boy whose time was, sadly, ripe."*

In Seoul, songs from *Thrill Me* were often performed in concerts by popular actors and singers. I was sent a recording of "Nothing Like a Fire" performed in English. The singer repeated half of a verse, just to make it longer. I really liked how that sounded.

So for the reunion performance with Doug, I decided to add that extra half-verse—but with new lyrics instead of a repeat. It was a bit of a challenge to try to match what I had written before.

The hardest part was that one verse ended with a metaphor about the smoke from the fire going *"straight to the stars,"* and the other ended with the smoke *"clouding the night"*—so I had to come up with a similarly themed third version. *"Hiding the moon."* Perfect!

I also finally found a way to fix a part of the title song that had always bothered me. The issue was that the last line of a verse ended with a wrongly stressed syllable, which any good lyricist should try to avoid. The word "sat-is-fy" had to be sung as "sat-is-FY." I tried for years to figure out a different word—even when we were in production the first time—but I just couldn't come up with anything.

At last I realized that, to make it work, I needed to change the entire verse around—not just the word. The new version would have the same meaning, just expressed in a slightly a different way.

So *"Why spoil my evening? / And why must you deny me? / I'll stop my complaining, / once you satisfy me!"* became *"Why spoil my evening? / What good are you gaining? / Once you start complying, / I'll stop my complaining!"* Why hadn't I thought of that in 2003?

I felt that "My Glasses/Just Lay Low" needed one more tweak. *"It's all starting to unravel, / the next sound we hear / will be the gavel,"* which I thought sounded a bit too casual for the moment, was reworked as *"My head's pounding like a gavel. / The whole thing, I fear, / will soon unravel."* I believed this new wording gave Nathan much more urgency.

213

There were also changes made for a much more significant reason. To be blunt, I felt that some of my lyrics and lines gave Richard a bit of a child molester vibe—and I feared they wouldn't age well. This was inspired by the real case. The police and coroners found possible clues that Bobby might have been sexually abused. But nothing was ever proven, and Leopold & Loeb vehemently denied it.

Way back in 1994 I wanted to be daring and edgy. But after nearly two and a half decades, I had a change of heart, and felt it would be best to soften things slightly. So *"No shortage of perverts"* became *"No shortage of misfits."* And *"We'll make it look like rape"* became *"We'll make a quick escape."*

Richard's dialogue about the proposed target which started as "Let's see…a ten or eleven-year-old" was bumped up slightly to an "eleven or twelve-year-old." Not that big of a difference, but it toned it down a notch in my mind. I don't think anything was truly lost by these adjustments.

The final change was the Parole Board. No, I didn't cut the recording and go back to monologues! But for the reunion, we had used just one Parole Board voice—for the sake of simplicity. I decided to make it the permanent approach.

Now there would be a single male voice going head to head with Older Nathan in the Parole Board scenes, which would contrast nicely against Richard going head to head with Nathan's younger self in the 1920s scenes. Two separate men in two separate times for Nathan to ultimately manipulate.

I also thought it might solve a production issue someday, just in case a theatre had limited resources. Now, in theory, the pianist could be the Parole Board voice—maybe even thematically costumed as such. Or the actor playing Richard could even do the lines on an offstage microphone, if needed. The recording would no longer be necessarily required.

* * *

I started offering a detailed list of these changes for any production to use if they wanted. While many companies *did* take me up on the offer,

I couldn't force them all to because they had every right to work with the original script that they had licensed. However, at this point, *all* new international productions that were not handled by Dramatists Play Service, Samuel French, or FBE (in other words, the ones still under my personal control) would receive only the revised version to use for their translation.

I managed to have a brand-new trade paper-back edition of the revised script published. Thank you, *Amazon*! The cover had the same wonderful red and black artwork that Mati Gordon created for the reunion poster. But since it wasn't connected to either of the licensing companies, it didn't solve the issue of productions continuing to receive the original version.

And just a short time later, the very first non-English language paperback of *Thrill Me*—also the revised version—was released. It was published in the Czech Republic to coincide with their production (the same one that streamed, not that first one on a boat). It included several gorgeous production photos. The only odd thing about the book was that for some reason it had the year I was born displayed in parentheses on the cover next to my name. I guess I should have demanded a "no personal details" clause!

* * *

I soon experienced major changes that I never could have foreseen. Within the span of about eighteen months, Samuel French was acquired by Concord Theatricals; Dramatists Play Service was acquired by Broadway Licensing; and Abrams Artists Agency— where Ron and Amy worked, went under new leadership that changed the name of the company to A3 Artists Agency.

It was a lot to swallow in such a short period of time. While things stayed exactly the same with Ron and Amy, the publishers would have new licensing teams, new procedures, and new priorities.

For the most part, the transition for *Thrill Me* went smoothly. And, in my opinion, I forged a great working relationship with both new companies.

There was just one little scare early on. Broadway Licensing, while putting the piano score into their new "house style," had reformatted it completely. This totally changed the layout.

What they didn't realize was that the difficulty of the near-constantly played score had been mitigated, way back in 2005, with very carefully placed page breaks. They were designed to make each page turn land at the most opportune spot possible.

This new format could be a disaster for the pianist. Forget three hands, *four* might now have been needed! Luckily, once I discovered this and reached out to the company, they simply reverted back to the original version. Crisis prevented! But I did feel bad for all the extra work they went through initially. I wished they would have let me know about the planned changes in advance.

Since everything seemed to be starting over again anyway, I finally got the chance I was waiting for. I decided to ask Broadway Licensing and Concord UK to redo their *Thrill Me* materials and put in all of the revisions, thus making them permanent once and for all. Both agreed. I appreciated it very much. They were under no obligation to do it.

For Concord UK, a brand-new published version of the script was created. But it was time to retire the photo of Doug and me and find something new. Mati's reunion version was already used for the trade paperback, so we had to think of something else.

I used to always be a little upset when any production would use Nathan's eyeglasses as a logo. I worried that it was giving away a major clue before the show even started. But after so many years, I stopped caring and we used a stunning new logo also created by Mati. It had the black outline of the glasses (the real ones) set against a red background with white and black text.

However, at Broadway Licensing, their procedure was to create rental packages for musicals. No more published paperbacks. And *no* cover art. All the new materials for *Thrill Me* looked great, and the revisions went in without issue.

In mid-2022, once both companies had issued their new materials, the original English language version of *Thrill Me* ceased to be available for performances—never to be offered again. While it felt a bit sentimental to "say goodbye" to some of my earliest ideas, I knew that I made the right call on every single change.

But since Broadway Licensing still used the Dramatists Play Service imprint for plays, the original version of the script would remain available as a "legacy version." Purchasable for reading, but not licensable for production. For some reason, the cover was adjusted to have much larger author billing. In industry terms, my name was now at "100% of the title!" Agents dream of getting that for their clients—and here it was without even asking.

Every now and then when I visit the New York Public Library for the Performing Arts at Lincoln Center, I still get a kick out of finding that Dramatists Play Service *Thrill Me* script on the shelves among all of the great musicals that start with "T."

Since the FBE script was in German, and I truly didn't know exactly how it was translated, I didn't request that their rental materials be revised. The same was true for the South Korean, Japanese, and Chinese translations. So all of these versions were still derived from the original script. Two Parole Board voices. Shorter "Nothing Like a Fire." And everything else.

* * *

The original versions of the songs would still live on via the Off-Broadway cast album. I never even considered re-recording or over-dubbing anything. I'm not even sure after all those years we could have made it match—and an all-new recording was out of the question.

But it was time to freshen it up a bit and bring it into the "modern age." Although it hadn't ever gone out of print, it was nevertheless re-released on CD. In order to match the trade edition of the script, this time the cover featured the same red and black artwork from the reunion performance. And, due to an overwhelming number of requests, it was also made available as a digital download for the first time.

For a while I thought there might never be more recordings of the *Thrill Me* score. The one with Doug and me was certainly enough, but

I also hoped that there would be international versions. It took longer than I expected, but eventually my hopes were fulfilled.

First came the release of three separate Japanese cast albums. They were recorded live at the theatre. Each one featured a different pair of actors, and each bore a cover featuring that ominous poisonous fruit.

For the tenth anniversary in Seoul, a deluxe South Korean cast album was released. It was a dual CD set. On the first disc were three different pairs of actors, each singing a third of the songs before the next pair took over. The second disc was the same thing all over again with another three pairs.

The whole set was made to look like a black evidence folder tied up with gold thread. Along with the discs inside, there were beautiful full-color photos on cardstock. A fold-out pamphlet of lyrics and credits was also included.

A German cast album would come a few years later. At my request, this one replicated the Off-Broadway version as close as possible. It included the same ad-libbed definitive endings of all the songs, and similar condensed dialogue within them.

* * *

There was suddenly a lot of new *Thrill Me* in the world, and I couldn't have been happier. It was clear that the early 2020s were full of surprises. And I was about to get a surprising opportunity to bring an even newer *Thrill Me* into existence.

17

THRILL ME'S HOLLYWOOD APPEAL

"If you want to see your son, / then you'll follow every rule."

Despite the small tweaks and changes that I had now made to *Thrill Me*, I thought that the major writing of the show was very far behind me. But in early 2022, I signed an agreement to write an entirely new version of the script. This time as a screenplay! Yeah, I was shocked too.

I was contacted by a fledgling film producer from Los Angeles who was interested in acquiring the rights to shop a film version of *Thrill Me* around Hollywood. This would be the type of option deal known in the industry as an "attachment agreement." It was a much different kind of contract than the one I had signed for the South Korean film rights years back.

In this deal I gave up no rights. I retained all ownership and control. The producer would spend an agreed upon period of time pitching the material until he found an interested studio, network, or production company. Only at *that* time, I would be obligated to separately make an agreement to sell both the film rights and the screenplay, and he would make an agreement with said entity for his producing services.

The producer was protected by a clause which stated that I couldn't enter into a deal independent of him—we were "attached." I knew going in that a movie of *Thrill Me* was a true longshot. Especially since it was a *musical*. Amy explained to me that in her experience, deals of this type had a failure rate of over 90%. The good part of the deal though was that it was very low risk.

And I was very much looking forward to writing the screenplay. But there was some concern from the producer that since I wasn't a professional screenwriter, with two or three produced credits, then I couldn't possibly be "qualified" to write it.

In my opinion, Hollywood types don't have as much imagination as theatre people do. Half of my degree from NYU was in screenwriting. A screenplay was my thesis. But it was true that I wasn't a professional screenwriter. Just a professional *Thrill Me* writer.

Amy explained to him that without a screenplay by me included in the agreement, his offer would be declined. As negotiations were happening, behind the scenes I just bit the bullet and started writing a screenplay "on spec."

There was no harm in trying, be it for this potential deal or just so I could prove to myself that I could do it. Once it was finished, I shared the draft with the producer and his mind was immediately changed! We signed the attachment agreement—which included the screenplay— soon after.

* * *

In adapting *Thrill Me* as a movie, I actually had a bit of a head start. There was already the Parole Board framing device—which was somewhat cinematic. And the scenes in the 1920s took place in many different locations. It wasn't like I was adapting a one-set play.

The producer didn't even insist that it would have to be a tiny low-budget film—he wanted me to feel free to "go big" if I wanted to. And I *did* want to. Why not? It meant that I would have to be willing to make significant changes in order to make everything more *visual*. But, still, I decided that it needed to at least retain what made *Thrill Me* "*Thrill Me*." After all, if the producer was just interested in a movie about Leopold & Loeb, he certainly didn't need the rights to my musical.

To me, among the most important elements was that the story was told from Nathan's point of view, and thus we could only ever see what Nathan would have seen. For example, there could be scenes featuring Nathan without Richard, but not the reverse. Also, *Thrill Me* was very much the story of only what went on between the two of them, with no other person mattering at all to the plot. But I couldn't write a realistic screenplay that had just two people in it.

The first thing I did was to decide on an overall concept. To start with, the Parole Board scenes would be greatly expanded. We would not only see the Parole Board room, but also scenes that would take place all throughout Joliet prison as Older Nathan (intended to be the same actor as "young" Nathan, wearing age make-up) was waiting to be taken to the Parole Board room before a series of sessions.

I created a new character that I dubbed the "Menacing Prisoner" who was always lurking around in the shadows, taunting Older Nathan, causing him to always have to look over his shoulder. This new character's face would never be seen until the end. The idea was to make the viewer think that the prisoner was Richard, having turned on Nathan—who now feared him. The truth of his identity would be a surprise reveal at the end.

The stage version's nonspecific Parole Board was turned into three men that I designated as "Stern Parole Man," "Bored Parole Man," and "Eager Parole Man." Their dialogue matched those traits. "Eager" was younger, and especially sympathetic to Older Nathan. There was a guard, a stenographer, a property sergeant, and other prisoners at Joliet. Most of them had a least a little bit of dialogue.

Once Older Nathan's first Parole hearing started, an ominous bird landed at the window to observe. As he sang "Why" over the opening credits, various newspaper headlines, crime scene photos, and police files would sweep across the screen.

When the flashbacks began, they would usually be tied to something that happened in the Parole Board room. For example, as the Eager Parole Man poured himself a glass of water, Older Nathan focused on the stream of liquid, which would then dissolve into the stream of gasoline being poured in front of the warehouse for the fire scene. Then the smoke from the burning building would transition into the smoke from a cigarette held by the Stern Parole Man, and we were back in the Parole Board room.

The 1920s scenes would be fully populated with many characters: Nathan's birdwatching club, both the Leopold and Loeb families, servants, shopkeepers, bartenders, patrons at a movie theatre, gruff players at a pool hall, men changing clothes in a locker room, Bobby Franks, Clarence Darrow, police, neighbors, you name it. But *none* of them would have any dialogue.

It wasn't written that they were mute or silent. The concept was that we would see everyone—sometimes prominently, sometimes in the background—but not hear them. Only the conversations of Nathan and Richard would be spoken on screen. I believed this would make it feel like a movie—yet still feel like *Thrill Me.*

To "open it up," the first 1920s scene now took place all across Jackson Park, including the pond, the flower garden, the monument area, and…the men's room. This was also finally my chance to change Nathan's binoculars into a camera to tie back to the photo of Richard at the end.

But instead, I wrote a later scene where Nathan steals a portrait photo from Richard's desk and hides it furtively. This photo is used to, ahem, aid in Nathan's fantasies. When Richard eventually calls him on the theft, it's a very embarrassing moment for Nathan.

As for the lyrics of "Everybody Wants Richard," there needed to be several modifications made. I felt that I needed to better explain the story of what had happened in the past, and what it was like for Nathan when they were apart.

So, to be clearer, the first verse of the song, *"Tell me, who can you have conversations with, / share your twisted observations with? / Who else has a roughly similar view, / if not me?"* became *"Richard, I thought I had gotten over you. / A feat which was extremely overdue / when you cut off all contact, / making me wait—yet again!"*

Next, the original verse *"You've played around with lots of losers / who ended up as cheats and users, / but who's been on the sidelines waiting for you, / if not me?"* became *"But I missed the days we'd laugh at losers / and turn our heads at plebes and users. / Survived that time away, / and now I tempt fate—yet again."*

Later in the song, the lines *"Tell me who's the girl in which sorority, /
I got word on good authority"* became *"Richard, you're quite smart and very
choosy, / so you picked me—and not some floozy!"* And then to really
hammer home the specifics of Nathan's feelings, *"And God knows why
I think you're so appealing, / or why you're always double crossing, double
dealing"* became *"For six whole months my lonely life lacked feeling. / But now
you're back to prove why you're still so appealing!"*

"A Written Contract" took place in Richard's luxurious bedroom
suite, starting with him in the bathtub. Then he and Nathan moved
to the bedroom, then onto his private balcony, then to his huge
dressing room—where he kept his knife.

When Nathan started typing on the Underwood, there were quick
cuts back and forth to the Parole Board in the 1950s, where the
stenographer was typing on her steno machine in a similar rhythm.
The song reached its dramatic vocal conclusion as Richard walked
Nathan back home on the street between their houses.

The title song started in the attic of the Leopold house—where
Nathan stowed the stolen goods near boxes of his late mother's
clothing. It then moved to the kitchen—where Nathan served
Richard root beer (I finally found a place for the root beer), when
he clearly would have preferred gin. Ultimately, it moved to
Nathan's bedroom—where he kept a pair of caged birds who liked
to watch them.

And what an eyeful those birds got during the climax of the song!
The producer had requested that I really amp up the sex and "the
naked," which would be a far cry from the stage version. I had no
problem with it, but since screenplays require everything to be
described in vivid detail, it was definitely a new type of writing for me.
As it ended up, the screenplay would unquestionably have led to an R-
rated movie. Make that an R-rated movie *musical!*

When Richard was pressing Nathan to go along with his idea for
"a superior crime," it started with a visual-only scene in the Leopold
back hallway. Nathan, his father, and brothers were enjoying a family
game night by setting up a long snake-like trail of dominos. A barging-

in Richard "accidentally" kicked them, causing them to topple prematurely, as he demanded Nathan come join him at the movies. No dialogue, just a pair of tickets in his outstretched arm. It could easily be seen on the faces of the other men of the Leopold family that they weren't fans of Richard.

This led to "The Plan." The song started in the backyard of the Loeb mansion on a swing set and then progressed to include a peek into brother John's bedroom, then a trip to the country club, a movie theatre, a library, and a ballroom where Richard swept Nathan onto the dance floor to the shock of family members and onlookers. As it continued, there would be a scene in a swimming pool where Richard would get the idea to kill "some random kid"—by watching a bunch of younger boys cavorting in the water.

All of these moments were simply visual enhancements. The songs and the dialogue within it remained almost exactly the same as the stage script. It just spanned more time and traversed more locations.

I ended "The Plan" in front of The Chicago Art Institute with Nathan finally acquiescing as he endures Richard stuffing a hot dog (I finally found a place for the hot dog), from a nearby cart, into his mouth. We would next see Nathan breaking into a hardware store to procure the murder weapons.

The "Way Too Far" scene would begin in the wine cellar of the Loeb mansion as Nathan and Richard furtively discussed what was to come next. Then it transitioned to scenes of Older Nathan, after having finished his first session with the Parole Board.

As the song was sung in voice-over, we would see him all through Joliet Prison—back in his cell, in the dining hall, and in the exercise yard. He was taunted by the "Menacing Prisoner" at every turn.

When "Roadster" is sung on stage, Richard is referring to a car off in the distance and he describes it vividly. But in the screenplay, he and Bobby would be right there in front of it.

That meant rewrites were needed. So *"would you like to see my roadster?"* was out, and *"I can see you like my roadster"* was in. Richard singing that it's *"a shiny Packard roadster"* would already be obvious to the onscreen Bobby. So I changed it to *"leather seats and metal dashboard."* Those impressive details couldn't necessarily be observed from the outside.

"See it sitting in the alley, / couldn't find a parking space. / We could open up the windows. / Wind will whip across your face." became *"Sure, it cost a pretty penny, / so I'm careful at the wheel. / We could, maybe, keep the top down. / Boy, how great the wind will feel!"*

To really emphasize that this was all Older Nathan's memory, the song would occasionally cut to *him* in front of the Parole Board singing a line or two of "Roadster" himself, then cut immediately back to the flashback with Richard singing. Of course, there also would be a few scenes actually inside the roadster as it drove through Chicago.

In the stage version, "Superior," which is sung immediately after the murder, starts with Nathan and Richard running in from the site where the body actually is. This is why Richard sings *"Twenty feet from here / in a culvert pipe, / lies a boy whose time was, sadly, ripe."*

But for a movie, they would need to be right there at the actual scene of the crime, not twenty feet away. So the verse was changed to *"In that culvert pipe, / thanks to your support, / lies a boy whose time was, sadly, short."* Yes, it was the second time I rewrote that line.

After "Ransom Note," we would see Nathan in front of the Franks house as he put the note into their mailbox. He stopped to watch the grieving parents through their window. I thought it was a very powerful moment for Nathan, especially considering the ending.

"My Glasses/Just Lay Low" began with scenes intercut back and forth between the two characters in their own homes. On Richard's tennis court, when he first learned from Nathan that the body was discovered, he would throw down his tennis racket (I finally found a place for the tennis racket) in a fit of anger.

The number also included a moment in which Nathan visited the grave of his mother. A groundskeeper walked by reading a newspaper with a huge headline about the search for the killers. The song would culminate with a clandestine meeting at the Chicago Harbor Lighthouse in the midst of a raging storm.

"I'm Trying to Think" started in the living room of the Leopold house. Many of Richard's ideas would be inspired by the items in the room. A copy of the Audubon Society Journal gave Richard the idea about Nathan dropping his glasses while birdwatching. A porcelain Gibson Girl doll gave him the idea of "the girl" as an alibi. A pink vase cued *"she wore something pink."* And when Richard pulled out a flask for a quick drink, Nathan added that she *"carried a flask!"* (this meant that I had to change the line before it from *"They'll want the details"* to *"Just say when they ask…"*).

The song culminated with Nathan at the police station. Crime scene evidence was presented to him judiciously. His eyeglasses were strategically placed in a bag before him—just out of reach.

The climatic fight scene—which on stage takes place back at Jackson Park—was set on the Michigan Avenue bridge. I didn't shy away from the possibility that Richard might actually throw Nathan off of it. I imagined a shot from Richard's point of view, in which he threated to let Nathan—who was precariously leaning backward over the railing (with the water raging beneath), fall. When he finally pulled him back up, Nathan would barely have time to catch his breath before the action continued.

To embellish the final scenes of the movie, I added a few new moments. While singing "Afraid," Richard looked at the gallows in the prison courtyard, from a high window in his cell. Then after the song, came a dramatic musically underscored courtroom scene depicting the judge pronouncing their sentence. The satisfied Clarence Darrow, the relieved men of the Leopold family, and the cold Loeb family all were watching—with no dialogue, of course.

Then Nathan and Richard were escorted from the courthouse, dodging photographers on the way to the police van. A dangerous near-accident in said van during "Life Plus Ninety-Nine Years" would give that song a startling jolt while leading into Richard's verse.

Older Nathan's final session with the Parole Board contained a painful, yet powerful, moment in which he recalls Richard's shower murder. It would be depicted *vividly* in flashback. We would see

Richard making a pass at inmate James Day, the stabbing, the blood, the steam from the shower, Nathan frozen in a corner watching it all happen—everything!

After his parole is granted, when Older Nathan gets his "things" back from the property sergeant, he had more flashbacks to when they were all in use. This would recall earlier moments from the movie. The items were expanded to include a small pair of foldable binoculars. The sergeant would mistake them for opera glasses, which Older Nathan found offensive.

And just as Older Nathan leaves Joliet, the "Menacing Prisoner" is revealed to be James Day—the man who stabbed Richard in the prison shower, and was feared by Nathan ever since. Older Nathan finally would stand up to this bully right before his release.

For the final moments, as Older Nathan waited at the bus stop outside Joliet, he would see a mirage of Richard across the street in front of him. And while running toward him, he would transform into his younger self again. But just as he reached to hug Richard, the mirage ended. He was old again, hugging nothing.

With binoculars in hand, Older Nathan would look up to a squawking flock of birds who were flying to race away from coming storm clouds. Then his final *"Thrill me"* would be sung directly into the camera—complete with evil grin—as the bus pulled up.

Some of Nathan and Richard's dialogue was changed to fit the needs of the screenplay. But, for the most part, it would be recognized as *Thrill Me* to anyone familiar with the musical. The expanded Parole Board/Joliet Prison scenes really made it feel like a movie. And since it was highly doubtful I could have talked the producer into having it scored with only one piano, there was no escaping the fact that, if it was ever filmed, this version would have *finally* required a lot more instruments.

* * *

I was extraordinarily pleased with how the screenplay turned out. In fact, I felt at that time that it was the best thing I had ever written. I truly believed that if the producer was actually able to strike a deal to get it made, my screenplay was a least a good starting point.

It showed that I was willing and able to add characters, scenes, and situations that weren't in my stage musical. I wasn't afraid to rewrite songs. And I had the imagination to make it bigger in scope and scale, while retaining what I believed were the most important hallmarks of the musical.

Throughout the time the agreement with the producer was in place, I would write a total of four drafts. The producer always had a lot of praise and insightful comments. And he never requested any changes. He only suggested very small additions for each draft, which were totally my prerogative to either agree or disagree with. It was still my property and every decision was still mine—because I wasn't yet working at the mercy of studio notes.

But after I turned in the fourth draft, everything changed. All of a sudden he asked me to add: a girlfriend for Nathan; a fantasy sequence for Loeb from *his* point of view during "The Plan," where he imagines killing his brother by maybe pushing him off a roller coaster and other things like that; and a line or two of dialogue for Nathan's father to be spoken somewhere around page eighty during "My Glasses/Just Lay Low" telling Nathan that the police had found the eyeglasses as a clue. While I have no doubt that the producer thought these would be improvements, my response was swift.

I reiterated to him that in *Thrill Me*, Nathan is presented as a gay man. I explained that the request to give him a girlfriend was not only offensive to me, but would be totally antithetical to the character's single-minded obsession for Richard.

Next I reminded him that the entire screenplay was from Older Nathan/Nathan's point of view, as was the musical. I felt that a sudden fantasy sequence from *Richard's* point of view would be extremely confusing.

Finally, I pointed out the obvious fact that for the entire movie no one in the 1920s had dialogue except for Nathan and Richard. So it literally made no sense to me that suddenly, out of nowhere, his father would say a line that could easily be depicted as a visual by Nathan reading a newspaper headline.

I would have never passed my screenwriting classes at NYU had I put incongruous things like those in any screenplay. The producer said that I shouldn't feel that I needed to "follow rules." Well, there are rules and there are *rules*.

I lamented to Amy that I now had a window into the movie that the producer had in mind, and it was unacceptable to me. She reminded me that he couldn't force me to implement his ideas, and advised me to just "stop writing." Under the terms of the attachment agreement, I had no actual obligation to have even written a second draft, much less a fifth.

I knew that if the movie really went into production, it wouldn't have mattered how many drafts I'd written. As per the norm for situations like this in Hollywood, once those cameras started rolling, as the writer I would lose control instantly. Nothing could stop the producer from finding someone else to write exactly what he wanted. And I would be miserable.

I hedged a bit and made it clear to the producer that I would do no further rewriting of the script unless an actual deal was made with a studio or network. This at least left the door open that further revisions, perhaps using his ideas, would be theoretically possible. To be honest, if I *really* believed an actual movie would come of this, I might have just held my nose and done the rewrites. But I *didn't* believe it.

Our agreement period was relatively short by industry standards. And when it came to an end, I wasn't unhappy. Still, I was very appreciative of the opportunity.

The good news was that I now had, what I considered to be, a fabulous screen adaptation of *Thrill Me* that I could be very proud of. It was written on *my* terms. And I'll have it forever. Who knows, maybe it'll come in handy someday.

* * *

As the decade moved toward its middle there was a beautifully designed, completely sold out production in Bangkok. The Thai lyrics were created by the same translator of Disney movies such as *Disenchanted, Frozen,* and *Encanto.* It was revealed to me that this version had a very attention-grabbing "pre-show."

The audience entered the theatre to hear a soundscape that started with muffled voices which segued into the chirping and flapping of birds, followed by a match being struck, then the sound of a crackling fire—which grew more and more intense. After that came a car engine revving up, then the sound of the car driving. Next there were footsteps, more sounds from the car, and finally the loud crash of a prison cell being slammed shut and locked.

Little did the crowd know that they were subliminally experiencing practically the entire story before the "Prelude" even began! It both amazed and gratified me that after so many years, a very creative director came up with a totally new and innovative idea for *Thrill Me* while still respecting the material.

There was also a highly successful Romanian tour—so successful that an extension began being discussed almost immediately after their first performance. Additionally, *Thrill Me* would have a new staging in Mexico City, an amateur version in Beijing, a potential opening in Taiwan, and more productions in the United States.

Of course, there were the ongoing productions and return engagements in Seoul and Tokyo, followed by another Japanese tour. The Ostrava, Czech Republic and Warsaw, Poland productions remained in repertory at their respective theatres. And Michael Park's brand-new Shanghai version would make its debut.

The world finally seemed to be back to normal. I worked on getting more productions of *Flames, Monster Makers,* and *Panic* on the boards. *Thrill Me* no longer needed my help in that regard. But, as always, I still had to keep track of it. And after three decades, there was more to keep track of than ever.

18

AND IT THRILLINGLY CONTINUES…

*"So I did what wasn't expected. / You never suspected. /
And now…we'll be together for / life plus ninety-nine years!"*

Well, actually make that life plus *seventy* years. That's currently how long
an author's copyright lasts. In the United States, at least. After that, a
work falls into the public domain and anyone can do whatever they
want with it—in other words, "my worst nightmare come true."

Maybe there will be interpretations of *Thrill Me* just like how
Shakespeare is done today. Like *Thrill Me* in outer space, or *Thrill Me*
in the Wild West or *Thrill Me* in, I don't know…a swimming pool? I'm
sure they might be very creatively done, but I'm glad I won't be alive
to see them.

At least, now that so much time has passed, I've mellowed on a
lot of the things that used to bother me. Even reviews don't matter
to me much anymore. It surprisingly took quite a while, but critics
eventually stopped scrutinizing *Thrill Me* as a new work and focused
more on the actors, the direction, and the production values—instead
of the writing and composing.

Usually, that is. In my opinion, it would be foolish for any critic
to suggest, for example, that "a new song should be written to convey
…" for a musical that had been in production for over twenty years.
But it actually happened. And I laughed it off.

I even keep my cool nowadays when production photos or videos
reveal things to me that I don't understand or agree with. Like
multiple costume changes—which I've always believed to be
superfluous. I once even saw Nathan and Richard changing into

prison uniforms to wear in the "Life Plus Ninety-Nine Years" scene—which takes place in a van after the verdict. If anything, they would be wearing formal suits!

And when a certain production added an actual, physical, real-life, prison guard—presumedly portrayed by the actor who was playing Richard—essentially escorting Older Nathan into the Parole Board room at the beginning of the show, I didn't complain. Though, frankly, I couldn't believe it when I watched the video. A character not in the script was *literally* added. "Oh but we didn't add any *lines!*" is what I imagine they would have claimed.

I even hold my tongue when I hear or read that a production is "fast-paced," though I believe that's the antithesis of how *Thrill Me* should be done. With no intermission, it's going to be short no matter what. So it doesn't need to be a race.

In my mind it should be roughly ninety minutes, certainly no less than eighty-five—which is what the Off-Broadway version usually clocked in at. In Seoul each performance runs close to one hundred minutes. In Tokyo it's sometimes nearly one hundred and ten minutes. There's never anything extra added to the text or music. It just breathes. For me, it can never be "too long," but it sure can be "too short."

When I saw a video of a production that ran less than *seventy* minutes, I thought they must have entered a contest to perform the world's fastest musical! In my opinion, what they were doing didn't give the audience the intended experience of *Thrill Me.* The staging was fine, but I felt that my writing just didn't come across well at such a speed.

What was I supposed to do, order them to slow down? Of course not. If I'm asked, I can share my opinion on the pacing. But if I'm not, I just can't let it be my concern...anymore.

Now just because I've relaxed a bit, it doesn't mean I still don't expect everyone to be working at the top of their game, and within the terms of their contract. I also continue to wish that all productions would place the emphasis on the acting and singing—not on the sets, costumes, and props. Sometimes those things can be overdone. The show was conceived to be simple, so why complicate it?

There was even a production that was intended to mark a significant milestone, but the producers *canceled* it due to a rented theatre not being able to accommodate every aspect of their planned lighting design. That said to me that the lighting was the *most* important element to them! I can only imagine how complicated the design was to have been.

But not long after this, I was pleased to discover that a particular production had massively succeeded based on the fact that they specifically followed my "simple" suggestions. Remember that reunion performance I did that had two chairs on a platform and nothing else? It was perhaps the most *uncomplicated* version ever. I had revised my author's notes in the new editions of the script to include a very detailed description of the "no scenery or props" concept. But it wasn't actually utilized until over half a decade later, when the Teddington Theatre Club produced the fourth separate version of the show to play London.

They got by with just lighting, sound effects, and the artistry of the cast, director, and crew. Their efforts were honored with The Judges' Award at the 2023 Swan Awards ceremony in the London borough of Richmond upon Thames. The citation specifically mentioned that their *Thrill Me* was "a masterclass in 'less is more.'" It went on to state "The silence and raptured attention of the audience said everything. Truly breathtaking, it left everyone very moved." And due to this success, their next small musical scheduled for 2024 was *Panic*. See? I rest my case!

I'm proud of myself for learning to live with all the things that aren't necessarily done "my way." It's not that I don't notice them. It's not that I don't question them. But it's now time for me to relax, enjoy, and be appreciative. And to be fair, while I do occasionally encounter aspects of productions that may make me raise an eyebrow, more often than not, I'm pleasantly surprised and awed by the talent involved.

* * *

As the thirtieth anniversary of starting to write *Thrill Me* and the one hundredth anniversary of the crime both approached, I took my third *Thrill Me*-related trip to Chicago to once again be filmed as an expert for a television program about Leopold & Loeb. I had unexpectedly received this generous invitation from one of the producers of a PBS documentary series called *Chicago Stories*.

For the program, they were interested in *Thrill Me* specifically and how I dramatized and musicalized the story. I was definitely an authority on *that* subject. They brought me to a beautiful wood-paneled room at Chicago's historic Newberry Library. When I was there, I realized that it was actually possible that the real Leopold & Loeb could have been in the building at some point over a hundred years earlier.

The interview itself went well. Though I would have no control over how I would end up being edited, I was hopeful that I would come across as confident and engaging. And, thankfully, this time I was allowed to wear black on camera!

* * *

Once I returned home, it was back to my usual *"Thrill Me* job." I've often been asked why I take such a "hands on" approach to all things *Thrill Me*. Wasn't my job essentially over after the script was finished? No. That was barely the end of "act one." As I used to sing when I was on stage as Nathan, *"It was impossible to run away."*

All I can say is that it just comes natural to me. Way back in the 1990s, *I* was the one who put up the first staged readings—there was no one to do it for me. In the early 2000s, *I* was the one who made the connections to first get the show on. The rest flowed from there.

I'm also lucky that it's not *only* me—it's a team effort. My agents and publishers do meaningful and exhaustive work on my behalf, and it's very much appreciated. But at the end of the day, no one could possibly focus on promoting my work as much as I do—or care as much about it as I do. That's why, when all is said and done, it's *my* job.

So, at this point, there were more and more licensing requests coming my way from around the world to consider. I usually approved most of them. As always, I made sure to study every word of every contract I signed. I knew exactly what rights every production company or theatre had. And, more importantly, what rights they *didn't* have.

In one single day I finalized the agreement for the Shanghai continuation; answered questions to alter the Romanian contract; gave permission for an archival video of a production to be recorded; got a confirmation of the payment for the Poland extension; received a request to provide a new program bio, greeting paragraph to the fans, and headshot for the Tokyo production; and contemplated a trip to see a production in the United States.

A couple of months later, over a holiday weekend, I took a meeting with the director of a very successful regional production that was just about to finish its run. He pitched me his idea to bring the show to New York City. I told him that I would be much more interested in having it be remounted at the theatre where it was such a big hit. I hope that happens at some point.

One morning around that time, I woke up to the news that the entire upcoming season of *Thrill Me* in Tokyo had completely sold out in advance, and standing room tickets would be offered at every single performance—I believe for the very first time.

A photo exhibit chronicling the first ten years of the Japanese production would be put on display at a café next to the theatre. While many shows have diminishing returns over the years, after over a decade in Tokyo, *Thrill Me* had become even stronger.

On another morning a few weeks later, I received an offer for a new Japanese streaming version of *Thrill Me* for late 2023. Since the first one had been such a success and didn't cut into the business of the stage version, a deal was immediately negotiated.

Then, about two hours later, I got a message from the producer of the original London production. Just as I had predicted after their last performance in 2018, he wanted to discuss the possible remounting of the show for another UK tour in 2024. Major business happening and it was only a Monday.

Later that same week, I had to delicately respond to a request from a producer who wanted permission to cast his production with a fifty-year-old actor as Nathan alongside an actor of around twenty as Richard. I could obviously understand what he was going for. And I'm certainly no ageist.

But the thought of intimate scenes between actors with a thirty-year age gap just didn't sit right with me. I felt it would add a subtext that I never intended. The script clearly states that the young actor embodies the older character, not the other way around. So that was what I hung my hat on and declined the request.

While in the midst of all of that, I met with Jim Kierstead one evening to pitch the idea of him producing a new Chicago production of the show to coincide with the centenary of the crime—so that the Windy City would get to experience *Thrill Me* to mark that historic occasion. Jim promised to add the possibility to his to-do list. I crossed my fingers!

One of the last major deals that Amy and I negotiated before the *second* thirty years of *Thrill Me* started was a big one. A major contract was signed to finally bring a professional production to *all* of Mainland China—not just Shanghai.

This large-scale tour would include performances in Mandarin, Cantonese, and English as part of an agreement that would last almost through the end of the decade. *Thrill Me* was already secure well into the future.

When not working on ironing out the details of a specific production or contract, my *Thrill Me* job includes tasks like reporting illegal uploads of the cast album on websites where people think it should be available for free streaming. As if it was *their* decision to make.

And I try to fight against those who've uploaded the complete piano score of *Thrill Me* that no one can possibly legitimately own—since it's only ever been available to rent for productions. Though a book of "Vocal Selections" was published.

I've even heard rumors about people who allegedly sell copies of unpublished or hard-to-find music, mine included, to actors for auditions. And they give no compensation to the writers.

In my opinion, that sounds akin to stealing. But chasing all of that down hasn't yet been a priority for me. So, like Nathan, *"I've held back and I've compromised."*

Curating my collection is also part of the job. In my desk drawers and under my bed I keep a huge assortment of *Thrill Me* branded merchandise, mostly from Japan, South Korea, and China, but there are a few items from other productions as well.

I have everything that I collected during the early years, plus newer items like adorable plush stuffed toys representing Nathan and Richard, zippered hoodies made to look like Older Nathan's prisoner uniform, embroidered towels, incense burners, custom boxes of Diamond matches, hand mirrors, make-up bags, pens, iPhone cases, note pads, scarves, handkerchiefs, eyeglass cases, buttons, notebooks, water bottles, passport covers, charm bracelets, decorative "washi" tape, stickers, AirPod cases, thumb drives, disposable cameras, and so much more. There were times when I was more excited about the latest merchandise than the actual show itself!

Since I don't have enough wall space, I have a nearly complete *Thrill Me* poster gallery reduced to refrigerator magnets in my kitchen. The fridge is so covered in them that I can hardly find the handle.

Incidentally, I've always hoped that one day I would see a poster with a logo of two birds in a cage—to tie to Nathan's "gotcha" line to Richard in their last scene. But so far it hasn't happened. If it does, I'll clear a special space for the magnet.

I also do my best to maintain my eponymous website by making sure it has an archive of posters, photos, reviews, and interviews available for anyone who wants to take a look. I organize the thousands of digital pieces of original Asian *Thrill Me* fan art that I've never stopped collecting.

And I even occasionally take a look at the official *Thrill Me* Asian fan fiction site. That's always a fascinating read, to say the least.

Perhaps the most rewarding part of my job is getting to greet members of *Thrill Me* productions from all around the world when they visit New York City. I've had the honor and privilege to meet many actors, directors, producers, musicians, and designers. We usually just chat about their experiences in the show over a meal at a restaurant—you guessed it, *near my apartment.*

Sometimes we actually discuss future business, which I've done with Michael Heller, regarding his German production; Damien Locqueneux, regarding his French language version in Belgium; and with Michael Park many times over the years to go over new aspects of his various Asian productions.

I enjoy yearly visits from Russ Wooley and Diana Wooley from the Lamb Theatre in Sioux City. We talk about all the latest theatre news from Iowa to New York! Moritz Staemmler of FBE in Germany comes to New York occasionally—it's great to catch up with him. And I'm always glad to meet up with my friend Miki Goto, who flies in from Japan all the time to see the latest Broadway shows.

I get to see Guy Retallack, the director from London, every now and then. His wife, Rachel Tucker, is an extraordinary West End and Broadway star. I saw her New York debut performance in *The Last Ship*, alongside the ultra-famous rock-star-turned-Broadway-composer Sting, and later in the hit *Come from Away.*

When Rachel was starring on Broadway as Elphaba in *Wicked*, Guy treated me to a ticket to the show. It was complete with a backstage visit to Rachel's dressing room—where she let me try on her pointed black witch hat. I think I looked fantastic!

I frequently receive correspondence from actors playing Nathan and Richard who I may never get to actually meet in real life. Many times their messages say that performing in the show was a life changing experience. I also hear from students and fledgling writers from all around the world who tell me that *Thrill Me* is an inspiration to them. All of that all means the world to me—and it's truly humbling—especially when I think back to where I started.

* * *

I've often wondered what would have happened if Martin Charnin wasn't assigned as my mentor for the Dramatist Guild Musical Theatre Program? What if I never met Jim Kierstead? What if I was too afraid to take over the role of Nathan Off-Broadway? What if Michael Park didn't have time to see the show in New York?

But there's no use speculating. It all *did* happen. And despite all of those lucky breaks, the key piece of my success was the fact that *I* took the chance and just *wrote* the damn thing! And it was *good*!

So my advice to anyone who might have an idea spinning around in their head is simply to "write it." Never be afraid to take the risk. It's the only way for goals to be achieved and for dreams to come true.

I would also tell any artist that they always must be able to stand behind their work and not be afraid to make unpopular decisions regarding it. It was for those reasons that I took all of my early pre-*Thrill Me* musicals out of circulation for production years ago, despite getting inquires on rare occasions. While I remain proud of them all, they no longer represent the way I wish to represent myself as a writer. And I would be uncomfortable having them performed again.

Even more importantly, I would also suggest that creation should only happen when one is ready and truly inspired. No timeline should have to be followed. Unless of course it's a commission or a specific commitment that's been agreed to in advance.

I wish I had a dime for every time some well-meaning person asked "What are you working on *now*?" or "Are you writing anything *new*?" As if the body of work I've already accomplished isn't enough. Well, it *is* enough for *me*.

The act of writing and composing a musical isn't a switch that I can just turn on anytime I want. I have to be totally enthusiastic about the subject—as I was with the story of Leopold & Loeb and everything else I've ever written. It requires my unwavering commitment and total immersion in the story to wake up every morning and be excited to see where the music…or lyrics…or dialogue…will take me. In short, I have to *love* it.

I may not be extremely prolific, but I feel that makes every musical I write all the more special. Every ounce of my heart and soul are deeply embedded into each one of them. That's what's most important to me.

So in case anyone is compelled to ask about my next project, for now I think that I've done *plenty* of work and I feel no obligation to ever write another musical again, unless and until the perfect idea comes along. And if or when that happens, everyone will know.

* * *

As for *Thrill Me* itself, what more can I say? My original goal was to create interesting characters, and a story that was improbably relatable. I feel that time proved that I succeeded. It wasn't always easy. But in those early days, I never stopped believing it could be accomplished.

I'm thankful that the first thirty years were filled with so many adventures, challenges, and *thrills*. What's left to be achieved? Maybe the South Korean movie will get made. Maybe my screenplay will be optioned again. Maybe the show will come to Broadway. At least I had my brushes with all of those exciting possibilities.

But none of those things really matter. I have nothing left to prove. And neither does *Thrill Me*. It continues to be a successful stage musical that entertains people all around the globe. Come to think of it, *Thrill Me* actually has a more exciting and exotic life than *I* do.

It's succeeded beyond my wildest dreams. Beyond the dreams of that little boy watching *Arsenic and Old Lace* with his grandparents, beyond the dreams of that young guy walking into Coliseum Books one fateful afternoon, and beyond the dreams of that excited writer spray-painting fake candlestick telephones in Jim Kierstead's backyard, a few days before his big premiere.

In New York, I may not be a household name theatre writer, and *Thrill Me* may not be a household name musical. But it's a cult hit in London and throughout Europe. And both *Thrill Me* and I are mainstream-famous in the world of Asian theatre. I dreamed of fame in the industry, but I guess I just didn't specify where. And that's okay!

240

I haven't stopped receiving invitations to attend performances of *Thrill Me* all around the globe. But, believe it or not, it isn't my favorite thing to do anymore! After over two hundred productions, I personally saw about twenty (in four separate countries). I also directed one myself. I played the role of Nathan on five different stages. And I performed songs from the show in beautiful countries that I never thought I would even get to visit as a tourist. I think that's already enough for one lifetime.

Truthfully, it doesn't matter if *I* see it. My only hope is that it continues to endure forever. So as far as I'm concerned, the only ones who need to be there are the *audiences*. Though I wouldn't rule anything out completely, it's possible that I've already seen *Thrill Me* live on stage for the last time with my own two eyes.

But the original costume pieces will always be lurking in my closet. The telephones, eyeglasses, and pocket watch will be waiting in storage. My one remaining near-empty jar of pomade from way-back-when will never leave my medicine cabinet. All of my precious souvenirs contain so much history and can instantly bring back so many memories. If I can't see *Thrill Me*, I can see all of these—anytime I want.

And thirty years later…thirty years *older*, that's exactly how I like it. I don't have to worry about tying the wingtip shoes or the blue paisley bow tie anymore. Or tie myself in knots hoping the show will be produced.

Thankfully, those days are long over. But sometimes, it's still hard for me to believe that so much time has gone by, and I get a little wistful—even misty-eyed, while thinking back on the past.

When I was in my mid-twenties, the fifty-four-year-old Nathan that I wrote about seemed so far removed from me. It was the younger version that I could relate to, even though I was technically already about half a decade older than the character. But thanks to *Thrill Me*, I got to play that nineteen-year-old on stage when my teenage years were *long* past me.

And now I'm just beyond the age of the real Nathan Leopold when he was paroled. In the script, my version of the character at that point is unambiguously described as an "old man." Well, I don't feel like an old man. In fact, I still feel like a teenager. I hope I always will.

* * *

As most of those involved in a production of any of my musicals will attest, the one consistent thing I recommend to them is simply to "have fun." So I decided to take my own advice when it came time to write this memoir.

I made sure it was fun for me. It was also difficult, scary, and cathartic—but definitely fun. And perhaps the *most* fun part was that my book was something that I was finally able to *fully* control myself.

While the creative input of many different artists has always been extremely important to make every production of *Thrill Me* sing—and I remain thankful to them all—no producers, directors, actors, designers, or pianists were needed to help bring *Thrill Maker* to life. This time every decision was mine and mine alone. Now, *that's* what I call a thrill!

THRILL ME

— Facts & Figures —

THRILL ME
COUNTRIES & LANGUAGES*

COUNTRIES

United States
Argentina
Australia
Austria
Belgium
Brazil
Canada
China
Czech Republic
England
Germany
Greece
Hong Kong
Hungary
Ireland
Italy**
Japan
Mexico
Poland
Romania
Scotland
Slovakia
South Korea
Spain
Thailand

LANGUAGES

English
Cantonese***
Czech
Dutch
French****
German
Greek
Hungarian
Italian**
Japanese
Korean
Mandarin
Polish
Portuguese
Romanian
Spanish
Thai

*As of January 2024.

**Workshop only, as of January 2024.

***Contracted but not yet performed, as of January 2024.

****Excerpts performed in Belgium, as of January 2024.

THRILL ME
INTERNATIONAL LANGUAGE TITLES*

Argentina-*El Pacto*, which translates to *The Pact*

Belgium, Dutch version-*Thrill Me*

Belgium, French version-*Thrill Me***

Brazil-*Pacto*, which translates to *Pact*

Czech Republic, 2015-*Thrill Me*; with the words *Spalující Vášeň* (*Burning Passion*) displayed underneath.

Czech Republic, 2019-*Thrill Me*; with the words *Vzruš Mé! (Excite Me!)* displayed next to it.

China-危险游戏, which translates to *Dangerous Game*. The words *Thrill Me* are displayed next to the Chinese characters in a smaller font.

Germany-*Thrill Me*

Greece-*Μέχρι Ο Έρωτας...*, which translates to *Until Love...*

Hungary-*Izgass Fel*, which translates to *Get Excited*

Italy-*Öltre Limite*, which translates to *Beyond the Limit****

Japan-*Thrill Me*; with スリルミー displayed next to it in a smaller font. It is phonetically pronounced as close to *Thrill Me* as it can be, but the phrase has no actual meaning.

Mexico, 2016-*Seduceme*, which translates to *Seduce Me*****

Mexico, 2019-*Estreméceme*, which translates to *Shock Me*

Mexico, 2023-*Prende Me*, which translates to *Turn Me On*

Poland-*Thrill Me*

Romania-*Thrill Me*

South Korea-쓰릴미, which is phonetically pronounced as close to "Thrill Me" as it can be, but the phrase has no actual meaning. The words *Thrill Me* are displayed next it in a smaller font.

Spain-*Excítame*, which translates to *Excite Me* (but in other Spanish speaking countries, that phrase is considered too sexual to use.)

Thailand-*Thrill Me*

*In most languages there is no word for "thrill," or any word with
the double meaning that ties to "thrill killers."
**Workshop in Belgium/French, no full production as of January 2024.
***Workshop in Italy, no full production as of January 2024.
****Production was canceled.

THRILL ME
PRODUCTION LIST*

2003-New York City, New York: Midtown International Theatre Festival, Abingdon Theatre

2004-New York City, New York: York Theatre Company

2004-Chicago, Illinois: Chicago Historical Society/Timeline Theatre

2005-Boston, Massachusetts: Stoneham Theatre

2005-Melbourne, Australia: Theatreworks, St. Kilda

2005-Orlando, Florida: Orlando International Fringe Festival, Orange Venue

2005-New York City, New York: Off-Broadway, The York Theatre

2006-Tampa Bay, Florida: Suncoast Theatre

2006-Chicago, Illinois: Bailiwick Repertory Theatre

2006-Orange County, California: Theatre Out at the Hunger Artists Theatre

2006-Dallas, Texas: Uptown Players

2007-Philadelphia, Pennsylvania: Media Theatre

2007-Richmond, Virginia: Richmond Triangle Players

2007-Seattle, Washington: ArtsWest

2007-Seoul, South Korea: Chungmu Art Hall

2007-Clarksville, Tennessee: Roxy Regional Theatre

2007-Sioux City, Iowa: Lamb Productions Theatre, The Box

2007-Seoul, South Korea: Artmadang

2007-Busan, South Korea: Pusan National University (*South Korean tour*)

2007-Cincinnati, Ohio: Know Theatre

2007-Buffalo, New York: New Phoenix Theatre

2008-Los Angeles, California: Havok Theatre Company, Hudson Backstage Theatre

2008-Bloomfield, New Jersey: Fully Flighted Productions, Pianos Bar & Grill

2008-Lincroft, New Jersey: Brookdale Community College Performing Arts Center

2008-San Francisco, California: New Conservatory Theatre Center

2008-Seoul, South Korea: Chungmu Art Hall

2008-New Orleans, Louisiana: Marigny Theatre, To Do Productions

2008-Athens, Greece: Livadas Theatrical Enterprises, Amiral Theatre

2008-Hongseong, South Korea: Chungwoon University

2009-Winston-Salem, North Carolina: Winston-Salem Theatre Alliance

2009-Fair Lawn, New Jersey: Fully Flighted Productions, Fair Lawn Community Center

2009-Seoul, South Korea: The Stage Theatre

2009-Madison, Wisconsin: Music Theatre of Madison

2009-Norwich, Connecticut: Spirit of Broadway Theatre

2010-Bakersfield, California: Empty Space Theatre

2010-Busan, South Korea: Open Drama Festival, Kyungsung University

2010-Sydney, Australia: The Seymour Centre

2010-Savannah, Georgia: Savannah College of Art and Design

2010-Seoul, South Korea: The Stage Theatre

2010-Kansas City, Missouri: Fishtank Theatre

2010-Seoul, South Korea: Sejong University

2010-St. Paul, Minnesota: Gustavus Adolphus College, Lowry Lab

2010-Milwaukee, Wisconsin: Theatrical Tendencies, Milwaukee Gay Arts Center

2010-Busan, South Korea: Lotte Art Hall (*South Korean tour*)

2011-Macomb, Illinois: Western Illinois University

2011-Seoul, South Korea: Seoul Institute of the Arts

2011-Washington, DC: Elden Street Players

2011-London, England: Tristan Bates Theatre

2011-London, England: Charing Cross Theatre (*Transfer*)

2011-Milwaukee Wisconsin: In Tandem Theatre

2011-St. Louis, Missouri: Max & Louie Productions, Gaslight Theater

2011-Tokyo, Japan: Atelier Fontaine Theatre

2011-Fort Lauderdale, Florida: Rising Action Theatre Company, Sunshine Cathedral

2011-Lexington, Kentucky: University of Kentucky

2011-Bloomington, Illinois: Wesleyan University, Phoenix Theatre

2011-Seoul, South Korea: Yonsei University

2011-Seoul, South Korea: Kyung Hee University

2011-Pocheon, South Korea: Daejin University

2011-Seoul, South Korea: Chungmu Art Hall, Black Theatre

2012-Seoul, South Korea: Chungmu Art Hall, Black Theatre *(Cont'd)*

2012-Tokyo, Japan: Atelier Fontaine Theatre

2012-Cheney, Washington: Eastern Washington University

2012-Tokyo, Japan: Galaxy Theatre

2012-Osaka, Japan: Sankei Hall Breeze (*Japanese tour*)

2012-Cambridge, England: Corpus Playroom

2012-Datteln, Germany: Katielli Theatre

2012-Oberlin, Ohio: Oberlin Student Theatre Association

2012-Vancouver, Canada: Fighting Chance Productions, Renegade Studios

2013-Tokyo, Japan: Galaxy Theatre

2013-Vancouver, Canada: Fighting Chance Productions, White Rock Players Club Festival

2013-Louisville, Kentucky: Pandora Productions. Henry Clay Theatre

2013-Seoul, South Korea: The Stage Theatre

2013-Cleveland, Ohio: Convergence Continuum

2013-Toronto, Ontario, Canada: Capricorn 9 Productions Red Sandcastle Theatre

2013-Busan, South Korea: Dongseo University, Sohyang Theater

2013-Hildesheim, Germany: Theater für Niedersachsen

2013-Rio De Janeiro, Brazil: Teatro Firjan SESI Centro

2013-Lauenburg, Germany: Theater Lauenburg

2013-San Francisco Bay, California: OMG, I Love That Show! Productions, Lesher Center

2014-Chicago, Illinois: University of Chicago, Noyes Theatre

2014-Tijuca, Brazil: SESC Tijuca

2014-Newnan, Georgia: Newnan Theatre Company

2014-San Diego, California: Diversionary Theatre

2014-Boca Raton, Florida: Outré Theatre Company, Mizner Park Cultural Arts Center

2014-Osnabrück, Germany: Theater Osnabrück, Emma Theater

2014-Seoul, South Korea: Uniplex Theatre

2014-Madrid, Spain: Fernán Gómez Centro Cultural de la Villa

2014-Edinburgh, Scotland: Edinburgh Festival Fringe

2014-London, England: Bridge House Theatre

2014-Tokyo, Japan: Galaxy Theatre

2014-Osaka, Japan: Sankei Hall Breeze (*Japanese tour*)

2015-Valladolid, Spain: Teatro Zorrilla (*Spanish tour*)

2015-Torrejón de Ardoz, Spain: Teatro José María Rodero (*Spanish tour*)

2015-Coruña, Spain: Teatro Rosalía de Castro (*Spanish tour*)

2015-Orense, Spain: Teatro Principal de Orense (*Spanish tour*)

2015-Alcorcón, Spain: Teatro Municipal Buero Vallejo (*Spanish tour*)

2015-Santander, Spain: Teatro Escena Miriñaque (*Spanish tour*)

2015-Getafe, Spain: Teatro Federico García Lorca (*Spanish tour*)

2015-Chiclana de la Frontera, Spain: Teatro Moderno (*Spanish tour*)

2015-Barcelona, Spain: Club Capitol (*Spanish tour*)

2015-Madrid, Spain: Nuevo Teatro Alcalá (*Spanish tour*)

2015-Seoul, South Korea: Daemyung Culture Factory

2015-Leuven, Belgium: 30 Cultural Center, Wagehuys Theatre (*Belgian tour*)

2015-Antwerp, Belgium: Zwarte Zaal, Fakkeltheater (*Belgian tour*)

2015-Ft. Worth, Texas: Out of the Loop Fringe Festival, WaterTower Theatre

2015-Coburg, Germany: Landestheater Coburg

2015-Shanghai, China: ET Space Theatre

2015-London, England: Greenwich Theatre

2015-Birmingham, England: The Old Rep (*UK tour*)

2015-Salford, England: The Lowry Theatre (*UK tour*)

2015-Halifax, England: Square Chapel (*UK tour*)

2015-Vienna, Austria: Off-Theater

2015-Hamburg, Germany: English Theatre of Hamburg

2015-Columbus, Ohio: Short North Stage

2015-Charleston, South Carolina: What If? Productions, Threshold Repertory Theatre

2015-Haddon Township, New Jersey: Ritz Theatre Company

2015-Gunpo, South Korea: Hansei University

2015-Prague, Czech Republic: Mystery Boat Theatre

2015-Ahrensburg, Germany: Alfred-Rust-Festsaal

2015-Ghent, Belgium: Bonbonnière, Tinnenpot Theatre (*Belgian tour*)

2015-Leuven, Belgium: Reynaert Theater Malpertuus (*Belgian tour*)

2015-Sint-Truiden, Belgium: Cultural Center De Bogaard, Club Theatre (*Belgian tour*)

2015-Antwerp, Belgium: Het Klokhuis Theatre (*Belgian tour*)

2015-Gablitz, Austria: Theater 82er-Haus

2015-Cape Cod, Massachusetts: Wellfleet Harbor Actors Theater, Julie Harris Stage

2015-West Orange, New Jersey: Luna Stage

2015-Bottrop, Germany: Spielraum

2015-Fort Lauderdale, Florida: Outré Theatre Company, Broward Center for the Performing Arts

2016-London, England: Jermyn Street Theatre

2016-Melbourne, Australia: Midsumma Festival, Chapel Off Chapel

2016-Datteln, Germany: Katielli Theater

2016-Ogden, Utah: Good Company Theatre

2016-Prague, Czech Republic: Mystery Boat Theatre

2016-Seoul, South Korea: Daemyung Culture Factory

2016-Mokpo, South Korea: Mokpo Culture & Art Center (*South Korean tour*)

2016-Rock Island, Illinois: The Speakeasy Theatre

2016-Shanghai, China: Shanghai Grand Theatre

2016-Bilzen, Belgium: Samaritan Musical Productions, Cultural Center De Kimpel

2016-Bree, Belgium: Samaritan Musical Productions, Cultural Center De Breughel (*Belgian tour*)

2016-Buenos Aires, Argentina: Border Theatre

2016-Wuppertal, Germany: Trio Theatre Company, TalTon Theater

2016-Shanghai, China: Malan Flower Theatre

2017-Sioux Falls, South Dakota: Augustana College

2017-Seoul, South Korea: Baekam Art Hall

2017-Busan, South Korea: Sohyang Art Hall (*South Korean tour*)

2017-Seoul, South Korea: Seoul Institute of the Arts

2017-Buenos Aires, Argentina: Border Teatro

2017-Denver, Colorado: Equinox Theatre Company

2017-Busan, South Korea: Dongseo University

2017-Icheon, South Korea: Chungkang College of Cultural Industries

2017-London, England: Bridge House Theatre

2017-Edinburgh, Scotland: Edinburgh Festival Fringe (*UK tour*)

2017-London, England: Arcola Theatre (*UK tour*)

2017-Seoul, South Korea: Kookmin University, Gwan 1st Theatre

2017-New York City, New York: The Cell Theatre

2017-Seoul, South Korea: Kyonggi University

2017-Goyang, South Korea: Joongbu University

2017-New Orleans, Louisiana: See 'Em On Stage Productions, AllWays Theatre

2018-York, England: Pick Me Up Theatre, Theatre@41

2018-Seoul, South Korea: Myongji University

2018-Berlin, Germany: OFFStage Germany, Admiralspalast Theatre (*German tour*)

2018-Hamburg, Germany: OFFStage Germany, First Stage Theater (*German tour*)

2018-Birmingham, England: Old Joint Stock Theatre

2018-Busan, South Korea: Busan International Performing Arts Festival (*UK tour*)

2018-London, England: The Other Palace (*UK tour*)

2018-Newtownabbey, Ireland: Theatre at the Mil (*UK tour*)

2018-Londonderry, Ireland: Waterside Theatre (*UK tour*)

2018-Shrewsbury, England: Theatre Severn (*UK tour*)

2018-Frome, England: Merlin Theatre (*UK tour*)

2018-São Paulo, Brazil: Porto Seguro Theater

2018-Tokyo, Japan: Metropolitan Theatre West

2019-Tokyo, Japan: Metropolitan Theatre West (*Cont'd*)

2019-Nagoya, Japan: Nagoya City Performing Art Center (*Japanese tour*)

2019-Osaka, Japan: Sankei Hall Breeze (*Japanese tour*)

2019-Gyeonggi, South Korea: Gyeonggi Arts High School, White Hall

2019-Toluca, Mexico: Casa de las Diligencias

2019-Seoul, South Korea: Hongik University

2019-London, England: Hope Theatre

2019-Ostrava, Czech Republic: National Moravian-Silesian Theatre, Theatre 12

2019-Seoul, South Korea: National High School of Traditional Korean Arts

2019-Budapest, Hungary: Hatszín Teátrum

2019-São Paulo, Brazil: Teatro Opus

2019-Kosice, Slovakia: Mala Scena Theatre (*Czech tour*)

2019-Prague, Czech Republic: Czechia-Studio Ypsilon (*Czech tour*)

2019-Cambridge, England: Cambridge University, Corpus Playroom

2019-Gyeonggi, South Korea: Kaywon University of Art & Design

2019-Seoul, South Korea: Yes24 Stage

2020-Seoul, South Korea: Yes24 Stage (*Continuation*)

2020-East Lansing, Michigan: Michigan State University-Wharton Center for Performing Arts

2020-Wuppertal, Germany: Trio Theatre Company, TalTon Theater

2020-Leuven, Belgium: 30 Cultural Center, Wagehuys Theatre (*Belgian tour*)

2020-Puurs, Belgium: Cultural Center Binder Theatre (*Belgian tour*)

2020-Czech Republic: Streaming version of the Ostrava production

2020-Budapest, Hungary: Hatszín Teátrum

2020-Warsaw, Poland: Mazowiecki Teatr Muzyczny im. Jana Kiepury

2020-Budapest, Hungary: TEMI Capital Cultural Center

2020-Shanghai, China: Gong Theatre

2021-Seoul, South Korea: Yes24 Stage

2021-Seoul, South Korea: Chungmu Art Center, Black Theatre

2021-Tokyo, Japan: Metropolitan Theatre West

2021-Gunma, Japan: Takasaki City Theatre Studio (*Japanese tour*)

2021-Nagoya, Japan: Winc Aichi Large Hall (*Japanese tour*)

2021-Ostrava, Czech Republic: National Moravian-Silesian Theatre, Theatre 12

2021-Shanghai, China: Gong Theatre

2021-Greensboro, North Carolina: Greensboro College

2021-Kielce, Poland: Kielce International Theatre Festival

2021-Japan: Streaming version of the Tokyo production

2021-Shanghai, China: Salute Theatre

2021-Germany: Streaming version of the Datteln/Katielli Theatre production

2021-Solingen, Germany: OFFStage Germany, Theater und Konzerthaus Solingen

2021-Warsaw, Poland: Mazowiecki Teatr Muzyczny im. Jana Kiepury

2021-New York City, New York: Little Red Light Theatre Company, NuBox Theatre

2022-Shanghai, China: Salute Theatre (*Continuous run*)

2022-London, England: Jermyn Street Theatre

2022-Seoul, South Korea: Project De:boun, Space Awul

2022-Ostrava, Czech Republic: National Moravian-Silesian Theatre, Theatre 12

2022-Seoul, South Korea: Showtime School, Yoloplay, R&J Theatre

2022-South Korea: Streaming version of the Seoul production

2022-Seoul, South Korea: Chungmu Art Center, Black Theatre

2022-Shanghai, China: Gong Theatre

2022-Warsaw, Poland: Mazowiecki Teatr Muzyczny im. Jana Kiepury

2022-Kraków, Poland: XII Miniature Theatre Festival

2022-Poznań, Poland: Time for Theatre Festival

2023-Shanghai, China: Salute Theatre (*Continuous run*)

2023-Shanghai, China: Gong Theatre

2023-London, England: Teddington Theatre Club, Hampton Hill Theatre

2023-Ostrava, Czech Republic: National Moravian-Silesian Theatre, Theatre 12

2023-Seoul, South Korea: Play En Dolphin, Daehakro Sundol Theater

2023-Beijing, China: Beijing Dong'an Music Laboratory School

2023-Hong Kong, China: Sheung Wan Civic Centre Theatre

2023-Struthers, Ohio: Selah Dessert Theatre

2023-Beijing, China: Lingyu Beast Tiger Bar

2023-Wilton Manors, Florida: Island City Stage

2023-Tokyo, Japan: Metropolitan Theatre West

2023-Osaka, Japan: Sankei Hall Breeze (*Japanese tour*)

2023-Hakata, Japan: Canal City Theatre (*Japanese tour*)

2023-Nagoya, Japan: Winc Aichi Large Hall (*Japanese tour*)

2023-Gunma, Japan: Takasaki City Theatre Studio (*Japanese tour*)

2023-Japan: Streaming version of the Tokyo production

2023-Bangkok, Thailand: Chulalongkorn University, Sodsai Pantoomkomol Theatre

2023-Bucharest, Romania: Teatrul ACT (*Romanian tour*)

2023-Brăila, Romania: Maria Filotti Theatre (*Romanian tour*)

2023-Cluj-Napoca, Romania: Cluj-Napoca National Theatre (*Romanian tour*)

2023-Warsaw, Poland: Mazowiecki Teatr Muzyczny im. Jana Kiepury

2024-Ostrava, Czech Republic: National Moravian-Silesian Theatre, Theatre 12

2024-Dongducheon, South Korea: Dongyang University

2024-Moline, Illinois: The Black Box Theatre

2024-Yongin, South Korea: Kyung Hee University

2024-Shanghai, China: MP & Company Productions

2024-Mexico City, Mexico: Ricardo Ian Productions, Wilberto Cantón Theater

2024-Seoul, South Korea: Yes24 Stage

2024-Bucharest, Romania: Metropolis Theatre

2024-Multiple Cities, China: C-Musicals (*Chinese Tour*)

*As of January 2024.

THRILL ME
AWARDS & NOMINATIONS*

NEW YORK/OFF-BROADWAY

2006-Drama Desk Award-Nominations: Outstanding Musical and Outstanding Music-Stephen Dolginoff

2006-Outer Critics Circle Award-Nomination: Outstanding Off-Broadway Musical

2006-ASCAP Plus Award-Winner: Stephen Dolginoff for Music & Lyrics

LONDON

2011-Off West End "Offie" Award-7 Nominations including Stephen Dolginoff for Best New Musical and Best Production

2011-Whatsonstage Award-Nomination: Best Off West End Production

2019-Off West End "Offie" Award-3 Nominations; Double Winner: Best Actor

2022-Off West End "Offie" Award-6 Nominations including Best Musical Production; Winner: Best Director

2023-Swan Awards-Nominations: Best Musical Production, Best Actor; Winner: Judges' Award

USA REGIONAL PRODUCTIONS

2005-Boston Irne Award-Nomination: Outstanding Production of a Musical

2006-Chicago Jefferson Award Recommendation

2007-Dallas Theatre Column Awards-Nomination: Best Musical

2007-Dallas Theatre League Award-Winner: Best Musical

2008-Los Angeles Ovation Award-Nomination: Best Musical

2008-Buffalo, New York Art Voice Artie Award-Nomination: Best Production of a Musical

2008-Cincinnati Entertainment Award-Nomination: Best Musical

2009-Los Angeles Garland Award-Honorable Mention: Musical Score by Stephen Dolginoff

2009-Los Angeles Garland Award-Winner: Best Ensemble Performance

2009-Los Angeles Ovation Award-Nomination: Best Production of a Musical

2009-Los Angeles Ovation Award-Nomination: Best Lighting

2009-Norwich, Connecticut Spirit of Broadway Award-Winner for Best Production of The Year

2009-San Francisco Bay Area Theatre Critics Award-Nomination: Best Musical

2009-New Orleans Big Easy Award-Nomination: Best Musical

2009-New Orleans Marquee Award-Winner: Best Musical

2014-Miami BroadwayWorld Award-Winner: Best Musical, Best Lighting, Best Ensemble Performance

2015-New Jersey BroadwayWorld Award-7 Nominations including Best Musical

2023-South Florida Silver Palm Award: Honoree for Outstanding Sound Design

ARGENTINA

2016-Premios Hugo Al Teatro Musical Awards-9 Nominations including Best Musical

AUSTRALIA

2005-Green Room Award-Nomination: Outstanding Musical

BRAZIL

2019-Bibi Ferreira Awards-3 Nominations including Best Actor and Best Duo

CANADA

2013-Vancouver Ovation Award-Nomination: Best Musical

2013-Greater Vancouver Zone Awards-Double Winner: Best Actor

CZECH REPUBLIC

2020-Amber Award-2 nominations: Best Actor

2020-Musical of the Year Award

JAPAN

2018-The Yomiuri Theatre Awards-Winner: Staff Excellence and Distinguished Newcomer

2021-Tokyo All About Musical Awards-Winner: Best Actor

POLAND

2021-Musical Viewers Awards-8 Nominations including Best Polish Premiere

2021-Jan Kiepura Theatre Music Awards-Winner: Best Set Design and Best Actor

SOUTH KOREA

2007-Korea Musical Awards-4 Nominations including Best Foreign Musical. Winner: Best Performance by a Leading Actor

2007-The Musical Awards-6 Nominations including Best Foreign Musical

2008-Korea Musical Awards-2 Nominations including Best Original Score-Stephen Dolginoff

SPAIN

2015-Teatro Musical Awards-10 Nominations. Winner: Best Direction, Best Actor, Best Lighting
2015-BroadwayWorld Awards-9 Nominations. Winner: Best Musical, Best Adaptation, Best Director, Best Lighting, Best Poster Design
2015-Mi Butaquita Awards-Winner: Best Musical
2015-Indifest-Winner: Audience Favorite Award

UNITED KINGDOM

2014-Broadway Baby "Bobby" Award-Winner, Best of Edinburgh Fringe

*Partial list only. As of January 2024.

THRILL ME
MENTIONED IN PUBLISHED BOOKS*

THEATRE RELATED

Blood on the Stage, 1950-1975 by Amnon Kabatchnik

Courtroom Dramas on the Stage Vol 2 by Amnon Kabatchnik

For the Gay Stage: A Guide to 456 Plays by Drewey Wayne Gunn

Gays on Broadway by Ethan Mordden

How Musicals Work by Julian Woolford

Let's Put on a Musical! by Peter Filichia

Modern Drama-Volume 66, No 1 Essay by Hyewon Kim

Murder Most Queer by Jordan Schildcrout

Musical Theatre: A History by John Kenrick

Out For Blood by Chris Adams

Teatro: Revista de Estudios Escénicos Vol. 35 Essay by José Romera Castillo

Tell it to the World: The Broadway Musical Abroad by David Savran

The Theatermania Guide to Musical Theatre Recordings Edited by Michael Portantiere; cast album review by Matthew Murray

Theatre World 2004-2005 by John Willis

Three Reasons Why the Musical 'Thrill Me' is Thrilling by Akikan

HISTORY RELATED

American Journal of Legal History-Volume 1, Number 2 Essay by Edward J. Larson

Arrested Adolescence by Erik Rebain

Chicago Portraits by June Skinner Sawyers

Crimes of The Centuries: Notorious Crimes, Criminals and Criminal Trials in American History Edited by Frankie Y. Bailey and Steven Chermak

For the Thrill of It by Simon Baatz

Journal of American Culture-Volume 34, Number 2 Essay by Jordan Schildcrout

Murder Among Friends by Candace Fleming

Murder in the Closet by Curtis Evans

Retrying Leopold and Loeb: A Neuropsychological Perspective by David L. Shapiro, Charles Golden and Sara Ferguson

The Leopold and Loeb Files by Nina Barrett

The Perfect Crime by Fergus Mason

Trial Stories by Michael E. Tigar and Angela J. Davis

*As of January 2024.

THRILL ME

— Review Quotes —

OFF-BROADWAY (2005)

"Stephen Dolginoff's pocket musical about the Leopold and Loeb murder case lands like a well-placed punch, arresting and a bit breathtaking. Others have told the tale in plays and films, but there is something brazenly satisfying about Mr. Dolginoff's rendition. It's a reminder that evil often looks and sounds beautiful. Credit the lean approach to the storytelling. The songs work nicely. "Nothing Like a Fire," sung after the two men have tried their hand at arson, has a subtle humor and passion; "Roadster" is a sinister hymn of child abduction." - **Neil Genzlinger, New York Times**

"Startling! Provocative! I can't get enough of this! Will keep you spellbound! *Thrill Me* freezes the blood and keeps you wanting more!" - **Rex Reed, NY Observer**

"Author Stephen Dolginoff has stepped into the role of Leopold, with exciting results. What was already a fascinating show is now even stronger, with richer layers of nuance. Ranging from nebbish to demon, Dolginoff's performance makes it clear that Leopold was not only every inch the monster Loeb is—in some ways, he was even more hateful. Dolginoff does this while creating moments of amazingly appropriate laughter. Not since Noel Coward has a composer-lyricist-librettist given New York such a remarkable performance in his own work. *Thrill Me* is even better than when I cheered it on two months ago. This intriguing show and its gifted creator give me real hope for the future of musical theatre." - **John Kenrick, Musicals101**

"The 1924 Leopold and Loeb murder case has been dramatized in several plays and films over the years and has now inspired a compelling Off-Broadway musical by Stephen Dolginoff, one of the rising new stars of the musical theater. Dolginoff wrote the book, music, and lyrics of *Thrill Me*, a York Theater Company production, and is playing Nathan Leopold in an extended run of the show... Dolginoff and Kreeger are perfectly cast as to type, and both are actors of emotional intensity, unafraid to depict scenes of uncompromising passion that can still be shocking in this era of anything goes sexuality. Leopold, of course, is the more sympathetic of the homicidal pair, but Dolginoff never holds back in portraying the weakness of Leopold's character." - **Frederick M. Winship, UPI**

"Dolginoff's portrayal of Nathan Leopold leaves plenty of room for sympathy and vocally he's trim and crisp. - **Russell Bouthiller, Fire Island Tide**

"Murder as a stylish musical! With a noir attitude, *Thrill Me* is a two-character slice of pulp fact-fiction by intriguing storyteller Stephen Dolginoff." - **Linda Winer, New York Newsday**

"A soaringly intense, propulsively melodic musical. Chillingly well-told, in all of its dark complexity. - **Jacques le Sourd, Gannet Newspapers**

"A taut, compelling, two-character musical. Stripping the event of the psychobabble that has surrounded it over the years, Dolginoff gets at the heart of it. The story sizzles!" - **Irene Backalenick, Backstage**

"Dangerously attractive! Keep an eye and especially an ear peeled for future shows by Stephen Dolginoff, a promising newcomer who has written the book, lyrics and music for *Thrill Me: The Leopold & Loeb Story*. Dolginoff is a smart craftsman with a knack for forging arresting tunes. He is capable of proficient musical theater construction, such as his extended sequence detailing how the murderers are tracked down over several days. He writes some alluring tunes, too. Loeb's crooning invitation to take his victim for a drive and the surging title number are compelling. Often using ascending and descending scales to powerful effect, the robust score does not echo the pop music of the 1920s, but is feverishly crafted in a more contemporary manner. - **Michael Sommers, New Jersey Star-Ledger**

"Dolginoff shows that unlikely musical subject matter can be mastered if the approach is strong enough. You will be intrigued!" - **Peter Filichia, Theatermania**

"How many modern musicals manage to remain thrilling—in the real, tingling sense of the word—years after you first encountered them? At best, it's a short list; chills dissipate faster in the theatre than anywhere else. Yet two years after its New York premiere, Stephen Dolginoff's *Thrill Me* still sends chills down the spine while it assaults with waves of violent and sexual heat…Here, the musical storytelling is suffocating in the best sense; Dolginoff pulls no punches in exploring the crimes of 1924 Chicago "thrill killers" Nathan Leopold and Richard Loeb. The York Theatre Company's production of the show is, like the story it's based on, uncompromising and intoxicating. It's also the best version of *Thrill Me* yet seen in New York. If you missed the show's first incarnation…don't fear. Dolginoff's adventurous benefactors at the York are helping him get the audience he needs to fulfill his promise as one of our next major composing talents. When he reaches that level, it will be due, in no small part, to this brilliant, unforgettable musical." - **Matthew Murray, Talkin' Broadway**

"I found the story fascinating. You must go see it!" - **David F. Richardson, WOR radio**

"The production values are kept rather simple. This minimalist design all works well-enough, but Dolginoff's material is what really fills the stage." - **Charles Battersby, Off-Boadway.com**

"A major accomplishment! To miss *Thrill Me* would be a crime! – **Ron Lasko, Broadway.com**

"The music is so hauntingly beautiful and what goes on in this musical is so arresting. They'll eventually be arrested for what they do but we're arrested in a different way about watching it…If *Thrill Me* turns up in your city, make sure you see it. Because it's certainly, as I say, arresting, with beautiful…beautiful…beautiful music and very precise lyrics. So Stephen Dolginoff is certainly a talent worth watching and I'm always interested in what he has to do. So I think you should be too!" - **Peter Filichia, Broadway Radio (New York Reunion, 2017)**

CHICAGO (2006)

"*Thrill Me* strikes chillingly insightful chords. Sometimes the simplest, most primal explanations make the most sense. That is precisely why *Thrill Me: The Leopold & Loeb Story*, Stephen Dolginoff's spare, compulsively engrossing two-man musical about the notorious Leopold and Loeb case—works so well." - **Hedy Weiss, Chicago Sun-Times**

"Author-composer-lyricist Stephen Dolginoff's portrait of the students whose abduction and murder of a randomly-selected child shocked American society in 1924 is not a docudrama, but a fable of seduction. We never see the victim or the brilliant attorney who delivers the killers from the death penalty or the hated father sparking Richard's antisocial impulses. Dolginoff, instead, presents us with the classic tale of a love-besotted nerd dazzled by his idealized paramour into abetting the latter in the violence comprising their sexual foreplay...since Leopold's the one recounting the story to his parole board, his account might be understandably—well, biased. Dolginoff's score is constructed along blatantly romantic lines, replete with pulsating tempos, sweetly symmetric harmonics and nary a Sondheim dissonance from overture to finale." - **Mary Shen Barnidge, Windy City Times**

"The best thing about *Thrill Me*, Stephen Dolginoff's 90-minute chamber musical about the twisted co-dependency of these proto-gays is its refusal to romanticize them as bold sexual outlaws...As the title promises, this is thrilling musical drama...No bitter irony goes untouched as Dolginoff brilliantly exploits the tension between secrecy and exposure that fuels these dirty deeds." - **Lawrence Bommer, Chicago Free Press**

"A psychological murder mystery, this tale can't help but fascinate because of its unusual subjects. And because it is well done and ends with a surprise twist, *Thrill Me* will hold your attention from beginning to end." - **Betty Mohr, Daily Southtown**

"Stephen Dolginoff, who starred as Leopold when the show opened Off-Broadway in New York, wrote the book, music, and lyrics for this

270

haunting, remarkable musical. In a somewhat Sondheimesque style, he has put together 14 songs that purposefully move the performance along with a minimum of dialogue. In the final analysis, however, this is a love story, with all the passion, longing, rejection, and disappointment as any other, but with the ominous message that uncontrolled obsessive love can lead to irrational acts with dire, tragic consequences." - **Julian K. Frazin, Chicago Lawyer/Law Bulletin**

LOS ANGELES (2008)

"For many, this story of senseless violence and tragic hubris among the offspring of Chicago's business elite would seem to be a poor candidate for a musical. But it is no obstacle to Stephen Dolginoff, who has created a dark little entertainment told in flashbacks that combines the extravagant emotions and ensemble couplings of verismo opera (complete with feverish kisses and embraces) with musical sounds and styles drawn from Broadway and the bittersweet ballads of Franz Schubert and Kurt Weill." - **Lawrence Vittes, The Hollywood Reporter**

"A hit off-Broadway, Stephen Dolginoff's two-character musical, *Thrill Me*, delves into the distinctive pathology of the youths' relationship, a homosexual attraction that devolved into a master-slave dynamic of deadly proportions." - **F. Kathleen Foley, Los Angeles Times**

"Ebulliently dark!" - **Steven Mikulan, LA Weekly**

"From its dark and dramatic prelude to the finale, the show's title tune, Dolginoff's piano-only score is packed with short, staccato songs that hit the audience like a sucker punch. While each song contributes a crucial piece of the puzzle, none is more chilling than "Roadster." The somber, slow number, in which Loeb seductively lures the boy into his car, resonates in today's pedophile-conscious world. All the more unsettling are the song's lyrics…Dolginoff uses pungent irony, too, as when, after the duo commits arson, Loeb coos. "There's nothing like a warm, romantic fire." - **Eric Marchese, Orange County Register**

"A dark, erotic love story. *I Do! I Do!* For the homicidal set!" - **Matt Sigl, The Simon.com**

USA REGIONAL

"Dolginoff's ingenious reworking of the familiar story never loses its grip on its audience…His taut dramatic structure, one that chronicles the peculiar symbiotic relationship between the men in a chilling fashion. His music has a striking, contemporary feel that run from the ironic ballad ("Nothing Like a Fire") sung as the two have sex in the glow of an arson fire they set, to Loeb's creepy "Roadster" in which he lures the unsuspecting Franks to his car, and the dynamic title song, an expression of sexual frustration on Leopold's part. Dolginoff offers a twist of his own that effectively brings his story full circle. Without giving too much away, let it be said that never underestimate a lover scorned." - **Robert Nesti, Edge Boston (2005)**

"Dolginoff's clever book and lyrics and moody score simultaneously propel the action, narrate the tale, and reveal the dynamics between two extremely bright but coldly warped boys driven into each other's arms by isolation and neglect. Songs like "Nothing Like a Fire" and "The Plan" use unexpected humor to expose Loeb's dark soul and lust for power, while "A Written Contract" and "Life Plus 99 Years" suggest that Leopold is not as innocent or easily manipulated as he seems. The most chilling number is "Roadster" in which Loeb lures young Franks into his car…The question posed in the opening number "Why?" may not be answered fully in *Thrill Me*, but "Roadster" brings us closer to understanding the thrill that Loeb gets from carrying out his heinous acts." - **Jan Nargi, BroadwayWorld Boston (2005)**

"In his portrayal of Leopold, Dolginoff expresses an author's subtle understanding of his character's intelligence and desperation." - **Tom Valeo, St. Petersburg Times (Tampa Bay, 2006)**

"Dolginoff, for his part, is delightful as well he should be, this being his baby. His Leopold is both adorable and abysmal, a tenor-voiced romantic whose apparent helplessness to resist Loeb may or may not stifle the nagging of his obviously superior intellect." - **Richard Morin, Seattle Weekly (2007)**

"Dolginoff plays Leopold, as he did in the original New York production. He's very good. He builds up layers of geek lust, criminal desperation, existential bleakness, insane craftiness and exhausted remorse." - **Joe Adcock, Seattle Post-Intelligencer (2007)**

"In his performance, the author imbues the character with great humor and mischievousness, which bubbles to the surface with unexpected vitality." - **Anthony Chase, Art Voice Buffalo (2007)**

"Strong performances make murder-based musical worthwhile. There are plenty of levels on which to enjoy the production. In this case, the primary reason is the pairing of Demerly and Dolginoff. The two embody a delicious kind of synergy, with the egotistical and domineering Demerly playing a perfect foil to Dolginoff's blubbering subservience. When the two sing, their voices produce a volatile mixture of murderous intent and intense, if one-sided, love. Such a mixture is uncomfortable to consider, but glorious to behold." - **Colin Dabkowski, Buffalo News (2007)**

"Let me count the thrills: a recent off-Broadway hit; a pair of fine young singer-actors; provocative work by a fresh talent in the world of musical theater. It's a bold and unflinching look at a heartless act, set to music." - **Susan Haubenstock, Richmond Times-Dispatch (2007)**

"A brilliant ride down a bumpy road that offers some of the best writing and acting that has been seen on a Richmond stage." – **John Porter, WCVE Radio (Richmond, 2007)**

"The music in itself is so seductive you have to shake yourself to remember the malevolent messages and intimations that the lyrics convey." - **Jerry Stein, Cincinnati Post (2007)**

"*Thrill Me* is intriguing, because Leopold and Loeb were so intriguing. Their story fascinates." - **Wendy Rosenfield, Philadelphia Inquirer (2007)**

"It's impossible to love the characters in *Thrill Me*, and impossible to resist probing their monstrous deed. - **Mark Cofta, Philadelphia City Paper (2007)**

"Most musicals are, almost by definition, hyper-emotional—people start singing when they're about to burst at the seams with feelings they simply can't express in normal speech. Such moments occur in composer/librettist Stephen Dolginoff's *Thrill Me*, but he also takes a distanced, almost anthropological view of his subjects—the infamous 1920s "thrill killers," Leopold and Loeb. The result is what might be called a cold-blooded musical. It's artfully made, thoughtfully written and oblivious to the viewers' collective need to sympathize on some level with the people onstage." - **Robert Trussell, The Kansas City Star (2010)**

"The songs are each perfect summations of how the characters are responding to each other and to the pressure cooker of the discovery of, first, their victim's body, and, then, Leopold's unique glasses. In real life, too, the glasses were the pair's downfall. Dolginoff's dark humor gives the cocksure Richard a line to lash out at Nathan: 'See what having the best gets you.' The book is just as sharply written as the songs and is necessary to provide the slivers of humor in a very tightly paced show of compact emotions." - **Kansas City Free Press (2010)**

"*Thrill Me* is a scream! With book, music, and lyrics by Stephen Dolginoff, is a truly thrilling piece of derring-do that gives us the sweep, horror and romance of one of the most chilling crimes of the last century. - **Sherri Rase, Qonstage.com (New Jersey, 2015)**

"One of the most satisfying aspect of *Thrill Me* is Dolginoff's refusal to exploit the homosexual aspect of their relationship; he shuns titillation and presents the gay attraction Defense attorney Clarence Darrow so wisely kept out of court (and the papers), to focus on the domination, manipulation and sexual pleasure to explain the *why* of this cold-blooded crime." - **Ruth Ross, NJArtsMaven (2015)**

"*Thrill Me* chills to the bone! The score contains most of the play's anguish, but is also playful at times, particularly in a duet that praises a warm, romantic fire as they embrace while watching the result of their arson. The most disturbing number is the wheedling attempts by Adam Berry's Loeb to lure the unseen boy to his death with the promise of riding in an expensive car. Both scenes are crucially enhanced by Bailey Costa's lighting design...*Thrill Me* is a chilling horror story indeed." - **Kathi Scrizzi, Cape Cod Times (2015)**

"At times disturbing, with its heinous crime being a constant undercurrent, the musical is first and foremost about an all-encompassing, addictive relationship, with its surprising power shifts and sly manipulations. It is therefore imperative that a believable relationship is developed in the two-man show between Leopold and Loeb. Under Jeffry George's tight direction, the two married actors could not be more convincing. Their natural intimacy and topnotch acting results in a thrilling and intoxicating ride, especially *Thrill Me*'s emotionally charged ending, with its cleverly unforeseen plot twists. - **Ellen Petry Whalen, Cape Cod Chronicle (2015)**

"Murder as Foreplay—Good Company Theater goes for the jugular ... Last night's opening of Good Company Theater's *Thrill Me* had the packed house alternately gasping and giggling as they watched two 'supermen' play with fire, and stolen goods, and dead bodies...'Murder is the only crime worthy of our talents,' Loeb tells Leopold at one point in the show. This show, in turns darkly hilarious and disturbing...Don't miss it." - **Autumn Barowski, Indie Ogden Utah (2016)**

"One of the most edgy, disturbing, and gasping-at-the-edge-of-your-seat musicals yet. One that grips you by the throat for 90 minutes...and never lets go." - **Mindy Leaf, South Florida Theatre Magazine (2023)**

"Murder has been the subject of many musicals, but there is something about the riveting Island City Stage production of *Thrill Me* that sets the show in a class of its own. It's intense material for a musical, but both Stephen Dolginoff's script and Island City Stage's production succeeds on all levels...scenes take intimacy to an operatic level, right up to an extremely satisfying conclusion, that, despite the brutality of the piece, is both haunting and beautiful." - **Mary Damiano, New Pelican (South Florida, 2023)**

LONDON

"*Thrill Me* is thrilling indeed! It's not difficult to see why *Thrill Me* (2003) was nominated for a hatful of awards when it played Off-Broadway. It's harder, though, to comprehend why this slick, sophisticated musical two-hander about the infamous Chicago "thrill killers" Leopold and Loeb has taken so long to reach our stages. I would be greatly surprised if Stephen Dolginoff's gripping work doesn't have a life beyond the tiny Tristan Bates." (**** 4 Stars) - **Fiona Mountford, Evening Standard (2011)**

"There is an edgy, Sondheimian quality to Dolginoff's music and lyrics which draws one inexorably into the warped world of the two damaged and dangerous misfits, to the extent that one soon begins to feel complicit in their revolting crime." (***** 5 Stars) - **Tim Walker, Sunday Telegraph (2011)**

"Dolginoff is good at charting the tiny changes in the balance of power. There are a couple of striking numbers. Such as "A Written Contract," played out to the tapping of the typewriter. And "I'm Trying to Think" as Nathan tries to think of plausible excuses to tell the police, if not quite enough musical variety." - **Georgina Brown, Sunday Mail (2011)**

"*Thrill Me* certainly thrilled me as well as chilled me as it recounted the true story of the Leopold and Loeb case of two teenagers who killed a young boy for kicks. It is performed with riveting intensity by Jye Frasca and George Maguire respectively." - **Mark Shenton, Sunday Express (2011)**

"A gripping ninety minutes of skillful musical theatre Stephen Dolginoff's words and music combine brilliantly to exert a vice like grip and this cast and production team give a great account of both" (****4 Stars) - **Phil Willmott, Attitude Magazine (2011)**

"A dark and unsettling production; boosted by a brooding piano score played beautifully by Tom Turner. The power dynamic between the characters is constantly changing, as it emerges that the seemingly vulnerable Nathan may have been pulling the strings all along. The score and lyrics are haunting and sharp, with some powerful harmonies between the two cast members. Due to the fluidity of the production the songs often blend into one but "Superior" and "Life Plus 99 Years" made a particular impression, combining macabre dramatic tension with intense music. If you're able to get over the eyebrow raising subject matter, *Thrill Me* can offer one of the most unusual and visceral theatrical experiences around. Disturbing but oddly moving and entrancing, it offers a unique look into the nature of evil and crime. Worth a visit, if only for a story to tell!" (**** 4 stars) - **Danny Coleman-Cooke, Britishtheatre.com (2016)**

"Based on an infamous true story, this superbly economical and gripping staging of the American composer Stephen Dolginoff's musical two-hander comes to London direct from the Edinburgh It is consistently melodic, intelligently written and marked with enough traces of grim humour to draw an audience in." (**** 4 stars) - **Donald Hutera, The Sunday Times (2017)**

"If you think this is an unlikely premise for a musical, think again. In this show, the audience will be taken on a journey into the minds of the two killers. *Thrill Me* is a beautiful, unsettling, dark and gripping production that makes us reflect about how far human nature can go in the name of love." (***** 5 Stars) - **London Theatre Reviews (2019)**

"Mesmerisingly sinister thriller in an Intensely intimate theatre! Musically, it is pitched just right, as the Hope Theatre is truly tiny and at times I could easily have touched either or both performers, so it was crucial that the singing was quite subtle and realistically delivered. The close proximity to the actors worked extremely well in this production, and I was mesmerised for the entire show." (**** 4 Stars) - **Deborah Jeffries, London Pub Theatres Magazine (2019)**

"Thrill Me certainly is thrilling. Based on the real-life case of Leopold and Loeb, the two lovers who killed a boy to prove that they were Nietzschean Supermen, this musical, despite its subject matter, is steamy and sexy. Rachel Ryan's set design transforms the theatre into a giant crime board, red thread connecting newspaper reports and photographs fixed to the walls. The trunks that the two actors push around the stage are full of surprises and Chris McDonnell's lights, while never quite dark enough, are creative." - **Richard Maguire, The Reviews Hub (2019)**

"With *Thrill Me*, writer and composer Stephen Dolginoff explores the psycho-sexual relationship between the two men, offering a twisted but dramatically satisfying ending to the deeply unpleasant story. *Thrill Me* proves the point that musical theatre can tackle any subject—no matter how macabre." (**** 4 Stars) - **Paul Vale, The Stage (2022)**

"Dialogue moves seamlessly into rhymed lyrics and song as feelings are heightened. Whether in their duetting demand of "Thrill Me!", Leopold's "Everyone wants Richard (but not the way I do)" or Loeb's tantalizing "Roadster" as he lures young Bobby into their car, these aren't the numbers of a traditional musical but a setting that feels like the obsessive repetition of the same insistent theme whilst musical director Benjamin McQuigg plays the through-written piano score which relentlessly underpins the action and sustains the tension. Powerful performances and carefully controlled staging make this a production that grips the attention for every one of its 80 minutes (there isn't an interval). It may leave you wondering who controls whom. *Thrill Me* kicks off the new season in style and is highly recommended. - **Howard Loxton, British Theatre Guide (2022)**

"Should you think that killing is not something to sing about, Stephen Dolginoff's chamber-of-horrors musical may change your mind…Dolginoff tightens the focus on the twisted, transactional relationship…the throbbing, urgent score both creates and propels the intense emotional subtext for Loeb's nerveless, intellectual exercise." (**** 4 Stars) - **Georgina Brown, Daily Mail (2022)**

"This musical thriller by Stephen Dolginoff is tantalising from the outset and feels like a secret glimpse into a murderer's psyche. *Thrill Me* is a superb one-act rollercoaster…Although you won't get every historical detail, there is no mistaking why this atmospheric trial for justice has been thrilling audiences since 2003." - **Paige Cochrane, BroadwayWorld London (2022)**

"The choice of *Thrill Me*, which is an unusual and off-beat two-hander, shows some remarkably brave programming...The bitter-sweet songs have hints of Sondheim and Kurt Weill and greatly add to the intensity of the story...This is an exquisite and haunting production which delivers a profound impact and is a gem not to be missed" - **Steve Mackrell, Theatre Thoughts (2023)**

UNITED KINGDOM

"Without giving any twists away, not everything is as it seems on the bubbling surface...Singing heightens drama, heightens tension, heightens self-expression, as inner thoughts burst out, and Stagnell and Hird are riveting to watch as Loeb and Leopold play out their dark plans in flashback." (***** 5 Stars) - **Charles Hutchinson, The York Press (2018)**

"For as much as *Thrill Me* did take me out of my comfort zone, it was also compulsive viewing. the intimacy of the Old Joint Stock Theatre works in favour of this production as I felt like a fly on the wall watching moments of tenderness between Nathan and Richard that felt more like I really shouldn't be there and times when I wanted to shout to Nathan "he's using you! For god's sake man, walk away from this toxic relationship."...In this wonderful theatre space the audience really does get to be close to the action, whether you like it or not...I did love the songs, at the end of the day this is still a top quality musical with a fabulous score with music, book and lyrics by Stephen Dolginoff. The songs all have a hauntingly simple melody and a warm, familiarity to them. Because of the subject matter, I found the music to be just the right amount of 'light relief' I needed to stop this play from being too difficult to watch. Yes's, it's a dark subject but it has been carefully crafted into a fabulously wicked musical. I honestly don't think I will ever forget seeing *Thrill Me*." - **Julie Wallis, Redandgoldweb (Cambridge, 2018)**

"Stephen Dolginoff's book and songs carry the narrative smoothly along with its own twisted logic, with songs that fit in seamlessly in this arc. We do feel that we get to know these characters, their dysfunctional relationship, their needs and motivations well as the story progresses. Not an easy watch: neither character is loveable, or even likeable, to the observer, but we can begin to understand why each asks the other to *Thrill Me*." - **Selwyn Knight, The Reviews Hub (Cambridge, 2018)**

"Stephen Dolginoff's creation of a psychological thriller musical is nothing short of genius and the creative team behind this staging have done more than justice to this show." - **Love Midlands Theatre (Cambridge, 2018)**

"While *Thrill Me* no doubt takes considerable license with its source tale, it is nevertheless a gritty examination of the human psyche, and the complex emotional and mental instabilities that could drive two young men, who seemingly had it all, to kill." (***** 5 stars) - **Samantha Creswick, The Cambridge Student (2019)**

"*Thrill Me* exceeded my expectations with its fast- paced plot, engaging actors, and catchy musical numbers." - **Carla Plieth, Varsity (Cambridge, 2019)**

AUSTRALIA

"Author-composer Stephen Dolginoff rises to the challenge remarkably well. His taut, tightly written two-hander tells the story and delineates the characters in 85 absorbing minutes and 15 impressive songs. Dolginoff's songs are not just ornaments to the play: they are its very backbone, ceaselessly exploring character and advancing plot. The striking, well-constructed score has strong melody lines, attractive harmonies and imaginative, rhythmic accompaniments. This is excellent contemporary music theatre." - **Jim Murphy, The Age Australia (2005)**

"This is really powerful theatre. The minimal set and stark, dramatic lighting serve to enhance the atmosphere of tension. At just under an hour and a half and with no interval, it is intense and sometimes uncomfortable viewing. Stephen Dolginoff avoids the clichés of the genre and delivers powerful songs and sparingly used dialogue to great effect." - **Rowena Scanlon Broadway Australia (2005)**

"This fascinating story certainly doesn't fail to captivate the audience from the very beginning. The real highlight of this show is the music. The contemporary musical theatre tunes are catchy and the performances are of high quality." - **Caitlin Wright, Aussietheatre.com (2010)**

"There's a psychological chiller of a musical playing at the Seymour Centre. Stephen Dolginoff's textured score, often in striking counterpoint to the dramatic action, provides essential distance and musical commentary. The humour is sparse, and again, placed for dramatic effect." - **Neil Litchfield, Stage Whispers (2010)**

"With *Thrill Me*, Stephen Dolginoff has created a dark chamber musical out of the Leopold and Loeb story. It's a tense and claustrophobic two-hander, with a diabolical twist, that delves into what was largely suppressed by the contemporary imagination. The musical succeeds through sharp, spare storytelling that lays bare the killers' deviant psychology." - **Cameron Woodhead, Sydney Morning Herald (2016)**

"This is a captivating story and what makes it more intriguing is that it is based on true events…I was kept engaged and was completely taken in to the 1920s with Nathan and Richard." - **Sara Gill, The Australia Times (2016)**

CANADA

"Thrill Me is a macabre love story with some fine vocal performances and a killer location…Playwright Dolginoff packs a lot into that short time, but judiciously concentrates on the bizarre motivations of his two characters as he presents the key facts of the murder. Told in a series of flashbacks as Leopold appears before a faceless parole board, we are offered a sometimes shocking explanation of the duo's relationship while walking a fine line between exploitation and fact." - **Mark Robins, GayVancouver.net (2012)**

"You walk down an unfamiliar alley and enter through a slightly ajar door at the back of a building. Inside is a warehouse with a large wooden staircase that goes up one wall. A series of mismatched seats are in three groups surrounding the playing area. The lights dim and a pianist at upright piano starts to pound out a grand overture in eerie minor keys. A single hanging light turns on and a handsome young actor steps into it...The overall evening, however, is effective, the venue is a fun adventure, the story is sadistically bent yet romantic and the actors bring a lot of passion to their performances and sing wonderfully. How often have you attended a chamber musical in an alley?" - **David C. Jones, The Charlebois Post (2012)**

"I didn't relish the idea of traipsing down a dark alley on a cold November night in search of the rear entrance to a former storage facility in the warehouse district of Main and Terminal. Also, not having ever seen this play before, I did wonder if the real life story of the murder of an innocent child by two over-achieving psychopaths was ideal fodder for musical theatre. However, my temerity paid off and I was rewarded with some fine musical drama that might even be described as modern opera." - **John Jane, ReviewVancouver (2012)**

"It is an entertaining story if very creepy. It focuses on a sexual relationship between the two as one of the driving forces behind the crime. The focus I'm most familiar with is that the two were geniuses and believed that they were 'supermen' as defined by Nietzsche and could commit the perfect crime. I enjoyed the performances and found the angle from which the story was approached very interesting." - **Sam Mooney, Mooney on Theatre (Toronto, 2013)**

OFF-BROADWAY CAST ALBUM (2006)

"While a musical about the infamous 1920s homosexual "thrill" killers Leopold & Loeb may sound bizarre, *Thrill Me* proved to be one of the most original and fascinating works to reach New York stages in several seasons. I raved about the 2005 York Theatre staging and felt the material benefited immensely when author/composer Stephen Dolginoff took over the role of Leopold partway through the run. He and co-star Doug Kreeger have preserved their finely nuanced performances in this excellent recording, which includes all of the melodic score and some crucial bits of dialog. Dolginoff examines the seductive power of evil, and suggests that arrogance can turn a puppeteer into an unsuspecting puppet. Regional and college theatres looking for a new, off-beat alternative to the usual musical theatre repertory should seriously consider *Thrill Me*, which despite its well-known subject packs a surprise ending, and provides solid entertainment along the way. This recording is a super memento of a first-class production." - **John Kenrick, Musicals101.com**

"For context, brief bits of dialogue work extremely well...setting up many of the songs. It adds to the dramatic tension, which hardly ever lets up. You can feel the tautness and the omnipresent sense of danger...The performances are the key here, and they make the most of the material...As the charismatic but coldly calculating Richard Loeb, Doug Kreeger is excellent throughout the recording, presenting a nuanced portrait that finds many shades of menace. He is especially successful in the solo "Roadster" where he is baiting his victim, making the most of each seductive phrase...Stephen Dolginoff turns in a compelling performance as actor-singer...His solo, "Way Too Far" is one of his best moments, underscoring the tragedy of realizing too late he has reached the point of no return, and the musical begins to feel like a Greek tragedy. The men's harmonies are striking and provide an oddly affecting balance to the harshness of the ugly realities that are the subject matter—murder, manipulation and deceit. The power and control one man has over the other and the unequal emotional and sexual investment they have with each other is convincing as played in their startling teamwork...An intriguing musical that is actually very accessible. It is unsettling without any doubt, but for it not to be would be a failure." - **Rob Lester, Talkin' Broadway.com**

"*Thrill Me* was an off Broadway show I somehow missed and sorry that was the case after listening to the excellent original cast. I had never heard of Stephen Dolginoff who wrote the book, music, lyrics and starred in this intriguing and disturbing story based on the maniacal duo Leopold and Loeb. Mr. Dolginoff's chillingly sinister lyrics focuses on the bizarre relationship and their evilness. Mr. Dolginoff and Doug Kreeger were the only stars and accompanied only by a piano. The cast recording is startlingly effective. Listening to the song "Roadster" in which Loeb entices the young man the twosome eventually murder is almost unbearably frightening. Hope to hear more from this very gifted young composer." - **Joseph Cervelli, Theatre.com**

"Legendary thrill killers Leopold & Loeb get the musical treatment in composer Stephen Dolginoff's *Thrill Me*, the latest re-telling of their shocking real-life exploits. Dolginoff's ambitious take on this seemingly sociopathic pair is that their crimes were driven by lust and infatuation with one another. The brooding intensity of both the score and Dolginoff and Doug Kreeger's performances...go a long way towards selling this idea. And, there are some truly surprising moments in *Thrill Me*: "A Written Contract," in which the duo craft their Faustian pact, the chilling "Roadster," which leads their innocent prey to his death, and the audacious jailhouse confession "Life Plus 99 Years," will make listeners' jaws drop in both shock and admiration. Kudos to Dolginoff for his brazen chutzpah in even attempting this—and, even more so for pulling it off." - **Michael Criscuolo, Nytheatre.com**

THRILL ME

– Original Notes –

NATHAN: My things?
(List them)

We could...
chloroform a fag
~~Steal My Father's gun~~
Borrow some old gun...

Tommy
John

RICHARD: I said NO.

Leopold & Loeb

NATHAN: Forget it
RICHARD: Scared?
(NATHAN doesn't respond)

~~The Thrill Killers~~
Thrill Me

~~SCENE ONE:~~
~~Lights up in a~~
~~Prison Shower Room~~

> THERE MAY HAVE BEEN A WITNESS NEAR THE LAKE!
> WE MIGHT HAVE LEFT A FOOTPRINT IN THE MUD!

FIRE
WARM, ROMANTIC
Roaring, Raging
Sound of Embers
Sparks Fly
Smoke In Sky
Intense Heat

DON'T THINK UP EXCUSES
THEY'LL NEVER PERSUADE ME
LET'S TURN ALL THE LIGHTS OFF
DON'T TRY TO EVADE ME,
THRILL ME!

"Quit watching
the stupid birds!"

RICHARD:
I KNOW YOU'VE GOT
        EXPECTATIONS
BUT I'M NOT
    IN THE MOOD!   >?
                                  ,

NATHAN:
I TOOK PART IN
    YOUR MACHINATIONS
        .... LEWD?
        SCREWED?
        (SUED)

WE'RE SUPERIOR
WE ARE SUPERMEN
SAYS MY NIETZCHE BOOK
CHAPTERS ONE THRU TEN!
AND AS SUPERMEN
WE COULD NOT GET CAUGHT...

~~LATE LAST NIGHT~~
~~You PROVED THAT~~ you
~~WERE FIT~~
YOU'RE NOT FIT TO
POUR ME BATH TUB
BOOZE!

~~Sports Car~~
Road Ster
Roll down all
the windows?

NATHAN (OLDER)

~~YOU'RE NOT THE FIRST~~
~~TO ASK ME,~~
~~BUT YOU DON'T CARE~~
~~WHY,~~
I'M SORRY IF I
STUMBLE.
THOUGH I'M TENSE,
I'LL TRY...

RICHARD
IF WE KILLED MY BROTHER ~~JOHN~~
        NATHAN
YOU COULD NEVER FACE YOUR ~~MOM!~~
                    MOTHER

       IT'S
~~THAT'S~~ ~~NO WAY TO~~ WHAT A WAY TO
MAKE YOUR MARK

RICHARD: ~~HOLD OUT YOUR~~ FINGER!
(SIGN IN BLOOD)

NATHAN: Now how about we do a little catchingup?

RICHARD: No. I've got a date.

NATHAN: A Date?

RICHARD: It needs more gasoline.

NATHAN: I'm Scared!

RICHARD: More gasoline, Nathan. Now!

(Nathan relents.)

ROLL CHICAGO LIKE A BALL

BACKED CHICAGO TO THE WALL

LET CHICAGO TAKE THE FALL

SMALL

THAT'S ALL

CALL

DON'T STALL

RICHARD: I've Changed my
mind.
Besides one of us
has to do the driving
while the other...
NATHAN: Has the fun?
RICHARD: Precisely

It's the only
Option I CAN PROFFER
Think it through
OR I'll Rescind the Offer
*(Switch "Proffer" and "Offer" =) *

NATHAN:
you've been reading (Magazines)
too many Detective Stories...
And↑ too much Nietzsche
(WAY)

Chicago
ALL of the City would ~~Condemn~~ Go Mad

But we're both Superior
MY Lad
Dear ~~Lad~~
~~Be~~ glad

> WASH THE BLOOD STAINS OUT / OFF ?
WIPE THE BLOOD STAINS OFF

I just polished
MY New ~~Sports Car~~
Raodster
~~It's A Brand New~~
~~Shiny Packard~~
Shiny Packard Roadster

YOU THOUGHT THAT   Enthused
    YOU USED ME
BUT MERELY AMUSED ME
I KNOW I'M STILL
    CUNNING AND
        DARING

DESPITE YOUR ENSNARING

AND NOW.. WE'LL BE
TOGETHER FOR LIFE PLUSS
            99 YEARS

YES I
~~DO YOU~~ Remember the Night *

Thrill Me
→ Impress ME ←
Undress Me
Caress me
→ Finesse Me ←

NATHAN
I'LL KEEP YOU
FOCUSED
NO OUTSIDE Forces?
Sources?

FOR LIFE PLUS 99 years.

RICHARD
You FINALLY STOPPED ME
You FINALLY TOPPED ME
Switch

I'M ONE ~~CHARACTER~~
~~WITNESS~~

* PERFECT ACCOMPLICE *
WHO'D NEVER BETRAY YOU
IF You ... THRILL ME ...
THRILL ME!
(Blackout)

ABOUT THE AUTHOR

Stephen Dolginoff is the writer, composer, and lyricist of the Off-Broadway musical *Thrill Me: The Leopold & Loeb Story*, for which he received Drama Desk Award nominations for Best Musical and Best Music, an Outer Critics Circle Award nomination for Best Off-Broadway musical, and won an ASCAP Music Award.

His musical suspense thriller, *Flames*; his horror movie musical homage, *Monster Makers*; and *Panic*, his musical based on the story behind the *War of the Worlds* broadcast, are continually performed all over the world. For his early musicals, Stephen received a Backstage Bistro Award for Outstanding Book, Music & Lyrics and a MAC Award nomination. Stephen holds a BFA in Dramatic Writing from NYU/Tisch School of the Arts. His musicals are published by Samuel French/Concord Theatricals and Dramatists Play Service/Broadway Licensing.

As an actor, Stephen played the role of Nathan Leopold in *Thrill Me* Off-Broadway, regionally, and on the cast album; originated the roles of Max Schreck, Boris Karloff, and Peter Cushing in the original New York production of *Monster Makers*; and portrayed Orson Welles in the New York premiere of *Panic*.

Thrill Maker is his first book.

Visit www.stephendolginoff.com

Made in the USA
Columbia, SC
11 February 2024

31595199R00172